Questions
Parents
Ask

Books from the Gesell Institute of Human Development

Your One-Year-Old
Ames, Ilg, and Haber

Your Two-Year-Old
Ames and Ilg

Your Three-Year-Old
Ames and Ilg

Your Four-Year-Old
Ames and Ilg

Your Five-Year-Old
Ames and Ilg

Your Six-Year-Old
Ames and Ilg

Your Seven-Year-Old
Ames and Haber

Your Eight-Year-Old
Ames and Haber

Your Nine-Year-Old
Ames and Haber

Your Ten- to Fourteen-Year-Old
Ames, Ilg, and Baker

Questions Parents Ask

Solutions to the most common parenting
problems from the author of the best-
selling Gesell Institute series on
child development

by Louise Bates Ames, Ph.D.

Gesell Institute of Human Development

Delta

A Delta Book
Published by
Dell Publishing
a division of
Bantam Doubleday Dell Publishing Group, Inc.
666 Fifth Avenue
New York, New York 10103

A detailed list of acknowledgments begins on page 295.

ISBN: 0-385-29902-8

Reprinted by arrangement with Clarkson N. Potter, Inc.

Printed in the United States of America

Published simultaneously in Canada

April 1990

10 9 8 7 6 5 4 3 2 1

BG

To my great-grandchildren:
Tommy, Doug, Greg, and Karen

Contents

Introduction:
Are Today's Children
Different?

Are children today really much different from what they used to be, as many people claim? It might seem so. A four-year-old of our acquaintance, not necessarily known as the best-behaved boy in his family, recently expressed his resolve to be a better boy: "I'm not going to hit my brothers. I'm not going to fight at the table. I'm not going to force the pieces in the jigsaw puzzle. I'm not going to tease at the grocery store. And if anybody offers me dope I'll just say no."

Nowadays we frequently see five- and six-year-olds deftly manipulating their Atari games in a way that quite astonishes their grandparents. And when a ten-year-old girl visiting the Gesell Institute overheard a little patient in the medical department crying loudly, she looked calmly at her father and explained, "They're probably giving his parents a child abuse test."

Even twenty years ago, most four-year-olds were not thinking about being offered dope; young children did not play with computers; and most ten-year-olds, unless themselves abused, did not know about child abuse.

So, admittedly, the world our children live in *is* different in many ways from the world that we, or even our earlier research subjects, grew up in. Television and radio bring children today into touch with life in other countries, space travel, the atomic bomb—all part of a distinctly different way of living from that of the past. Communities are less supportive than they were, and crime is definitely on the rise.

Life for many children is far more exciting, and also far less safe and protective than it used to be. But everyday observation as well as research findings lead us to the conclusion that human behavior not only still develops in a patterned, largely predictable manner, but also that the pattern it follows as it develops is very much the same as that which held for earlier generations.

Basic biological changes in behavior, changes that come with age, do not seem to be substantially different from what they have been in decades past. Babies are still managing first to roll over, then to sit, crawl, creep, stand, and eventually walk, in that order.

When we describe to parents our observations about behavior that is characteristic of the various age levels, they frequently comment, "That's my son to a tee. You could have been living at our house." We get this response even though some of our earlier observations were made originally when the parents themselves were children.

Though in general it does seem that life is harder, or at least not as comfortable, for children today, a cheerful note comes from the reports of children themselves. In a recent large-scale "National Survey of Children" conducted by Temple University with government support, over two thousand boys and girls aged seven to eleven were interviewed. Of these, more than 75 percent expressed agreement with the statement, "I am lucky," and 90 percent said, "I like being the way I am." Also on the positive side, nine out of ten children pointed to a happy face to convey how they feel about their families, though eight out of ten reported that they sometimes worry about their families.

However, reflecting our troubled times, more than two-thirds of the children said they feel afraid "that somebody bad might get into my house." One-quarter responded affirmatively to the question, "When you go outside, are you afraid someone might hurt you?" More than 40 percent of the children reported being bothered by older children, and more than one out of eight by adults.

Whereas nearly 60 percent of the parents rated their neighborhoods as "very good" or "excellent" places to raise children, in no type of American community did a majority of children interviewed describe their neighborhoods as "a very good" place to grow up. Even in affluent suburbs, the proportion answering "very good" was only 40 percent.

It isn't just neighborhoods that are less secure and stable than they used to be. It is families themselves. The average child is much less likely than a child from an earlier generation to end up living with the two parents he started out with, though most children would prefer to remain with their two original parents, even if the family unit is less than ideal.

The very structure of the home also tends to be different from what it was just a few years ago. When Mother works outside the home, no matter how satisfactory the arrangements for child care may be, family life will inevitably differ from what it was in the days when most mothers stayed at home.

The role of fathers, too, is changing. Not too many years ago, Father in most families was the supreme authority, rather than an active participant in day-to-day household responsibilities. As one little boy put it, "I'm the boss of Jim [his younger brother]. Joan [his older sister] is the boss of me. Mom is the boss of Joan. Dad is the boss of Mom. But who is the boss of Dad?" However, many more fathers today than in times past *do* change diapers. (I recently overheard a father of two explaining to his brother, a brand-new father, "It's really not so bad.") They also may sit with the children when Mother is out, and I have known divorced or widowed fathers who were marvels of affection and efficiency with their sons or daughters.

In some families parents stagger their working hours so that one or the other is always at home with the children. And on still rarer occasions, fathers actually take on the traditional mothering role and keep house and take care of the children.

If in this volume we seem to include rather more criticisms of fathers than of mothers, it is possibly because when things go wrong in a family it tends to be Mother rather than Father who consults a columnist, psychologist, or pediatrician. While very few fathers write to us to complain about their wives, many mothers write to complain about their husband's poor handling of the children.

These days there are more questions about family problems in general. With the increase in divorce, stepfamilies, and single-parent families, relatively more parents now ask about how to handle the special kinds of problems that their situations raise as opposed to questions that relate specifically to child behavior.

The fact that the world around our children today is very different does make for somewhat different questions and concerns on the part of parents. Questions about eating, for instance, which were once so numerous, have taken a new turn. Parents used to feel that their children were not eating *enough*. Now many realize that appetites differ and that most children do eat a sufficient amount to keep themselves going. Today the concern is more about what kinds of food children eat. There is greater awareness of the harmfulness of junk food and the need to avoid foods to which the child may be allergic.

Toilet-training questions are now fewer. Most parents start the training later than they used to, and with the older child who is naturally more capable of being trained success often comes relatively soon after efforts start. Children who don't sleep well, or who make a big fuss at bedtime, however, remain a major concern in many families.

Questions about school have changed to some extent from wondering how to make the child study harder, to expressing a reasonable concern that perhaps a child is failing because he is overplaced and too much is expected of him. Questions about discipline are always with us, but now they are somewhat more desperate, as the firm discipline that many parents maintained is weakening and, it must be admitted, children on the whole do not behave as well as they used to. Certainly they are less afraid of their parents. At the same time, now that parents are more aware of the various stages (some good, some bad) that normal children go though, there is much more patience with the contrary behavior of the two-and-a-half-year-old, the wildness of the four-year-old, the rudeness of the six-year-old.

It is when children reach their teens that parents' questions are most different from what they used to be. Parents used to worry that their teenagers were rude and fresh, unfriendly and disobedient, "growing away from the family." Now the concerns of many parents are much more serious—about the use of drugs, promiscuity, just plain refusal to obey house rules. Teenagers no longer simply mumble and slouch around. Now many are in serious difficulties, which parents and school alike find hard to handle. It's fair to say that the older the child, the more different parents' questions are from what they used to be.

So much for questions. How about our answers? Basically they have not changed conspicuously over the years. Our position is, and always has been, that any child's behavior tends to be determined by three main factors—his age, his basic individuality, and his awareness of the world he is living in. The control of environment customarily provided by school, church, and family is not as consistently strong and effective as it has been in the past. Parents do have a harder time making things work out happily than they used to have. That's why they need all the help they can get. It is our hope that the parent problems presented in this book, culled from letters to my column in the *New Haven Register* during the last thirty years, and our own suggested solutions to these problems may be of use to you in bringing up your own family.

—Louise Bates Ames
The Gesell Institute
New Haven, Connecticut

On Infants and Toddlers

Are You in Danger of Spoiling Your Baby?

My husband and I are the proud parents of a two-month-old baby girl, Amanda. She is the joy of our lives and we think we are going to be good parents. However, my mother-in-law insists that we are spoiling her and that if we keep this up we are going to have a rotten kid on our hands.

The problem is mostly about her feeding. Grandma insists that when she was bringing up her babies they were on a strict schedule—they were fed every four hours—and this taught them that they couldn't get anything they wanted, whenever they wanted it, just by crying. . . . Our pediatrician seems to us more modern. He says, though we shouldn't pick Mandy up the minute she cries, or every single time she cries, that crying is her way of communicating with us and that it will not spoil her if we respond to her needs.

We don't want to have a spoiled baby on our hands. But it is hard for us not to respond to her. She is so tiny and so dear. And for the most part a very smiley little girl.

Fortunately for babies, most parents nowadays worry very little about spoiling their baby. It could be done, presumably, but you would really have to go out of your way to do it.

If you *always* picked your baby up the *minute* she cried or if you fed her every single time she cried, you would probably be spoiling her. However most parents and most pediatricians have come a long way beyond the old idea that babies *have to learn to wait* and that you *build up their characters* by making them "cry it out."

Eating, sleeping, and eliminating are among the main activities of the very young infant. All parents accept the fact that the baby has no control over its elimination functions, so that, as a rule, is not a problem. Even though it would be convenient if the baby slept well, especially at night, most parents appreciate that it takes a while for a baby to learn, or adapt to, our own notion that one wakes in the daytime, and sleeps at night. Few parents go too far in trying to control this function.

It is in relation to feeding that parents usually put in their greatest efforts at helping their baby to be "reasonable" in its demands. In the 1940s many parents, at their pediatrician's suggestion, began to substitute what is called a self-demand feeding schedule for the old every four- (or whatever) hour schedule. So instead of making babies who might be hungry every three hours cry for an hour till the scheduled feeding, parents adapted, within reason, to the child's own bodily timetable.

This might seem like spoiling to those who are ignorant of the fact that a self-demand feeding schedule has a second part that is called self-regulation. This means that unless the baby's demands for food are excessively frequent, one does more or less feed him, during the first months, when he is hungry. But little by little, the parent does expect the baby to wait a little longer. Thus you adapt to him but he adapts to you.

One might consider a baby spoiled if he had the upper hand and the parent would do *anything* to keep him from crying. One would not consider a baby spoiled if you and he worked things out together. You respond, lovingly and willingly, to the baby's demands, but little by little the baby becomes more independent and more able to wait for your response.

Living with a baby, though often demanding, can be a vast pleasure. I, myself, would worry very little about spoiling an infant.

Playpen—Good or Bad?

As the mother of a nine-month-old baby who is just beginning to creep, I swear by my good old reliable playpen, which also saved my sanity when my four-year-old was just getting to the creeping stage.

Now I hear that some psychologists are against *playpens. What is the story? And what is your opinion?*

I personally am very much in favor of playpens. The criticism you have heard is very likely from one Burton White of Boston. He feels that there is no way of keeping most children from being bored in a playpen for longer than a very brief period of time, perhaps ten to twenty minutes. And that to bore a child on a daily basis by regular use of a playpen is a very poor child-rearing practice in terms of the child's educational needs.

This may be a psychologist speaking, but most mothers whom I know consider the playpen truly a godsend. Certainly you don't just put a baby in it and let him stay there for hours, unentertained. But in between his walk and his feeding, his bath and his nap, and the periods when you are actively playing with him and enjoying him, there come those times when *you,* the caretaker, are busy with other concerns.

The ordinarily lively and intelligent baby does not have to be entertained by others during *all* his waking hours. And the ordinarily intelligent and lively mother knows how to embellish the playpen with reasonably interesting toys. When a baby is first getting about the house on his own steam, everybody is better off if he spends some time in his playpen.

If he is not too demanding, the pen can be within sight of Mother. Most babies will play with their toys, or with their fingers or feet, and then, if like most nine-monthers they are able to pull to a standing position by the side of their pen and cruise about it their own motor activity will keep them quite happily entertained for reasonably long periods.

So, let your baby play away in his nice, safe playpen to his heart's content till the time comes all too soon when he will have outgrown it.

Sixteen Months Is Not an Easy Time

I am deeply concerned about my sixteen-month-old grandson, Billy. He was always an enthusiastic, responsive, happy-seeming baby and a pleasure to be with.

Now he looks like a little waif or orphan. The sad expression on his little face is breaking my heart. And he is so demanding—wants to be carried around all the time and he is heavy!

Also he used to be so responsive—a big smile for everyone. Now his main word is no *and his chief gesture a vigorous negative shake of his head.*

I do have to admit that there is one extenuating circumstance—there is a new baby in the family. But it seems to me that his parents go out of their way to show him that he is still loved and appreciated. And they spend a great deal of time alone with him.

Do I have cause to worry?

If you mean just ordinary grandmotherly fretting, *yes.* But if you mean do I think there is necessarily anything wrong with Billy, *no.*

Even without the advent of the new baby, fifteen to twenty-one months is a very difficult time in the lives of many young children. Earlier, admittedly, they are almost totally dependent on those around them. They cry when they want something and, more often than not, their wants are answered (often, perhaps, before they are even fully aware of what it is they want).

By fifteen months or so, most children's demands are very strong and definite. They know what they want (the blue bib instead of the white one, a food different from what is being offered, to go for a carriage ride instead of being rocked). And they know what they don't want, too. They don't want their diaper changed, their shoes and socks put on, *anything* that goes on and off over their head. But except for gestures and crying, they have little way of making these exact wants known to other people because they don't have the words. Their appreciation of their own vulnerability may in part account for that waiflike expression that you mention.

Since Billy enjoys being carried around, chances are that like many others of his age he appreciates motion. So see to it, or suggest that his parents see to it, that he has as many carriage rides and car rides as possible. And within reason, try to interpret his gestures and demands, and so far as you can, give him what he wants.

Language will come in soon and will solve many of his problems.

Her Eighteen-Monther Is Hard to Handle

I have an eighteen-month-old son, Geoffrey, who is death on wheels. Hardly anything seems to influence him. He bumbles through his days, disruptive behavior alternating with temper tantrums. He hits, cries, breaks things, and is never still.

One of his less charming habits is that he hits me, his mother. Recently I read a columnist's advice that if your eighteen-monther hits you, you should make him sit on a chair, without toys or anything to interest him, for half an hour.

This of course is ridiculous. Did you ever see an eighteen-monther who would sit on a chair for half an hour? Other advice I have received from various sources has been equally unhelpful. And he absolutely ignores me when I say no.

You're quite right, of course. The usual eighteen-monther would not sit still in a chair for half an hour unless you tied him to the chair. And even then he would probably manage to tip it over.

A hitter is admittedly hard to handle. But since the eighteen-monther has no good time sense and is only influenced by the immediate present, your best bet, if you can't duck quickly enough, is to hold the hands of a hitter and simply tell him, "No hitting."

This may work and it may not. As in the case of temper tantrums, your best bet is preventive. Try to find out why he is angry and unhappy, or tired and tense, and do what you can to keep his life smoother.

We have found that discipline as we usually think of it does not work too well at this age. In general, you get furthest by using what we call preschool techniques. And at this age, these techniques must be rather gross and physical.

You control the eighteen-monther by controlling his surroundings, just not having too many things around that will get him into trouble. Or you control his activity by a harness, or simply by picking him up and putting him where you want him to be, without words and with no big fuss.

Our best recommendations for getting the eighteen-monther to come to you, for instance, are not to call him but rather to pick him up from behind and put him where you want him to be, lure him with a bit of food or a favorite toy, or turn your back on him and make an interesting sound, as crumpling paper. (He will come to see what it is that you are doing.)

Language in general is not, as it will be later, a good motivator. If you do use language to motivate your child keep it very simple and use words of one syllable, such as "Coat—hat—out." And keep in mind one mother's comment, "You program him as if he were a robot." This was not said unfeelingly; merely in full appreciation of the typical eighteen-monther's definite immaturities.

You say that your son ignores you when you say no. So, keep in mind that no is the eighteen-monther's word, not his mother's. As a friend of ours once commented of her son, "He puts all the force of his personality into his nos. He really means them and will stick with them to the bitter end." You, on the other hand, mean no for the time being but tend soon to move on to something else.

So, try to cut down the number of times you use the word and it may be more effective when you do. Also try to say no in ways other than in words. If you don't want your son to fall down the cellar stairs, instead of saying no, no when he approaches them, either keep the door locked or protect the stairs with a gate. Do the same for the kitchen or for fragile parts of the living room. Gates are much more effective than words.

In fact, you may well find that distraction goes a lot further than a verbal no. If you move quickly and cleverly, you may find that quite a lot of the time you can get a child of your son's age to do more or less what you want him to without giving him the opportunity to ignore your no or to express his own.

Dos and Don'ts for Parents of Twos

All too often, mothers of terrible two-and-a-half-year-old children (boys especially) complain of exhaustion. Pediatricians sometimes tell them that "This, too, will pass," but they can't wait. Here is some specific, practical advice that might help you get through this trying time.

• DO use techniques whenever you can, so that if your son does not comply with your wishes, you can drop the situation. Thus whenever you can, in giving commands, give yourself an "out." Avoid such directives as "You have to pick up all your toys before we go for our walk." Instead try, "How about picking up your toys?" or "Let's pick up your toys." If he doesn't do his fair share, no issue need be made.

• DO keep things the same: "After your nap we go for our walk," or whatever. Children of this age like everything to be just the way it was before and just where it was before. Then they know what to expect and may very likely go along with what you have planned.

• DO keep your family living as settled as possible. This is not a good time to move, unless you absolutely have to—nor is it a good time to take a nice vacation trip, even to Disneyland.

• DO, when trouble threatens, try to distract your child's attention from the specific problem at hand. And try not to meet resistance head on. You don't have to work everything through. Just shift, distract, change the subject or the situation. Fortunately children at this age have short memories.

• DO put valuable or highly breakable objects out of sight or at least out of reach. Your child is still not old enough to learn not to touch. (An exception would be that he must not touch the hot stove. There can be certain other absolute nontouchables. But don't waste time teaching him, right now, not to touch valuable vases, ashtrays, and other ornaments that do not need to be left within reach.)

• DO try to appreciate that the child of this age has very little inhibition. So you provide the necessary inhibition, when you can, by rearranging the environment.

• Above all, keep an ever-hopeful eye out for improvement in any sector of behavior—eating, sleeping, elimination. Time will bring improvement in these important areas. Don't expect too much, but be grateful for anything that begins to go a little better —as it almost certainly will as your son approaches the often-delightful age of three.

• DON'T expect all daily routines to go smoothly. As you have discovered, your child will not always cooperate.

- DON'T introduce any sudden changes in routines without warning or some cushioning buildup. Your child will prefer that things always be the same.
- Avoid any questions that can be answered by no—such as, "Do you want to have your bath now?" And *don't* give choices if the answer matters. You *can* use choices if it's just a case of "Do you want the red one or the blue one?"
- DON'T expect your child to wait for things, but you may have to wait for him.
- DON'T give ultimatums such as, "You have to eat all your lunch before you can go out to play." Give commands gently and so far as you can rather inconspicuously.
- Try not to be upset by your son's rigid ways. Try to see his behavior not as badness but as immaturity. Your doctor actually is right, even if it may not be much help—this, too, *will* pass.
- DON'T, whatever you do, deprive a child of this age of any security measures he may have worked up—his thumb, his blanket, his teddy bear.
- DON'T feel guilty when and if you have to punish. There will be many rough spots during any day with a child of this age. Neither you nor he is to blame when things don't go smoothly. That's just the way it is. You will find that isolating your child when things are at their worst will help you a lot.
- DON'T get mixed up in your boy's "Mummy do, Daddy do" routine. Children of this age often want whoever is not helping them to be the one to help. Just ignore his demands and commands (as much as you can) and go on dressing him, or feeding him, or whatever you are doing. Especially *don't* let your feelings be hurt if he seems to prefer somebody else to you. If you ignore this kind of emotional blackmail, which even a two-year-old may use, he will soon learn that it doesn't work.
- DON'T expect a child of this age to wait his turn, to share toys with others, or to play nicely with other children. *Do* give the help he needs, such as asking, "What else could you use?" Or assure him that "Johnny needs that tricycle now." Or promise, hopefully, "Pretty soon it will be your turn."
- Children of this age, difficult as they may be at times, tend to be more predictable in their behavior than they will be later on. Thus often even rather simple techniques tend to work with

them, over and over again. Life can be difficult at this age, but more often than not you have the upper hand, if only you have the patience and ingenuity to use it.

Two-and-a-Half-Year-Old Is Constantly Demanding

*M*y toddler, Mike, aged two and a half, is running me ragged. He demands my constant attention except for fifteen minutes in the morning when I lock him in his room (with plenty of toys, of course) and about two hours in the afternoon when he naps. Otherwise he wants me almost every minute of the day.

Here is an example of one of his less demanding times of day. He decides to play songs on the piano but needs my help in finding notes. We play "Had a Little Nut Tree" (three minutes). He then runs to the kitchen and wants a pear. I cut the pear for him but he wants a different bib from the one I try to put on him. He eats the pear (two minutes). Runs to record player, needs help with record. Also has to be chased for me to wipe his sticky hands. Listens to record (three minutes). Then he wants to be read to (five minutes), etc.

I mostly give in to avoid confrontation as he is very prone to temper tantrums. I would enjoy playing with Mike for perhaps two or even three hours a day. Beyond that, it is too much. I never get anything done around the house or for myself. Also by midafternoon the older children are at home and they, too, need attention. How can I be fair to myself, my family, and to Mike?

Yours, alas, is the typical story. An active, lively preschooler demands just about 100 percent of some adult's time. That is the discouraging thing—that after having played "nicely" with him for an hour or so, you still have so many hours to go. His two-hour nap is obviously the best time of the day for you.

Since Mike will accept fifteen minutes locked in his room, even though he calls out to you, could you expand this to half an hour, or to two fifteen-minute periods?

Could you possibly engage a babysitter for either an hour a day or for one or two mornings a week? Or if your house is small, since it might be difficult to detach Mike from you even if there were a sitter available, could you find somebody in the neighborhood who would accept him in her house for short but predictable periods?

You are wise to appreciate that constant but directed activity of a preschooler is not necessarily so-called hyperactivity. I can assure you that your boy's constant activity and constant demands of you are not unusual, but of course that is not too much help.

Since your son is so very demanding of personal attention, and you are very sympathetically responsive, your best bet is obviously for you and Mike to be physically separated as much as possible. Nursery school, if you can find and afford it, has saved many a mother's sanity.

Should Parents Go on Vacation Without Their Toddler?

O ur son and his wife are planning to take a week's vacation away from their two-and-a-half-year-old son, Benjy. The plan is that he will spend the first three days of this time with his maternal grandparents, in their home, which he is familiar with. Then he will spend the rest of the week with us. He knows us but has never visited our home.

Our question is, is it right for parents of such a young child to take a vacation away from him? Won't it make him feel insecure and anxious? My wife and I are very dubious about the wisdom of this plan.

T o begin with, regardless of how you and your wife feel, your son and *his* wife are the child's parents and it is up to them, not to you, to decide whether or not they will take a vacation without him.

True, children at his age tend to be very set in their ways and *any* change in routine is likely to upset them. But, parents, even of preschoolers, are not prisoners and if they want to take a vacation it is really their privilege.

Possibly the ideal solution, if parents must be away, is to leave the child in his own home and to have somebody (grandparents or others) come into that home to take care of him. Then at least his surroundings, except for his parents, will remain those he is used to.

Since the plan to have Benjy visit his maternal grandparents in their home (which he is familiar with) has already been made, it would be my recommendation to go ahead with that for the first few days.

But for the last few days of the week, it would be my choice to have him go back to his own home, and you and his grandmother take care of him there. You may ask, wouldn't he be upset to return home and not find his parents there? Well, possibly. But this should be taken care of, as much as one can take care of it, by your going over and over the plans with him.

His parents, you, and the other grandparents should go over and over the fact that Mummy and Daddy are going away and that Benjy will be going to visit Grandma and Grandpa X in their house, where he can play with his cousins, etc., etc. And then he will go back to his own house and Grandma and Grandpa Y will be there to take care of him. And then in two more days (or whatever) Mummy and Daddy will come home.

Benjy may not be wild about all this and you should expect a few tears and possibly tantrums. But after all, he is not being sent to the stockades. One thing that sometimes helps in situations like this is if every night somebody provides a "surprise," left by his parents for him. This will give something to look forward to, and assure him that they haven't forgotten him. Also, with some children, frequent phone calls from the parents work out; with others they may make things more difficult.

Keep in mind, normally endowed children tend to be extremely resilient. Benjy may indeed show some anxiety, after his parents return, that they may go away again and they might expect him to be a little unusually clinging. But I do believe that he will survive.

On Preschoolers

Techniques for Handling a Three-Year-Old

My daughter, Doreen, is now three and a half and she is more than a handful. Any general suggestions you could give to make our lives more comfortable would be more than appreciated.

Here you are. Three-year-olds, as you may have discovered, tend to be reasonably easy to get on with, but not so three-and-a-halfs. Then comes trouble. Techniques can, if you are fortunate, work wonders in smoothing over the rough spots of a mother's day.

First of all, try to face the fact that at this age the child's big emotional struggle is with her mother. She is the one who matters most to her, so she is the one she needs to rebel against. Almost any young child is at her best and worst with Mother. So, your best bet is, if at all possible, to enlist a good baby-sitter for as much of the time as possible.

A similar suggestion, which also may seem like an easy way out but nevertheless can work wonders, is to send your child to a good nursery school. This gets her away from you. And the stimulation provided can make it less necessary for her to get her excitement by rebelling against you.

Simplify and streamline. Buy her clothes that do not have to come off over the head. Think about not having a bath every day unless the child is especially dirty. Keep mealtime as simple as possible, and try not to insist that your child consume either certain kinds of food or certain quantities of food.

Remember that it takes two to quarrel. Try to stay as emotionally calm as you can when trouble arises. Walk away.

Give commands in a loose manner. Try not to say "You have to," but rather try, "How about?" "Let's," or other ways of speaking that allow you to retreat, if need be.

Keep in mind that routines are the hardest part of your day. In order to keep up your pleasant feelings about your child, spend some time with her not in going through these difficult routines but in pleasurable play. At his or her best the child of this age can be an imaginative and enjoyable companion.

Give lots of loving, physical attention. Hug the child a lot. Tell her what a good child she is. There is much insecurity at this age. Try to dispel it whenever you reasonably can.

If some bit of behavior gives trouble, try to think up some master plan that will help out, instead of going through the same difficulty every day. For instance early morning wakers will sometimes refrain from waking parents if you lay out a "surprise" for them the night before. Tell them that they can have the surprise every day that they do not bother you before you get up.

These little tricks should make life with your three-and-a-half-year-old easier and less trying.

Easy Ages and Difficult Ages

For the informed parent, the many odd behaviors that the child exhibits as he grows do not come as a complete surprise, do not seem to be the signs that something is necessarily wrong with the child. "Now I know he's normal," say parents who find their own boy's or girl's sometimes peculiar behavior described on a printed page and labeled "customary." You don't have to like everything your growing child does. But your concern can at least be lessened if you know that he is not alone.

The following diagram and table illustrate overall changes in the basic kinds of behavior that occur as the child alternates between stages of equilibrium and stages of disequilibrium with maturing age. We think of development as a kind of spiraling of growth. Once a child has reached a "good" stage, or stage of equilibrium, in his behavior, unfortunately he cannot seem to then move on to a new and more mature stage of equilibrium without having the behavior break up into what we call a stage of disequilibrium. These two kinds of behavior alternate rather systematically during the ages between eighteen months and sixteen years, as the diagram illustrates.

THE GROWTH SPIRAL

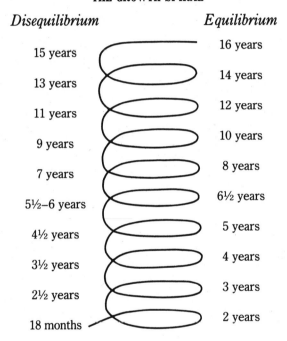

Disequilibrium	*Equilibrium*
15 years	16 years
13 years	14 years
11 years	12 years
9 years	10 years
7 years	8 years
5½–6 years	6½ years
4½ years	5 years
3½ years	4 years
2½ years	3 years
18 months	2 years

More than this, we have determined a six-step pattern of development that repeats itself three times between the ages of two and sixteen. These steps are: smooth behavior, breakup of behavior, balanced behavior, inwardized behavior, expansive behavior, troubled or neurotic behavior, and then once again smooth behavior. The table gives the basic story of these behavior changes.

If parents find it interesting to know what, in general, is going to happen, norms can be helpful. But say we tell you that good ages tend to alternate with difficult ages and that around two

CYCLES OF CHANGE IN THE EARLY YEARS						
Smooth	*Breakup*	*Balanced*	*Inwardized*	*Expansive*	*Troubled*	*Smooth*
2 yrs.	2½ yrs.	3 yrs.	3½ yrs.	4 yrs.	4½ yrs.	5 yrs.
5	5½–6	6½	7	8	9	10
10	11.	12	13	14	15	16

you may hope that your child will find life easy—and around two and a half it may be more difficult for him. You own child's good period might occur earlier or later. Also in some children, good periods are few and far between, whereas other children are more or less comfortable and contented much of the time.

Thus a parent shouldn't worry, as some do, if his child does *not* hit a difficult stage around two and a half, an out-of-bounds stage around four. But let us hope it may be helpful to any parent to have a bird's-eye view of the way behavior tends to change in the early years of life.

What to Do About Whining

My three-and-a-half-year-old daughter, Chris, is a terrible whiner. Seems to me that she whines all day and even her father, who of course is not with her as many hours as I am, admits that her whining gets on his nerves. Do you have any suggestions about what to do with a whiny child?

Whining is a very hard thing to handle because it is so general. Say a child hits a baby sibling—that is more specific and can be dealt with as such. But in your daughter's case, whining can go on all day and does not seem to be about any special thing—just about everything.

Three-and-a-half tends to be an especially whiny age. Many around four burst out from whining into wildness—so that is something to look forward to, if you think of it that way.

Much whining occurs because the child is tired, sleepy, hungry, or restless. So food sometimes helps, or possibly an earlier naptime—

assuming your child still naps. Whining also occurs because a child wants more attention from you. Some mothers find that it takes less time in the long run, and is less wearing, to stop whatever they may be doing and devote a certain amount of time directly to the child. You can then say, with a clear conscience, "Now we played together and now *you* play by yourself"—presenting your child with something specific to do, since many children cannot figure this out for themselves.

Some parents just leave the room when their child whines. (Of course she may follow unless you go into another room and lock the door.) Others try saying, in a calm, friendly way, "I can't hear you when you whine. It hurts my ears. Just talk to me in a nice voice and then I'll see if I can help you."

Or, instead of your leaving the room, you can send the child to her own room to stay either till the timer rings, or till she thinks she can come out and talk in a "normal" voice.

Of course, some children are by nature whinier than others. Some, instead of whining, become very vigorous and get into trouble, either with people or things.

And sometimes whining is a sign that the child does not feel well. If a normally cheerful child all of a sudden becomes whiny, it may indeed be a sign that something is wrong with her health.

Whatever the reason for it, whining is one of the things that annoys parents most and many find that the sooner you can cut into it, the less it gets to be something of a habit that resists all efforts to turn it off.

All of a Sudden Teresa Is Stubborn as a Mule

*M*y three-and-a-half-year-old daughter, Teresa, has become quite a puzzle to me. She is a dear little girl though she has always been rather strong-minded. What puzzles me is that we can be having such a good time together, going along happily at whatever we are doing, when suddenly she turns obstinate and contrary and just sets herself against me.

For instance we'll be having a nice lunch and all of a sudden she absolutely refuses to eat another bite. Or if we're going for a friendly walk, for absolutely no reason that I can make out, she stands stock-still and refuses to take another step.

She is a regular Dr. Jekyll and Mr. Hyde. What causes these sudden shifts in behavior, and what can I do about it?

The behavior you describe could occur at any time during the preschool years, but it does seem especially conspicuous around three and a half. Few of us can penetrate the mind of a child of this age, or fully understand why shadow follows sunshine so frequently and so erratically.

We don't always understand but we can protect ourselves by knowing that this is the way that very young children often act. So instead of trying to make sense of it, we probably do best by recognizing its inevitability and remaining very calm. Ignore stubbornness when you can, as in eating. If Teresa doesn't want to eat any more, or doesn't want to eat some particular food, just skip it. Few children starve themselves to death.

As to that all too frequent refusal to budge another step, sometimes if you shrug and say okay and walk away, the child will finally give up and follow you. If she doesn't, *you* will have to give in and go back and pick her up and carry her—unless you can think of a nice lure, such as some splendid thing you will do when you get home.

If your baby falls down a lot when first learning to walk, you don't feel that he is failing at walking. You just realize that he isn't quite ready to walk securely. And so with other physical immaturities.

Emotional security also has to grow, as with this three-and-a-half-year-old, and it takes its own time. Older children often behave badly, too. But usually their behavior is not quite as baffling as that of the preschooler who goes from compliant to totally noncompliant in the bat of an eyelash.

Children of this age are really very amusing in their mood swings—if you are not in too much of a hurry and their obstinacy is not ruining your day.

At any rate, a very light touch and seeming indifference will make *you* feel more comfortable with Teresa's mood swings. And be encouraged to know that a few months more will bring another whole and different set of problems. Every age has its quirks.

There's Nothing Wrong with
Having an Imaginary Companion

*M*y husband and I are somewhat older parents of an only child, a three-and-a-half-year-old boy named Jonathan. He has been a delight to us and we try to be good parents though sometimes we feel we don't know as much as we should about children.

Only one aspect of his behavior troubles us, and has done so for the past eight months. Though Jonathan has plenty of friends to play with in the neighborhood, he devotes most of his time, and his interest, to a purely imaginary playmate named Tulipka. Tulipka not only takes up vast amounts of his time but she rules our household.

If Tulipka won't go on a walk or auto ride, Jonathan won't go either. If Tulipka doesn't like a certain food, Jonathan won't eat it either. This goes on all day long, every day.

Our friends and our pediatrician give widely differing advice about this strange phenomenon. This varies as follows:

    a. The behavior is normal,

    b. It is a sign that Jonathan is emotionally disturbed since he can't distinguish reality from unreality,

    c. Jonathan plays this way because he is an only child and thus lonely.

Some feel we should permit the behavior (or even encourage it); others say we should stop it. Can you help?

We vote for *a*—that is, we believe the behavior is normal. It is by no means a sign that Jonathan is lonely but rather suggests that he is a highly imaginative and probably intelligent youngster who is clinging, a bit long and hard, to an extremely typical three-and-a-half-year-old kind of behavior. Some of the most superior boys and girls we have known enjoy their imaginary companions.

We can practically guarantee that the behavior will drop out, or most certainly diminish, within the next few months. (Imaginary companions, though more individual and personal, in many respects resemble Santa Claus. When the child is good and ready, he will "know" that beloved Santa Claus is not really real.) In the meantime, take advantage of it while it lasts. If you want him to do something, tell him—quickly, before

Tulipka has a chance to object—that Tulipka does this particular thing very nicely. Or suggest that "You and Tulipka might like to come for a nice walk." Use her as an ally, not an enemy. And don't worry.

Perhaps the whole point of having an imaginary companion is that he or she *is* a figment of the child's imagination but that he seems real to the child. It would be no fun if the child kept in mind all the time that his friend was *only* imaginary. The very young child has the whole world to sort out. For many, it will be a long time before this sorting is completed.

So imaginary companions can be extremely comforting to children, amusing to parents (if you take it that way), and often can be used as good examples whom you can encourage your child to imitate.

Her Four-Year-Old Clings

O *ur four-year-old son, Sammy, has for the last few months been afraid to leave my side. He refuses even to be in another room. It isn't just that he demands that I play with him constantly. He won't even let me shut the bathroom door without his crying. When I do shut the door he waits, a pathetic little lump, just outside. You would think the world would end if he didn't have his eyes on me every minute. I am a prisoner in my own home.*

At night he insists that either my husband or I stay in his room till he falls asleep. No amount of affection or reassurance seems to help.

When asked why he is afraid, he talks about monsters and so forth. Other than Sammy's being so fearful, his behavior seems relatively normal. I have enrolled him in a preschool two afternoons a week. Other than that he sees little of other children.

S ammy sounds like a perfectly normal but somewhat immature little boy. His behavior with you is quite typical of some three-and-a-half-year-olds who develop a super-strong attachment to their mothers. Many won't let her out of their sight, as you say, even to allow her to go to the bathroom.

With most of these children, the more you satisfy the strong need and desire for their mothers, the more quickly they will move on to independence. This independence usually comes as part of the outgoing expansiveness of *four*. Sammy is just a wee bit slow in this department.

You don't say whether you have to stay with him during his time in nursery school. But the mere fact that he will attend preschool suggests that he may be on his way to letting you go. Could you expand the number of weekly sessions to three?

Also, fortunately, it appears that Sammy will accept his father in place of you for prebedtime comfort. It would be a good idea to have Father take over as your substitute sometimes during the daytime. The more you spread your son out away from you, in any direction or to any other person, obviously the better.

Gradually you might be able to introduce a baby-sitter. At first the sitter might have to be there *in addition to you*. But eventually you might be able to go into the house when he is outdoors, for instance, leaving him alone for brief periods with the sitter.

In short, you should accept the fact that his strong demand for your presence is not too unusual and probably should be given in to for the time being. But seize every opportunity or pretext for spreading him out beyond your immediate and constant presence.

Techniques for Handling a Four-Year-Old

I think I have been a pretty good mother, though it has been far from easy. But now that Ronnie is four he is so fresh, so wild, so defiant, it is all I can do to keep my temper with him. If I can't control him now when he is only four, whatever will I do in the years that follow?

He is a sweet little boy but so out-of-bounds. He boasts and brags and lies, and though we are a soft-spoken family, he is even sometimes profane. Any suggestions would be appreciated.

It sounds as though this is your first child. It also sounds as if you may not be too familiar with the typical ways of the four-year-old.

Wildness, though quite naturally a parent doesn't always see it that way, is one of the amusing things about this age. Since wild, exuberant ages tend to alternate with calm, quiet ages, if Ronnie were not wild at four, he might be almost too passive and quiet when the usual calm-down at five arrives.

As to his defiance, it's quite possible that you expect just to give a command and your son will obey you right away. As you have discovered, it doesn't always work that way.

So for wildness, defiance, naughty language, whatever, here are some of the techniques that we have found useful in living with and still managing to love that remarkable little creature—your four-year-old.

One of the best approaches is to keep the child's life full of excitement. Fours love adventures, and fortunately even rather small things seem like adventures to them. Just a walk around the neighborhood can entertain a four-year-old, especially if by good luck there is some building (or tearing down) going on.

When he acts really wild—boasts or swears—just ignore him. It's not much fun to perform without an audience. Or, if you are in a particularly good mood and he tells some ridiculously tall tale, go him one better and tell an even more outlandish story.

Or if he's acting silly, *you* can act silly too. Make up a silly story of your own or read from any one of the beautifully silly books that have been written for four-year-olds, such as *I Want to Paint My Bathroom Blue* by Ruth Kraus.

Since the child of this age does go out of bounds, it's important to establish acceptable physical limits for his activity. Gates and closed doors don't work as well as they did earlier. But fours do respond, often, to verbal limitations: "As far as the corner," "Just up to the fence."

Do your best to avoid head-on collisions. Try to get through the day's routines casually, as if you took it for granted that all would go well, without too much *talk* about what he must or must not do.

However, many children at this age respond very well to the dogmatic statement that "It's the rule that you do so and so." And sometimes you can prime a child in advance, as when visiting somebody you explain to him that he is the *guest* and guests behave in certain (attractive) ways.

Even though your son is already four, you might get to know the way of the four-year-old better than you now do by reading our own book—*Your Four-Year-Old: Wild and Wonderful* by Ames and Ilg.

Sheila Takes Things That Don't Belong to Her

We have moved to a new neighborhood and my four-year-old daughter, Sheila, has made great friends with the little girl next door. Imagine my embarrassment, then, to discover that Sheila has been stealing candy from this little girl's house.

I talked to Sheila very seriously about this and she promised not to do it again, but she did do it again—and again. Now she has come home with some paper stars. She says her friend gave them to her, but the friend says she didn't. I slapped Sheila's hand and really hurt her. Again, the promises came pouring out.

My husband and I are at our wits' end. We can't believe that our daughter is a thief, but apparently she is. Even though it is only candy and paper stars, we can't help but feel that this situation is a dire one. Please advise.

I advise you strongly not to make a big, big issue out of what may be a relatively small thing. You have just moved to a new neighborhood. Sheila may be more upset about the move than you realize.

Admittedly she does have taking ways but this is not too unusual for a child as young as she. We do not think you should call Sheila a thief. This is a very harsh word for a (so far) minor misdemeanor.

As you have found, forcing her to promise not to take things is not getting you anywhere. Your best bet is to keep small, attractive objects out of sight or locked up. If your neighbor can't do the same, and very likely she can't, have Sheila return each thing that she takes. All of this should be done without any atmosphere of moral horror.

Your daughter just needs a little more help in distinguishing between mine and thine. Chances are that when she discovers that taking things not only incurs your displeasure but that she is also going to have to return everything she takes, she may soon give up her taking ways.

Sheila may be old enough for you to plan with her that for any week when she doesn't take something that doesn't belong to her, there will be, at the end of the week, some pretty, desirable reward. A chart kept with a star for each day when nothing is taken could be used to keep her weekly record.

Right through six years of age, many children do take things that don't belong to them. Locking things up, careful supervision, requiring that they return things taken, plus the inevitable moral lectures (you will not be able to restrain yourself entirely from these), are sufficient for most children to help them toward the honesty that most of us so treasure.

What to Do About Those Embarrassing Remarks

What do you do when your children make some terribly embarrassing personal remark about a stranger, in public?

The other day as I got on the bus with my two little boys, aged four and five, they spied a man with crutches and only one leg. Seth piped up, "Oh look! That man broke his leg!" Simon made things worse by shrilling, "He broke it right off!"

I felt terrible, but the best I could do was walk ahead of them as if I hadn't overheard, and as soon as we sat down I started talking to them animatedly about the fact that we were on our way to the beach and what a good time we were going to have. So the man's missing leg was forgotten.

Later on, I did explain to them that it is best not to make personal remarks about people, especially about strangers, and especially in public. But I feel that this advice was rather abstract and have no doubt that some similar incident will happen again.

Since we *do* want our children to be honest and open, it tends to be very difficult to make very young boys and girls understand the fine line between tact and truthfulness. That is, you *do* tell the truth, but many things are better not said in the first place.

Fortunately, most people who have children or who *know* about children do appreciate that almost any young child is liable to say almost anything at any time. Those who do know this, even when their feelings may be a little hurt by some overfrank appraisal—"That lady has a big nose, doesn't she?" or "Why does that man have only one arm?" will not be too surprised. And they will not *blame* either a mother or her children.

Around the age of three and a half to four many children are much bothered by anything that isn't whole, or that appears to be broken. Or even by people who look different from those they are used to. Thus it is not surprising that your sons noticed and commented about the man with only one leg.

You did the best thing possible under the circumstances by appearing to overlook their comments and changing the subject quickly. Scolding your child or children just makes things more conspicuous and embarrassing for those around you. Apologizing to the person who has been commented on also tends to make things worse.

I believe most parents agree that in this kind of situation the less said probably the better.

They Spent Too Long at the Zoo

J ust recently, I took my daughter-in-law and my two little grandchildren, Frank, aged five, and Frannie, three, to the zoo. Admittedly it was rather a long afternoon.

The zoo we visited seemed to have the animals up in their cages, quite a distance from the viewers. So the whole thing may have been somewhat of a disappointment to the children.

Perhaps predictably, it wasn't long before Frank wanted something to eat. Then he wanted a balloon. Both these wishes were granted.

Finally, we got into the car to go home and Frank started fussing for a drink. Well we didn't have anything to drink in the car and his mother told him so.

He went into a real tantrum and after saying several very unpleasant things (which would never have been allowed in my own children) he yelled, "I wish we hadn't gone to the zoo. I hate everybody in this car!"

To my amazement, his mother ignored this whole outburst. Believe me, any child of mine who spoke that way would have gotten a good sound spanking right on the spot. And I told my daughter-in-law so. Don't you think I was right?

W ell, actually, no. Shouting, "I hate you" for a five- or six-year-old is a lot like having a temper tantrum for a preschooler.

Both behaviors tell us things have gone too far and the child is exploding in the only way he or she knows how.

Nobody likes to be told "I hate you" but when it is said by the very young child it usually means little more than "I'm unhappy, sad, mixed up, tired, frustrated and I'm going to take it out on anybody or everybody in sight."

It definitely does not mean, as a rule, "I have thought things over carefully and I really do hate you."

I think your daughter-in-law did right to ignore her son's outburst. The chances are that the whole zoo trip was a little too long and too demanding for a five-year-old, let alone for a three-year-old.

The path of wisdom might be to keep all excursions short and not too frequent.

Interest in Bathroom Behavior Not Too Unusual

L ately my son, David, aged five and a half, who acts young for his age and whom I held out of school for a year, has become fascinated by urination. He makes "pee pee" jokes a lot and laughs about it. Unfortunately several youngsters on our block are allowed to urinate out of doors. One named Jarvis even did this on a little girl. David seemed to think that very amusing.

It is only when with Jarvis that David himself behaves like this. David gets along well in school and likes it. He is an only child and doesn't like babies—even picks on them. He says they break his toys.

David teethed late, walked late, was toilet trained very late. Even now he has not lost any of his baby teeth, but he can read a little and do math. Mostly he is a very good boy, but I worry about him a good deal.

S o far as I can tell from what you say, David does not seem abnormal in his behavior. He does seem young for his age, but fortunately you say you had him start school late.

In many ways he seems more like a four-year-old. Boys of this age tend to be extremely interested in bathrooms—bathrooms themselves, bathroom behavior, bathroom jokes. They often particularly delight in urinating out of doors, and in the presence of other children.

It's too bad your neighbor's boy is permitted to urinate out of doors, but you can still assure your son that in your family this is *not* permitted. This may not stop him entirely, but it definitely should slow him down.

This kind of behavior is rather like sex play. Parents are often much disturbed by it, but it is quite usual and probably does little harm. It is very important for parents to stay calm. Since David gets good reports from school, and much of the time is contented and happy, I would not assume that he is in trouble and would not seek professional help at this time.

If unsuitable behavior continues to take place when your son is with Jarvis, you may eventually have to forbid him to play with the boy. But the likelihood is that time will take care of the problem.

On School-Age Children

Techniques for Handling a Rebellious Six-Year-Old

Help! My six-year-old son, David, has turned into a monster. He used to be such a darling boy, especially last year when he was five. Now nothing goes right and we just yell at each other all day long. He won't do a thing I say—in fact he seems to delight in refusing to do the simplest thing. Now everything is "No, I won't," or "Try and make me."

And he talks so mean to me—even tells me he hates me. The other day he said, "Why don't you get a job? Then you wouldn't be hanging around here all the time, bothering me." That night he apologized. He said, "I really love you and I don't want you to get a job."

Can this behavior be normal? Is it my fault? What can I do about it, if anything?

David, I suspect, is one of those many children who hits all the ages hard. Unfortunately his behavior is highly typical of such children. He was sweet, loving and friendly at five; now he is terrible at six.

The typical five-year-old is fun to be with because to him his parents, especially his mother, are the center of the world. To the typical six-year-old he, himself, is the center. He wants everything for himself, doesn't care about the feelings of others, and to a large extent works against others and especially against his mother. As one mother put it, "I seem to be the center of all his problems." Another once told me, "Every morning I get up and vow that I won't fight with my daughter; but we seldom get past breakfast without a bang-up fight."

So the kind of behavior that David is exhibiting is normal. And even though you seem to be mixed up in it, it is not your fault. Is there anything you can do about it? Yes, there is.

Since in his normally rebellious way, this child will often challenge your suggestions or directives with "No, I won't" or "Try and make me," one must be prepared to meet this challenge. Be calm. Do not rise to the bait. Appreciate that many six-year-olds use up all the defiance they have with their initial refusal. So give him a chance to comply. To begin with, give him several chances. If you ask him to do something and he says he won't do it, remain calm and say, "Well, I guess you're going to need three chances on that one." Most, having expressed their rebelliousness, will obey on the second or third opportunity.

Second, try counting. If your child rebels when you ask him to do something, again remain calm, ignore his refusal, and say, "And let's see if you can do it by the time I count to ten." (Or twenty, or thirty, depending on how strong you consider his resistance.)

Ignore. This is one of your very best bets. You don't have time or strength to punish every disobedience, so now and then, when things don't really matter, just pretend you haven't noticed some misbehavior or disobedience.

Similarly, try sidestepping or changing the subject. Just move on to something else.

Or, if it doesn't offend you to do so, try a little bargaining. Certainly you shouldn't have to bargain for everything, but now and then it does no harm to say that just as soon as he does something you have requested, you will do something nice for him.

Time out is now very in with parents. Don't necessarily give time out as a punishment. Merely point out that he seems cross and tired and suggest that he go to his room for ten minutes (A timer can mark the end of the time-out period).

Above all, try praise and praise and praise and praise. Most any six-year-old will break off right in the middle of quite naughty behavior if you start telling him what a good boy he is and how well he did something or other.

You *can* manage a six-year-old. It just takes vast patience and considerable skill. A very helpful technique is to spend as much time apart as possible. If you can, get a baby-sitter for some afternoons. On weekends, see if your husband will take David out for a little expedition.

The usual six-year-old, for all he may seem so bold and brash and oppositional, actually is a relatively easy person to deal with, much of the time, if only you have a few good tricks up your sleeve.

Rachel Is Not Very Good in Department Stores

I am an inveterate shopper—I just love to shop. My problem is that I have to take my six-year-old daughter, Rachel, along with me since I have nobody to leave her with. And she is terrible in a department store.

She is very quick, so she usually runs ahead of me. Then she grabs things, one by one, from the counters. She can get as many as three or four bracelets on her wrist before I can catch up with her.

Needless to say we attract many nasty looks, and I am embarrassed and don't enjoy my shopping.

I'm afraid that both you and your daughter need a little more discipline. And if Rachel at six behaves as you say she does, it is very clear that your own methods of discipline have been either ineffective or nonexistent.

For the time being it seems clear that you should discipline yourself to cut down on your shopping for pleasure. Shopping that must be done, since for some reason no baby-sitter is available, will probably have to be done in the evening when your husband can take care of Rachel.

Next, you could start preparing your daughter to take part in shopping trips in a normal manner. Even a six-year-old can learn to behave, in a department store or elsewhere, in a manner that doesn't drive everybody up the wall.

You could, at home, play "department store," helping Rachel to practice walking by desirable objects without touching them. (Some mothers of very grabby children suggest that they walk through a store holding their hands behind them.)

Then when you think the time has come, try a very short and simple expedition through a store that's preferably not too cluttered and tempting.

An effort of this sort will be most successful if some reward is offered for success. A child should not have to be rewarded for every bit of good behavior, but when he or she is just starting out on the path of virtue, it helps.

So, a practice visit to a not-too-large store or the offer of some kind of food may help Rachel to success, or near success.

Clearly you are going to have to be much clearer and much firmer in your demands than you have been in the past. But there is no reason to assume that Rachel is hopeless, or that she cannot in time, young as she is, learn to be an acceptable shopping companion.

Donny Is So Self-Centered!

I have a six-year-old grandson, Donny, who is so terribly self-centered, it drives me out of my mind. Up till now he has been a very nice little boy. But now he seems to think of nothing but Donny. He has to be the center of everything, has to win, has to be first, has to have the most of everything. Can this be normal?

Yes it is normal, even though not very nice. Some years ago, Dr. Ilg and I made a list as to who actually was the center of the child's world at different ages. It came out like this:

> 5 years: Mother is the center of his world.
> 6 years: Child himself is the center of his world.
> 7 years: Child is still the center of his world, but he may no longer act this out. He is not competitive or angry.
> 8 years: Child and mother; or child and friend are working out relationships in which both share.
> 9–10 years: The child's friends, or the group in general, are quite as important to him as he is to himself.

Similarly, we have a list of age-changes in the person the child quotes as authorities. At five the child tells you, "My mother says," as if she were the final authority. At six he is apt to say, "My teacher says." By seven he may tell you, "My big brother says." By nine he tells you what his friend says.

Whom does he boast about as the years go by?

> 4 years: Boasts about both parents.
> 5 years: Boasts about mother.
> 7 years: Boasts about older siblings, if any.
> 9 years: May show hero worship of some slightly older friend.
> 10 years: Hero worship of father. Father is "everything" to the usual ten-year-old.
> 12 years: Crush on some adult—scoutmaster, teacher, TV star.

And so as you will see, all these things change with age. My guess is that your grandson will be a lot more acceptable to you in even one more year.

Albert Thinks Somebody Is Always Watching Him

My seven-year-old son, Albert, is so suspicious. He thinks that everybody is against him, everybody is talking about him, everybody is mean to him, nobody likes him. Recently he has expressed a feeling that something is always watching him, wherever he is, whatever he is doing. I asked him whether this was a good feeling or a bad one. He said it was bad.

Albert starts second grade this fall. He has done well in school and has lots of friends. He eats and sleeps well. He is outgoing and verbal and has exhibited no signs of emotional disturbance up to now.

I am concerned about his anxious feelings, but since he eats, sleeps, and plays as usual I am hoping they are really not dangerous or harmful. What do you think about it? Are these common feelings at seven? Does all this have anything to do with his new awareness of God, which has come in lately?

Yes, these feelings that you say your son experiences are, indeed, common at seven years of age. However, Albert, though you say he has shown no earlier signs of emotional disturbance, may nevertheless be a naturally anxious or apprehensive little boy. His suspiciousness is normal at this age. But chances are that his anxiety about being watched could stem from somebody's thoughtless remark. Religious-minded people, in all good faith, often say a great many things that scare small children.

Whether it was you or his father, his schoolteacher, or church teacher, chances are—since you mention his "new awareness of God"—that somebody has made an anxiety-provoking remark. Saying that God is watching us, as some adults do, is intended to give a feeling of security, but quite often it produces the opposite effect.

Most of Albert's life seems to be going nicely, and you will probably be able to develop a more comfortable and less personal notion of the deity in the course of a series of bedtime chats.

But it is true that seven is in many a somewhat suspicious and paranoid age, even under the best of circumstances. Children quite often feel that people are mean to them, don't like them, are talking about them, or even plotting against them. A little supportive talk from you, and added age, may remove at least part of Albert's anxiety.

But for any child there comes a time when we can no longer shrug off a behavior as "just a stage." If Albert's anxiety continues into his eighth year and still bothers him, you would be well advised to check with a child psychologist or clinic.

Today's worry (a child's own worry or even your own worry about your child) is apt to be gone tomorrow. But if the problem persists, get help!

Friend Tells Melissa There Is No Santa Claus

My seven-year-old Melissa came home from school today quite upset. It seems that one of her friends had told her there wasn't any Santa Claus.

Actually I may have been more upset than Melissa, since Santa has always meant so much to her. Now she isn't certain, and I hate to see her filled with doubt.

Of course I knew she wouldn't always believe, but I had counted on this one more year for her. Don't you feel that parents should warn their children not to disillusion younger children about Santa Claus?

Not really. During these years, usually through six, when belief is very strong, a child can seldom be shaken no matter what the other children say.

By seven, many children begin to have doubts on their own, even without outside interference. But if belief is strong enough, it is hard to shake it even then.

We know of one seven-year-old who was told by a friend that there was no Santa. "That's ridiculous," he replied, his faith unshaken, "How could your mother and father buy you all those presents? They couldn't afford it—and when would they have the time to buy them, anyway?"

Or, we know of a little girl of seven who had been grossly overplaced in school, and was in third grade. She told me that most of the kids in her class didn't believe in Santa Claus, that she and her girlfriend were the only ones who did. It didn't matter to her what the other children thought, even though there were twenty-six children in that particular class who did not believe and only two who did.

And my guess is that your Melissa will still put out the milk and cookies on Christmas Eve as she probably has done in the past.

So I don't feel that parents should warn their children not to tell younger children that there is no Santa Claus. They're almost bound to, anyway. It is so exciting (even though sad) to most children when they catch on that Santa really is a myth, that it would be difficult indeed to supervise their conversation to an extent that would prevent them from sharing this discovery. But how about a more general question—Is it right to tell your children the usual lie that there is a Santa Claus? I don't think of it as a lie. Maybe a slight stretching of the literal truth. But as Dr. Gesell used to say, "Generations of children have assimilated, adored, and in time come to deny the concept of Santa Claus without suffering any scars of disillusionment."

What do you do when your child begins to disbelieve and tries to pin you down to whether or not Santa really is real? No problem. You can turn the questions back to him—"What do *you* think?" Or by the time the child is seven or so you can quite easily switch your story from a round, fat Santa to the spirit of Christmas or the spirit of giving.

Now, what if, as is usually the case, your children have so many Christmas wishes you know you're not going to begin to give them everything they want. How do you prevent Christmas day from being a major disappointment?

In most cases, that should not be too difficult. True, some children never seem satisfied no matter what you do. Others are remarkably gratified even with rather minor presents. Like the seven-year-old who was given a box of pencils. "Pencils!" he exclaimed in a tone of delight. And then as he examined them he added rapturously, "With my *name* on them!"

At any rate, it is sensible to encourage your children to make their lists, and then to assure them that of course Santa (or you) can't give them everything they might like but that he (or you) will do the best possible.

Most especially, if something is *big* this year—Cabbage Patch dolls, Pet Rocks, Slinkys—remember that you really do not have to fall for it. But if you do wish to go along with any current fad, say the object costs thirty-five dollars and that is all you have to spend for your child's entire Christmas, you can explain to him or her that that will be all he or she can have. The child may agree at the time and then fuss afterward—but that is the child's problem, not yours.

And lastly, how do you prevent the commercialization of Christmas?

You can't, really. But in your own household you certainly can emphasize the notion that Christmas is a time for unselfish loving and giving. Adults quite reasonably resent the commercialization of Christmas. Children, especially your own, will be more influenced by the emphasis you yourself put on it than by what goes on outside your home.

Clarice Is Her Mother's Shadow

Help! My eight-year-old daughter, Clarice, won't let me breathe. At least not unless she is breathing right there beside me. Up till now she has always been a reasonably independent little girl. Now she haunts me. It's as if she were my shadow.

I love my daughter and I enjoy being with her, talking to her, playing games with her. But not 100 percent of the time. Things are made worse by the fact that I am a working mother and have recently, due to a very unhappy divorce, become a single parent. Clarice is more clinging than ever since the divorce. I suppose she figures that if her dad left her, I might do the same thing.

I feel so guilty when I have to tell my daughter that enough is enough, that I have to go to work, do my housework, even (sometimes) see friends of my own. Do you feel that my divorce has harmed my daughter irreparably

*or do you think she will get over it eventually? And in the meantime what
do I do about her need for my constant company and attention?*

It doesn't necessarily change things for you to know that Clarice is
behaving like a great many other eight-year-olds, many of whose
mothers do not work and whose fathers are still a part of the family.
Eight-year-olds can have any or all of the problems we find at other ages.
But this clinging bit is something so strongly characteristic of the age
that we can assure you that there's a very, very good chance that in
just another few months, with any sort of luck, it will be a thing of the
past.

Believing that it is probably temporary may help you to show that
extra bit of patience that is needed right now. Busy as you undoubtedly
are, do your very best to spend as much time as you possibly can with
your daughter. Since it will never be enough—from her point of view—
we recommend the following. Tell her in advance that you are going to
spend the next half hour playing exclusively with her. And then, barring
some act of God, do just that.

Most children at this age are better satisfied with a big block of time
during which they can enjoy your entire attention, than with longer periods in which you have half a mind on them and the other half on other
activities or the demands of others in the household.

Keep firmly in mind that Clarice is *not* making these extra demands on
your time and attention just because you are a working mother or just
because you are a single parent. At any rate I'm practically willing to bet
that by the time your daughter is nine, she will be much less demanding
of you.

Techniques for Handling an Eight-Year-Old

*I have read and reread all you have written on eight-year-old behavior.
Ours is a textbook case! My particular problem is the defiance—and
what sounds like sheer hatred toward me—every time it is necessary for me*

to correct him, or to forbid something that will either hurt him, or someone else, or someone's property, all of which seems to happen all day long. I often end up with giving in to him, when he shrieks at me about not loving him, or not caring about "what makes him happy." Then I hate myself for not sticking to my convictions.

He is a sensitive child and feels many things very deeply. And he loves his father, thank goodness, and respects his authority. He seems to feel so bitter toward me. Yet he won't let me out of his sight. He spends many Saturdays with his father in the office. This he adores, and is good from morning till night, pleasing his father at every turn.

He is a bright, intelligent child, gentle in so many ways and good at heart. But any refusal that I must give him is always met with a torrent of condemnation of his mother as the "meanest person around, who doesn't care even about what I like . . ." and so on.

Should I just look forward to the better age of nine? Or is there something I can do now to make him feel that the world, and especially his mother, isn't against him?

There are many good things about your son's situation. One of the best, of course, is his excellent relationship with his father. This will do more than anything else to get him through this difficult eight-year-old period.

As you know from your reading, eight-year-olds are quite normally all mixed up with their mothers. The mother-child relationship at this age is one of the strongest, deepest, most demanding and yet most tangled to date. The apparent strength of their occasional seeming hatred for their mother often tends to mark the strength of their dependence on her. Even by nine, most children are a little more ready to let their mothers be and not take everything out on them.

About the best a mother can do is to lovingly adopt a rather hard-boiled attitude toward a boy of this age. Whenever his own behavior will allow it, be as completely understanding as you can. But when he starts "taking things out" on you, let him see, if you can possibly steel yourself to it, that this is not crushing you. It is no fun to take things out on somebody who is not harmed.

Of course, this dual course is hard to steer. Because at the same time that you have to protect yourself against him, he needs to know that you really love him, understand him, sympathize with him. It is a tangle that usually only age solves. But it doesn't help the tangle if you get all mixed up, too.

Have him with his father or otherwise away from home as much as you can manage for the next few months. While you and he are together try to have it be in situations where you can devote pretty nearly 100 percent of your time and attention to him, and try to be doing positive things together.

She Takes Everything Out on Her Mother

I have four children. I find that my relationship with three of them is good but am having a very difficult time with my nine-year-old daughter. She is intelligent and healthy and quite pretty. She does well in school and is evidently well behaved there. She loves pretty clothes and is very choosy about what she will wear, even at home. Her hair, also, is a source of friction. She wants it to be pretty but almost fights me when I have to put it up, wash it, or brush it out. She insists on curls.

But what bothers me most is the way she shouts at me when the slightest thing goes wrong. Everything is my fault. When she can't find something she wants to know where I put it. If she forgets to put her clothes in the laundry and she wants a special pair of socks, it's all my fault, even if she finds them later under her bed. Her room is always in a mess. Her bed is never made until I insist on it (forcefully). She does no chores until I say she has to now—or else.

She is good with her father. He seldom has to scold her, and when he's at home she speaks more respectfully to me. What do you think I have done wrong? I love her just as dearly as the other three. She has nice friends, both girls and boys. I seem to be her only "enemy." Where have I failed her?

There are many little girls like this, especially in the age range between eight and twelve. Your daughter may be a little nicer with you when she is ten. We are almost certain that she will be much worse when she is eleven. This taking everything out on Mother is a most unattractive behavior, common to a great many children, especially growing girls. It is very hard to curb. You can make rules that she not be allowed certain outward expressions of this reaction, but you can hardly curb the reaction itself.

This kind of behavior is not a sign that you have necessarily done anything wrong or that you have failed. The best way that we know of to handle it is by divorcing yourself emotionally from the situation as much as you can. Try if you can to get over feeling that things ought to be better, but be hopeful that eventually you can make them better. Of course you do care; but try to act as if it doesn't matter too much. Be friendly but serene—if you can. This won't change her behavior over-night. But it is less satisfactory to quarrel with someone who won't get into a quarrel with you.

That a child of nine still blames her mother for everything is immature. And in recognizing this immaturity we have sometimes suggested to mothers that they pretend they are someone else—the housekeeper or Mrs. Jones. This sometimes shifts the scene into role-playing and re-lieves the tension. By "becoming" someone else you may be a little less involved yourself and therefore ready to give in on unimportant things. Maybe her hair can be a bit messy at times. Or maybe you could let her room stay messy.

Whatever you do, it may be some comfort to you to know that Boston pediatrician T. Berry Brazelton points out that some mother-child cou-ples just naturally click and others don't. You and this particular daughter may never be as good friends as you and your other three children. Three out of four isn't bad!

Nine-Year-Old Girl Worried About School

I have a nine-and-a-half-year-old daughter who is very self-reliant, bright, normal, lovable, helpful, and an independent little girl. She is very outspoken and expresses herself very clearly. My only problem is that she is very fearful. Every night as I kiss her at bedtime, she tells me she is afraid of school, of science, and especially of arithmetic.

Any new venture she participates in at school she fears and sometimes she even cries—in spite of the fact that all her work is done accurately and neatly. She has received all A's on her report card. I try to impress upon her that her mental attitude is more important than her A's in school.

I also tell her that I was afraid when I was a child, but that conditions will change as she grows older and she will be braver. Hearing this seems to help her some.

She loves poetry and constantly writes it. Here is a poem she wrote yesterday: "Dear Mother and Dad: I am full of fright and fear. Please give me your love and cheer. For you know I love you dears. Please try to take away my fright and fears."

If there is any way that I can help her overcome her fears I would be very grateful.

We can almost see this little girl as we read your letter. We have known others like her. We suspect that she is one of those well-organized little girls who appears to get on well in school, and who puts up such a good front that nobody outside the family knows that she is really troubled.

Often with fourth-grade girls we do get this difficulty in arithmetic. We frequently recommend that the teacher cut down on the amount of math they are required to do. Or at least be sure that she understands the arithmetic process the child is using so that she can straighten things out if they are wrong. Also the teacher should try to stick to reality in math as much as possible and not make the problems too abstract.

This is a good age for you to start explaining your daughter's personality to her. Explain to her that new things are hard for her, and that they always may be to some extent. (The teacher can help, too, by warning her in advance of new things.)

The personality you describe will probably always be your daughter's basic personality pattern. It is most fortunate that she has the outlet of poetry. This can be an organizing medium for her.

Things should be quite a lot better when she is ten, but she will need support, help, and much understanding all along the way. With a child like this it is nearly always helpful to let her know—as you have done—that things were much the same for you when you were a girl, and that you eventually outgrew your own fears. Teenagers are usually quite uninterested in things that happened to their parents when the parents were young, but younger children often like to hear your stories.

Jerome Is Too Young for Fifth Grade

My husband and I would be grateful for any advice you could offer concerning our son and his school progress. Jerome is nine and in fifth grade at parochial school. Since first grade he has had more difficulty in his schoolwork than all our other children combined. The trouble seems to be his reading.

His teacher says his attitude is one of unconcern; that he is happy-go-lucky and seems just as contented with a low mark as a high one. Sister also said she caught him cheating on a test, which surprises us because he seems fair-minded in work and play. He's been sick and out of school a lot.

My husband feels there may be an emotional problem behind his lack of interest and poor schoolwork. The school is small so that classes are doubled. The fifth and sixth grade are in the same room, taught by the same teacher.

We are also surprised by the difference in his behavior at home and at school. At home he is moody and sulky if things don't go his way. At school he seems happy-go-lucky, cheerful and confident. How can we help him?

We don't see how Jerome got into the fifth grade if he's only nine. Even under our present system of pushing children too fast, most are ten by the time they're in the fifth grade, and most would be better off if they were eleven. If you're right about his age, Jerome is miles ahead of himself.

It's probably lucky his attitude is one of unconcern. This may be better than his being worried to death. We're almost certain fifth-grade demands are too much for him if he's only nine.

Cheating in school is often a sign that school demands are too much for a child, not necessarily that he's a cheater.

You say he's been sick and out of school a lot, and that to add to the confusion, there are some sixth-graders in his classroom. This obviously makes matters worse.

It's not unusual for children to show quite different faces at home and at school. We can't always explain why some are angels at home, devils abroad, but we know that's the way things happen.

As you see, we seriously question Jerome's placement in fifth grade— we think he should be only in fourth. Would your school check his performances and then make the adjustment if this is indicated? If not, would you consider putting him in a public school in a lower grade?

We can't say from this distance, of course, but it's hard for us to imagine a nine-year-old ready to do fifth-grade work in either public or parochial school.

Robert's Temper Is a Horrible Problem

E *ver since birth, my nine-year-old son, Robert, who was a very colicky baby and then had problems with vomiting, has had a terrible temper. He even killed his dog with a trowel when he was a preschooler. He disrupts Sunday school, behaves badly in regular school. A good stiff beating seems to be the only thing that will calm him down.*

One of his biggest troubles is his total inability to take the blame for anything he has done, ever. If he can't blame his troubles on somebody else, even when he is obviously the one at fault, he ends up telling me, "I hate you and you hate me." He is breaking my heart for I love him so much. Yet I am deathly afraid that I'll maim him or that he will maim somebody else.

My husband and my parents refuse to recognize the fact that he is developing into a definitely disturbed individual or that he needs professional help. And I don't know where to get it even if they would permit.

Y ou mention in your letter that Robert had terrible colic in the early months of his life and once the colic was over, excessive vomiting. We are beginning to relate these early extreme feeding difficulties to poor emotional organization. Later on many of these children need protection from their own emotions, just as early they needed special feeding formulas.

Since Robert is having so much trouble in school, some special plan must be worked out with the school. Try for instance to have him out of school one day a week, maybe Wednesdays, and to devote a lot of time to him on that day. Explain to him that this will help him be better in school on the other days. Then arrange with the school that as soon as trouble occurs, you should be sent for to take him home. Explain to him that this means he isn't ready for school full time. Children like your son need to know that school attendance is a privilege to be earned. Sometimes a pep talk before they go to school, repeated each morning, will improve their school behavior.

How much time do you really spend with him alone? Is he a boy who likes cooking? Could he help you make breakfast instead of fighting with his brothers and sisters? Do you have a chatting time with him before he goes to bed at night?

Robert is obviously the kind of boy who needs a very firm hand. We can understand why you were driven to spanking him, even though we're sure you realize that spanking provides no real solution. In general these boys (and we have known many) are at their worst in the preschool years; pretty bad from five to ten; and then if they don't go off the track entirely (and some do) easier after ten.

However, we suspect that this is not a problem you can, or should, be expected to solve all by yourself. You need help from a specialist. The big question is, what kind of specialist. We would try to find a skilled physician who practices what is called orthomolecular medicine. Such doctors have found that difficult and out-of-bounds behavior, such as Robert exhibits, may frequently be the result of something the child is eating, drinking, or inhaling to which he is allergic. Or, conversely, he may *not* be getting some food, vitamin, mineral that he needs. Much uncomfortable behavior (uncomfortable both for the child who exhibits it and for those around him) may be due to one or both of these causes.

Though not all doctors agree with this approach, it is one we ourselves practice, and it can be very effective. So try to find such a physician.

On First, Middle, Youngest, and Only Children

Advantages of Being an Only

*M*y husband and I are among the many parents who, happy with just one child, are being pestered and badgered not only by family but by friends to have another. We figure it is nobody's business but our own. However, all these people tell us such horrendous tales of spoiled only children, and insist that we are harming our daughter by bringing her up as an only, that we are almost on the verge of weakening.

We've heard that you think it is okay to bring up an only child. Can you give us some support?

I can indeed. I can assure you that it is okay with me if you stop at one. It would be wrong, in my opinion, to have a second child whom you don't really want, just in order to prevent you from doing some unspecified and largely imagined harm to the one you already have.

First of all, an only child is spared the pleasures but also the agonies of sibling rivalry. He or she does not need to use up a great deal of emotional energy in competing for a parent's love and attention, because there is nobody to compete with.

Also, there is nobody for his parents to compare him with. He does not have to listen to "Why can't you be more like your sister?"

He has privacy for himself and for his possessions. There is nobody to get into and disturb his "things."

His parents can usually give him more material things than they could if he were one of several. But more important than material advantages, his parents can give him more of themselves. And whereas they might not be able, or willing, to take several children along when they go on outings, they often are comfortable with taking along one. Thus in general he may be more experiences and adventures than he otherwise would.

As one only child reportedly remarked with pleasure, "It was so great because they let me be a part of them. I never felt left out!"

As to disadvantages and the fear that you are spoiling your only child, a parent, if discipline is weak, could spoil more than one child quite as easily as he or she could an only one.

However, we can give a few warnings. The main one is to be certain not to live through your child. Don't let his successes and/or failures, the reports he gets from school, his athletic accomplishments, mean too much to you.

Always remember, no matter how much you include him, that he is the child and you are the adults. As much as you may share with him, allow him to lead a life of his own. In fact, as he grows older and, as any child normally will, turns away from you to some extent and toward his friends, grant him this freedom.

And while he is still young, allow him to be a child. Just because he may spend quite a bit of his time with adults, don't treat him as if he were an adult. Lead your own lives, too, all the way along. Then it will not be too hard for you to let him go when the time comes.

How to Be a Good Parent to Your First, Second, and Third Child

If, as you seem to believe, a child's position in his family (oldest, middle, youngest) influences his personality and behavior, what can you suggest to us parents that we should keep in mind in parenting these three different children. Presumably if they are quite different, we should approach each one in a different way.

Right you are. First, let's look at the characteristics these three kinds of children are thought to have. Oldest children are considered capable, strong-willed, and achievement-oriented, and to have a strong sense of responsibility—they want to do things right.

Seconds are less highly driven toward accomplishment and often seem more spontaneous and easygoing, more tactful, more adaptable, more relaxed. They compete in indirect ways and may even be a little tricky or sneaky.

Thirds tend to be more passive, more accepting of domination, more babyish, less driven toward accomplishment, more dependent and, often, easier to get along with.

Keeping all this in mind (if it fits with what you yourself have observed of your children), here's how you apply it.

For the oldest: Try not to be too stern, demanding, and authoritative lest he or she later on adopt that role with others. Help him not to be too bossy and domineering. Forgive his lapses from perfection. Help him relax so that he will not overdo the "good, responsible child" role. He will demand quite enough of himself without your adding to that demand. Now and then baby him as you baby your youngest.

For the middle: Be sure that your middle child does not get lost in the shuffle. Occasionally single him out for special attention, but do not worry unduly because he is a middle child. That is, try not to feel that "middleness" is a special problem.

Be sure that your middle does not spend so much time adapting to the needs of others that he never gets a chance to be himself.

For the youngest: Don't let your older children treat the youngest as if he or she were a toy. Try to avoid letting them tease him, even though this may ostensibly be done good-naturedly.

Discourage his efforts to control by complaining and tattling. Help him learn to give as well as to receive.

And do what you can to encourage him to behave in increasingly mature, responsible ways. Try at times to give him some of the responsibility you give your oldest.

Last of all, if your oldest expresses jealousy of the younger one, point out to him the privileges and responsibilities that age and competence bring. Then ask him if he would like to switch roles. Any such "experiment" is likely to be very short-lived, as the older child rather quickly appreciates the disadvantages of being treated as though he were younger.

Is Middleness Really a Disadvantage?

*W*hoever started that myth of the middle child anyway? So many speak
of middleness as if it were some sort of handicap. I consider that for
my own middle child, Jason, aged five, being the middle one in the family
has many advantages. Being two years younger than his older brother, he
was at home all the time for two years while the older boy was in school. So
he had all that extra attention and care.

*My older boy Sammy is always complaining about having so many re-
sponsibilities: "Do I always have to do these things? Can't he do anything
for himself?" I think if Sammy had the choice, he might indeed prefer to be
the middle one.*

*Also, don't forget, each child is an individual and whereas some children
might feel squelched to be in the middle, others enjoy this relatively incon-
spicuous position.*

I agree. Each child is indeed an individual and different children do react
differently to each family position. Many do enjoy being in the middle;
others feel deprived.

The general picture on middleness that many child specialists offer is
that they seem less often than the firstborn to be highly successful and
seem to have somewhat less of a need to achieve. They do not seem to
need to hold a certain role of dominance in relation to others to be
happy.

In general they are found to be less dominant, more patient, more
emotionally responsive. Middle children seem often able to balance opposing forces. They are frequently gregarious and friendly and get on
well with others, especially with the opposite sex (some say). In fact,
some people consider them to be good matrimonial risks since they tend
to be both adaptable and sharing.

In a work situation, middle children tend to be tactful, though they are
often not interested in being leaders or in assuming positions of great
responsibility.

Some do find middle children a little sly, as if they have had to learn to
play both ends against the middle and to attain their goals by stealth
rather than by dominating (as do firstborns) or by depending on others
(as do the very youngest).

So, we agree with the implication of your letter. The myth of "middle-ness" as if it were some sort of disease or handicap has probably been greatly exaggerated.

On Twins

Dos and Don'ts for Parents of Twins

One of the most useful pamphlets available is called *And Then There Were Two—A Handbook for Mothers and Fathers of Twins* by The Twin Mothers Club of Bergen County, New Jersey.

This pamphlet offers the following general Dos and Don'ts.

• DON'T group your twins together, in conversation or in your own thinking, as "the Twins." Do treat them as individuals.

• DON'T compare performance. Do realize that each twin, even when they are identical, has his own special abilities and interests.

• DON'T expect twins to share everything. Do see to it that each has some personal possessions of his own.

• DON'T feel that you must dress them alike, though it probably does no harm in the very early years.

• DO try to encourage each child to develop special talents and interests on his own. Don't feel that everything they do must be a duet.

• DON'T punish both when you're sure only one was to blame. Do try to see the humor in some of their naughtiness, and you'll be punishing them less often.

• DO, especially when they are young, try to sandwich in sleep for yourself whenever and wherever you can. Don't be constantly tired and irritable.

• DO let your twins enjoy the close relationship with each other but don't let their closeness reach a point where one feels lost without the other.

- If one twin seems to need special attention, *do* give it to him, but *don't* take it for granted that it will be plain sailing for the other indefinitely. Sometimes it may be one, sometimes it may be the other, who needs the special attention.

- DON'T skip companionship with your twins because there is so little time. Playing with them is just as important as getting through the daily routines.

One of the best books I know of about twins is *The Psychology of Twins: A Practical Handbook for Parents* by Dr. Herbert L. Collier. However, in general, there is remarkably little good advice available in book form for the parents of twins. Your best bet probably is to join a parents-of-twins group if you are lucky enough to have one in your community.

Should You Name Twins Alike?

I'm expecting a baby, or actually babies, next month and that is the problem. Like most parents-to-be, my husband and I talk a lot about their names. I like the idea of matching names—John and June, Donald and Dennis, or Sue and Sharon as the case may be. But my husband thinks that the names should be as different as possible in order to help the children preserve their identities.

Also, and I suppose this is really part of the same question, should I dress them alike? And when the time comes—I realize it is rather far in the future—for them to start school, should they be in the same classroom or in separate rooms?

It's always a temptation to name twins alike, and if you and your husband both wanted to do so, it's your privilege. But I have to admit that perhaps the majority of child specialists tend to agree with your husband that it may be best to give them different-sounding names.

Also most everybody seems to feel that it is important for twins to grow up as separate individuals, even though much of the time they may be very close to each other. Matching or very similar names obviously stress their similarity; quite different names help people to remember that they are separate people.

The same goes for clothes. Twins look so nice, to many older people, when they are dressed alike. And certainly an occasional similar outfit is not going to warp their personalities. But again, most people nowadays seem to feel that being dressed differently does help the children themselves, and others, to see them as individuals.

Some people suggest, though, that as they grow older, if they prefer to dress alike, they should be permitted to do so, but perhaps be encouraged at least to wear different colors.

Actually, neither names nor clothes (alike or different) are as important as the family attitude toward the children. You could dress or name them alike but still treat them as individuals. You could dress them differently but still treat them as a pair.

As to school, if they seem mature for their age and nicely independent, it might be just as well to have them in different rooms right from the start. This is especially true of fraternal twins who may have quite different academic abilities and who should definitely *not* be compared with each other.

In fact, here is a very special warning. It may be, especially if one twin is a girl and the other a boy, that the girl may be ready for kindergarten before the boy is. This will be a hard thing to put across, but keep in mind—every child should be placed in school where he or she belongs, not just in relationship to where some other child in the family is placed. If you are fortunate that the two *are* of different sexes, it may help to explain to your son that young girls do grow up a little faster than young boys and it by no means implies that one is better or smarter than the other.

At any rate, if twins are especially immature, or shy, or extremely dependent on each other (but at approximately the same level of maturity) it may be best to start them off together and separate them only in second grade. Whether twins stand out as individuals or cling pretty close as a twosome may finally depend as much on *their own* temperaments as on the way you as parents treat them.

Bigger Twin Beats Up on His Brother

*M*y problem is my one-year-old twins. One of them, Alden, seems almost twice as big as his brother (well maybe a slight exaggeration, but he is big). From the beginning, he would grab his bottle away from him, and now he is very rough and frightens him.

The result is that the little one, Peter, seems scared to death. He cries a lot and clings to me almost all the time—just hangs onto my legs. He can't walk yet, but he can hang on to me and pull himself up. It is hard for me to get my work done with him clinging and crying so. Yet I hate to reject him for fear he will be more unhappy than ever. What do I do?

Your problem is a very difficult one. It is not unusual for a larger and older sibling to be very cruel and aggressive to younger ones, but often as time goes on, school separates them when the older one starts sooner.

Unfortunately poor little Peter is really stuck with Alden, and you'll be lucky if one day actual physical harm does not result. For the time being, just for another month or two, I would allow Peter the comfort of clinging to you, even if it does slow up your housework. In fact for some of the time you might forget the housework and concentrate on doing positive, and fun, things with Peter.

However, do what you can to stagger their schedules. Or at least have them nap in different rooms. If you can afford a baby-sitter, have him or her take Alden out of the house and leave Peter with you. Give him all the time away from his brother that you can manage.

In another month or two, Peter will probably be walking. This will help him to feel secure and by then you really will have to begin to detach yourself, physically. Just unglue him and move on about your work, but let him stay in the room if he wishes. If you ignore his crying and complaining, it should eventually lessen.

When that lovely time comes that the twins are old enough for nursery school, you might try to have them go to different schools, even though this would double your transportation problem. Or if you should be lucky enough to find a school that permits every-other-day attendance, perhaps they could go on different days. Or perhaps, especially if Alden is so big, he may also be more mature than Peter, the school would just put them in different groups.

When Alden is old enough to respond to things you say and to have conversations with you, you may to some extent be able to help him not to be so aggressive with Peter. Also you and your husband both can begin to use the kind of discipline that is appropriate for preschoolers though not as appropriate for babies, and help Alden realize that bad, aggressive behavior brings punishment or deprivation of privileges.

On Personality

Daughter Was Easy but Son Is Hard

We have a girl of three and a boy of just eighteen months. Our daughter, Marilyn, is a sunny, sweet, adorable, cooperative child. However our son, Tabor, is completely different.

At six months he was operated on for pyloric stenosis and while we have been assured that the constant vomiting would not affect his temperament, I can't help wondering if it did. Temperamentally he is just the opposite of his sister. He is stubborn, uncooperative, easily frustrated. Even a little dog that plays with him and then goes away causes him to cry.

That is the big problem now—he cries almost all day. My time is arranged so that each child is alone with me part of the day and they also have a loving, devoted, calm, and patient father who takes over when he is at home.

Each day with Tabor is a difficult thing for me. He cries when his toys annoy him; he cries if I leave him even for a minute. He cannot accept any frustration, and everything frustrates him.

Having been so spoiled by my lovable daughter, I am at a loss as to how to handle this stubborn, difficult little boy.

Tabor's illness did not help, but his early vomiting was probably more a part of a personality pattern than a cause of it.

One of our own books, *Infant and Child in the Culture of Today,* by Gesell, Ilg, and Ames, might help you understand the different stages your son will go through—and especially his present stage.

You will need to be very clever about simplifying his environment so that he can handle things without so much frustration. Have you tried feeding him in a lower chair? If he throws his food, this will cut it down.

Does he have his own room and a place in other rooms for special possessions? Do you take him on walking excursions? Boys like Tabor are often easier to manage out of doors. Give him a chance to climb steps, for instance.

Sometimes a sitter does better with these boys than does their own mother. Try a high-school-boy sitter, afternoons. And since he had so much vomiting in infancy, be very careful about his diet. Allergy to certain foods may be causing part of his irritability.

Your son's personality will not change markedly, so you need to analyze each day to find out the danger points and what could be relief points. Of course at present it may seem that every point is a danger point, but gradually the islands of safety will increase.

Why Are Boys So Noisy?

Why are boys so noisy? So active and so loud? I look with envy at my friends who have only girls. I love my three little boys, but our house is so full of sound and action. You seldom see girls wrestling and rough-housing, yet this goes on all day with us. And then somebody always gets hurt. And howls. I must say it does get very tiresome.

The answer is very simple if one believes in the biology of behavior. Boys, on the average, have more mesomorphy (heavy muscle) than do girls. And the more mesomorphy, the more noise and action. So if you have a strong-looking, muscular boy, the chances are that he will be loud and noisy and seldom still. (In your case multiply this by three.)

This doesn't mean that girls have no mesomorphy at all. In fact, it would be possible to find a girl who was more mesomorphic than one of her brothers. But on the average boys are more muscular, and thus more active and more noisy. As another mother of three once commented, "You can hear the decibel level rise when the boys come home from school."

Some Children Are Just Naturally Difficult

You'll think I am a terrible mother, but there are times when I could literally kill my oldest son, Anthony. Tony, now four, has been a difficult individual almost from the moment he was born. (In fact, my pregnancy itself was no picnic.) I thought we would never get his sleep and feeding schedule straightened out when he was a baby. Toilet training was also very hard.

He is so precise, so persnickety, so demanding that other people do things just so. Yet, at the opposite extreme, he is very temperamental and much given to striking out. Taking him to a new place, in fact taking him anywhere in public, is a nightmare. I am always in hot water with the neighbors over him; and his nursery-school teachers also have complained a very great deal.

It seems as if I am always picking on the poor child. I don't mean to, but he does so many things wrong. Sometimes it's almost more than I can stand. Fortunately, he started kindergarten this year so he is out of the house part of the day. But all too soon, home he comes and the battle begins again. Help!

Unfortunately, there are all too many children like Tony—difficult from the word go. But it is only fairly recently that psychologists and pediatricians have started speaking as if this were an identifiable personality type—"the difficult child." Among the characteristics of this type of child are irregularity in biological functions such as sleep-wake cycles; having negative reactions to new situations; and accepting any change slowly. The child with such a temperament is at high risk for developing serious personality problems, though not all do so. Our recommendations have always been: don't blame yourself for your reaction to a child like this, and get away from him as much as you can. Arrange for baby-sitters. Arrange for him to play at other people's houses (if they will agree). Arrange for him to visit any willing relatives.

Child specialists recommend a quiet, patient, but consistent parental approach to the child's intense negative reactions. The child should be exposed to new situations, but only one or two at a time and the parents might as well anticipate an intense negative reaction to begin with. So don't push for a quick acceptance, but, if the situation is one that the child needs to meet, try again, and again.

Such children tend to be highly destructive and also highly sensitive. They are the ones who complain about their clothes because they are too tight or are uncomfortable. Girls of this temperament often have a terrible time with their hair—their braids are too tight or hurt them in some other way.

Children like this, of course, should not be allowed to rule the household. Parents do need to make reasonable demands and to stick to them, but they must also anticipate that often things will go far from smoothly. Appeasing such a child can be disastrous, but showing great patience *is* necessary.

And, while Tony is at home, do everything you possibly can to focus on and emphasize his good behaviors rather than his bad. Your basic impression and feeling may be that Tony is *never* good. But, if you should take the pains to chart his behaviors, you would actually find that a lot of the time he may be behaving in a quite acceptable manner.

Say that hitting out (at you, his brother, or his friends) is the thing that bothers you most; instead of merely jumping at him, or punishing him whenever this happens, concentrate on the times when he is *not* hitting anybody.

If at his worst he hits out nearly every hour (and it is probably less often that this) make a nice big chart divided off into fifteen-minute intervals. Then, for every fifteen minutes when he doesn't hit, make a mark. Call his attention to what you are doing, and praise him for every mark you make. When he achieves a certain number, plan that there will be some minor reward.

That is, focus on the positive and not on the negative. It won't change your son overnight, but it may make him just a tiny bit easier to live with.

Do Lefties Have More Trouble?

My husband and I are the parents of five children. Our middle child, Scott, now seven years of age, is the only one who is left-handed, and, so far, the only one who gives us substantial trouble. You name it and Scott has had it. Life just seems a whole lot harder for him than for the others.

Is there any scientific evidence to bear out the old wives' tale that left-handed children in general do have a harder time with life than right-handers?

There seems to be. Psychologist Theodor Blau, who studied more than five hundred left-handers between the ages of four and seventeen, notes that more than the expected number of children whom he saw in a private outpatient clinic were left-handed. While an estimated 6 to 11 percent of the general population is left-handed, nearly sixteen percent of Blau's patients were.

His findings, in brief, were as follows.

Left-handed children are more likely to have significant physical problems and behavioral difficulties during the first five years of life than are right-handed children.

They are more likely to have preschool adjustment problems and first-grade behavioral and achievement problems.

Their intellectual performance is likely to be more variable.

They are more likely to show performance below the anticipated potential.

They have a tendency to prefer swimming under water more than do right-handed children. (Now, that is an odd observation!)

They are more likely to exhibit socially unacceptable behavioral traits.

They are more likely to show symptoms of poor sleep, headaches, and dizziness.

But, happily, they *are* more likely to be imaginative and creative.

Thus Blau's research conclusions fit in with what many people have always thought about left-handed children. It is very customary to believe that they tend to be especially imaginative and creative.

There isn't too much you can do about all this. At least you can't, and shouldn't try to, change your son's "handedness." But knowing that he may indeed be supervulnerable will I hope encourage you to give him that extra attention and extra protection he seems to need.

Jasper Lacks Self-Confidence

*M*y *eight-year-old son, Jasper, seems entirely lacking in confidence. Whenever anything new comes up he thinks he can't do it. He thinks people don't like him. He just has no zip. Do you have any suggestions for helping a very insecure little boy to feel a higher self-esteem?*

Y ou have described a typical seven-year-old, so one can hope that just possibly Jasper is merely a little young for his age. That would be your best hope because if that should be the case, added age will improve things. However, unfortunately, there are all too many girls and boys of any age who are just like your son.

There are two somewhat conflicting opinions among child specialists as to where the child's sense of worth comes from. Some, like me, have observed that there can be big differences, from infancy and the pre-school years on. Some children at any age just seem to live on top of the world—sure and secure. Others, often with greater actual advantages and attributes, just don't seem to think very much of themselves.

But not everybody agrees with this interpretation. Some believe that a child's self-esteem, or sense of worth, depends almost entirely on how he is treated, especially by his parents. And certainly regardless of how secure or insecure a child is by nature, his parents' treatment of him does make a big difference.

We agree heartily with the following good rules offered by Earl Grollman and Gerri Sweder for things you might especially try with a child who seems to lack self-esteem. (Possibly you are doing many of them already.)

Act in a loving, caring manner, even when you are disappointed in your child.

Create an emotionally supportive household environment.

Voice pleasure at just being your child's parent.

Tell your children that they are special and cherished.

Show acceptance for their limitations as well as their strengths.

Offer praise freely but sincerely.

Treat every child with respect.

Express confidence in every child's abilities.

As Grollman and Sweder point out, when you take the time to express confidence in their abilities, you create an atmosphere in which young-sters are encouraged to value their own achievements. They feel espe-cially good when you compliment them on daily homework efforts. Such simple statements as "You've really worked hard tonight," or "That looked like a difficult math assignment you just finished," or "Your history paper shows a lot of thought," carry a powerful message. Your children want to please you and fulfill your expectations. If you tell them how proud you are of their performance, usually they try even harder.

As one little girl reported, "My mom and dad always tell me how proud they are of me and the work I do for school. They make me think I can do most anything."

Our own suggestion for developing self-confidence in any child is to do your best to see that he is put into situations where he can succeed. He may not always believe your words of praise, but real success, in school or in social situations, speaks for itself.

James Has No Drive

My husband and I have three seemingly quite normal children, and then we have James. James is now ten years old and he has not one bit of oomph. No zip. No get-up-and-go. What he really likes to do best is sit in front of the television set and even this he does in a sort of apathetic way.

Even when we take him on family weekends, boating, skiing, he sort of flops around. I don't mean that he is totally uncoordinated, just that he shows no drive. I don't think he is really an unhappy boy but we would like for once to see a normal display of energy.

Apathetic behavior is always trying for a parent. We assume that you have already tried the usual things: good diet, plenty of sleep, pro-viding the kinds of situations in which he can succeed. We also trust that you have checked with a capable physician to discount the possibility that there is some correctable physical cause (minimal allergy or some such) behind James's lack of energy.

If you haven't done all these things, you should. But the chances are great, since this apathy has lasted so long, that your son is just one of the many children who does not have a great deal of drive or energy. Some children, and some adults, all their lives have and display tremendous amounts of energy. Others have only a modest amount, and some seem to have only the minimum.

If energy output varies, at least you have a chance, because you can note those situations, or conditions, when it comes up to your expectations. But if your child almost never shows what seems to you like normal energy output, you may have to accept the fact that this is a basic personality characteristic. And then try to encourage him toward activities that can be accomplished by a low-drive individual who, alas, is also often very slow moving.

Family weekends may not really be the thing for James. Could you make some other arrangement for him while the rest of your family skis and boats? Is it possible that your son may have abilities, or at least potentials, that you have overlooked, or that haven't had a chance to express themselves? Sometimes young people who are not physically active show considerable intellectual or creative ability, if you can steer them in these directions. Sometimes it is the very quiet ones who later on do so well as writers, in the theater, or in other creative fields.

Could you try to stop thinking of your son in a negative way and begin to find some area where success is possible without a great expenditure of physical energy?

Is Violence Inherited?

Do you think that violence is inherited? I have a very violent husband. His father, too, was violent. And now our son shows every evidence of carrying on this family trait.

I won't go into details—you have probably heard it all. But this child, though only two years of age, absolutely tyrannizes our household. He bellows with rage at the slightest frustration. His ability to wait is nonexistent. His temper tantrums are so long and loud that he often causes himself to have nosebleeds, let alone large bumps on his forehead from hitting his head on the floor.

Our pediatrician takes all this very lightly and says that's the way boys are. Should we, and can we, do something about our very violent son?

It is our impression that a tendency toward violent behavior *is* inherited. One sees it perhaps most in extremely mesomorphic (well-muscled) masculine boys, but a child of any physique could be violent.

It often does seem to run in families, and we see it more in boys than in girls. We *do* recommend that you start now and make every attempt to help your boy overcome or contain his rage.

Mothers of such boys who, like you, have violent husbands often hope that by good handling they *can* help their sons to be more comfortable with themselves and less violent than their fathers. Sometimes they have success. Sometimes not.

In the preschool years, the most you can usually do is to try to plan your child's life so that he is frustrated as little as possible. This may indeed mean giving in a lot more than you would like to.

Soon he may be old enough that your own doctor (or a different doctor, if your own takes all of this too lightly) may be willing to prescribe medication to calm things down. I hope that whichever doctor you seek will also be willing to give you practical suggestions for ways in which diet control can help to calm down rages. Something as simple as a taste of sugar can induce overactive or violent behavior in some children.

If you are lucky enough to have a good child-guidance clinic in your town, you should consult there by the time your boy is three or four. You are going to need every bit of support you can get (and then some) in controlling your son's rages and in helping him, as he grows older, to control himself. It is a hard job, but the important thing is to accept the seriousness of your problem, and not waste time in hoping vainly that time will change things. Because the chances are, it won't.

Shy Children May Be Born That Way

My youngest son, Alex, is so terribly shy that it worries his father and me. He is very awkward around other children and if, for instance, he goes to a birthday party he doesn't take part in the games. He never speaks up for himself. We have done all we can to get him to put himself forward, but to no avail. Do you have any suggestions?

Most parents, except possibly those who are extremely shy themselves, are more comfortable if their children are outgoing and friendly, if they speak up, if they join groups easily and make themselves heard. They tend to feel that there is something the matter if the child is quiet and shy.

Yet our own studies and current research by Jerome Kagan of Harvard, as well as common sense, tell us that some children will be shy, and some outgoing. According to Kagan, there is a biological contribution to shyness—that is, some children are just born to be shy. He feels, as we do, that the environment can alter the degree of inhibition, but it can't change basic personality.

Thus parents of shy children should try to help them feel comfortable, and perhaps more secure, by putting them in situations they hope will not be overwhelming. Or they should encourage them in fields in which they are good—athletics, music, or whatever their particular talent—and then compliment them on successes.

Keep in mind that the shy nursery-school child who does not join readily in the games but watches the others, taking in things with his eyes even though he does not participate vigorously, may enjoy school quite as much as the joiner.

At any rate, Kagan tells us that the "inborn temperamental differences in children may be the result of neural circuitry that makes them more reactive to stress." Among the shy children he has studied, an unfamiliar person or a mild intellectual challenge such as a memory task actually produces a rise in the child's heart rate, dilation of pupils, and tension in the vocal cords.

So we believe that there is a biological basis for shyness, and that the quiet child may be just as satisfactory a person, and may have just as good a life, as the one who is outgoing and bold.

Don't forget, the main things *not* to do are to nag at your child for being shy, insist that he speak up, ask him if he doesn't have anything to say, tell other people in his presence that he is terribly shy and you just don't know what to do about it.

Stay away from the topic as a topic. Just do things that will make him feel more comfortable, if you can. And try to enjoy him for what he is, a naturally quiet and not terribly outgoing individual.

Nobody Likes Billy

A very hurtful thing has occurred in our family. Our only son, Billy, nearly eight, is not popular. Though one of the oldest in first grade he is one of the least mature, and by far one of the poorest students. The other children don't play with him much, either at school or after school.

He does fairly well with very young children, especially girls, and a few boys. But in an effort to help him find boys of more or less his own age to play with, I recently encouraged him to phone and invite one of his class-mates over, a boy named Steve. This boy came over and they had a good time. Billy and I were both delighted. Imagine my shock, surprise, and disappointment, when next day Steven's mother phoned and said she didn't see why her son, who was very popular and had plenty of friends, had to be the one to come and play with Billy, just because nobody liked Billy.

You can imagine how that made me feel. I'm afraid I won't have the courage to try again to help Billy make friends. But what do I do now?

First of all, don't give up. Steven's mother is, if you report her conversation correctly, a rat of the first order. Chances of running into another mother like her are one in a thousand.

Mothers of popular children are, of course, not actually responsible for the unpopular children, but most will show compassion. I would try again. But not too hard.

Most any mother of a seven-year-old boy would prefer that he play with some boys, and not just with little girls. But, for the time being your Billy may be most comfortable in this kind of play situation.

Sometimes a concerned father can plan some kind of outdoor party or outing to which quite a few boys could be invited. But parents can do only so much.

Boys like your son tend to do better socially when they are a little older, and tend to do best in supervised groups, such as in the Cub Scouts or at the Y, where activities are programmed, an adult is in charge, and when the not very social child is at less of a disadvantage than in the freer group situations.

Some children are very slow about coming into their own socially, but most do make it, more or less, eventually.

Child Rejected Because He Is in Trouble

My problem is our nine-year-old son, Thad. The other children don't like him. We have had terrible luck in this respect. In fact, we even went so far as to move because the children in our former neighborhood and at his former school were so unfriendly.

To our dismay, they are just as bad here. He almost never is able to make a friend and even when he does the friendship never lasts.

Needless to say, all this rejection is having a terrible effect on Thad's personality. He has just about given up. My husband and I do all we can to help him feel that he is loved and valued, at least by us, but this makes little impact in view of the obvious fact that he is vastly unpopular.

Perhaps only a few very fortunate children have as many and as "suitable" friends as their parents might wish. But from everything you say, your boy is one of the truly rejected.

You feel, and quite realistically, that this presents a sad and serious practical problem, and that if the other children would just play with your boy he would be all right.

I'm sorry to tell you—and this won't cheer you up very much—that children like your son are not primarily in trouble because they are rejected. *They are rejected because they are in trouble.*

Children, as I suppose you know, are quite naturally cruel. Unless discouraged from doing so by parents and/or teachers, all but the really nicest tend to pick on, reject, or neglect the child who is in trouble in almost any respect. It is as if they fear that difficulties are catching.

So perhaps the most important thing you can do for Thad is to try to find out what it is about him that the others don't like, and then help him to change it. Sometimes you can do this yourselves, by looking at your child *very* objectively and trying to figure out where his difficulty lies. Sometimes you may need the help of a specialist to make this discovery.

The problem may be as simple as that he is overplaced in school and the other children recognize and resent his relative babyishness. It may lie much deeper and be far more complex.

It is extremely important for all concerned to appreciate that some boys and girls will never be wildly popular. But every child needs *some* friends. Recognizing that part of your son's problem may lie in himself and not just in other people could be your first step toward helping him.

How to Deal with a Lonely Child

The lonely child cannot easily pick up the communication skills that come naturally to many of us. He may, indeed, need to be taught many things that more popular boys and girls seem to know instinctively. Here are some suggestions for parents of an unpopular girl or boy from Ernest, Rita, and Paul Siegel's practical and sympathetic book, *Help for the Lonely Child: Strengthening Social Perception.*

According to the Siegels, people communicate in two ways. One is through words. The other is through nonverbal communication. When another person is talking, most of us act interested, enthusiastic, supportive.

The unpopular child is often one who does not respond in these usual ways. But he can be taught to behave in ways that will make people comfortable with him and will make people like him.

Poor social perception can cause loneliness and rejection. With proper efforts, we can sometimes change or improve the lonely person's social perception.

The lonely child, say the Siegels, cannot pinpoint the source of his discomfort. His loneliness is not bound by a single incident, but is related to a whole history of failure in dealing with people.

The lonely child often has to be taught even the most basic rules of communicating effectively with others. Here are some of the things you may need to teach him:

1. Don't interrupt other people when they are talking.
2. At least attempt to show interest in what other people are saying.
3. Stand in a way and try to assume a facial expression that communicates interest, or at least one that does not communicate apathy and disinterest.
4. Don't talk too loudly.
5. Don't stand too near other people.
6. A boy or girl who is dressed attractively and one who is well groomed is more likely to be accepted than one who is not.

On Gender

Children's Sex Play Upsets Their Parents

My five-year-old son, Jake, is an only child so he always enjoys a chance to play with his four-year-old cousin, Drexel. They have always been very close and recently they have been exploring each other's bodies. This discovery has Drexel's parents very concerned because they consider that it is bad and something has to be done about it.

The first time the boys were "caught," one was exploring the possibility of putting his penis in the other's anus. The last time, one was putting his penis in the other's belly button.

I am not really worried but what does concern me is Drexel's parents' attitude. Since my son is the older, he seems to be viewed as the instigator. I have suggested that we organize and supervise their play more than we have been doing and that we introduce some (apparently needed) sex education.

I quite agree with you that what is going on with these two little boys is by no means "bad." In fact, it is more or less typical of the play of most children, at least if they are left alone, unsupervised. Trouble is introduced when the parents become overemotional about the whole thing.

Most older parents, and some younger ones, do not feel comfortable with this kind of behavior. And most of us (though not all) do feel that it should be discouraged. This is quite easily done, as a rule, by making simple rules such as no playing in the bedrooms, or in the garage, or in fact anywhere with closed doors. A little more supervision plus other more interesting things to do can cut down on this kind of behavior quite readily.

Plus, as you suggest, a little more sex education, which will answer the children's questions in ways that are to us more acceptable. It is *very* important not to blame one of the two children so engaged—as if this "bad" child had lured the "good" child into unacceptable behavior.

Actually, the behavior of these two little boys is relatively amusing since it illustrates how unsexy, from the child's point of view, it probably is. Experimenting with belly buttons usually does not upset the adult, because most of us don't think of belly buttons as terribly sexy. The other behavior described does upset many adults because, in the adult, it has, for many, adverse connotations. But to the boys, one act was probably at about the same level as the other—they were trying to see what fits.

However, if Drexel's parents are upset, that is their privilege and they are not alone. So I would simply suggest less unsupervised play for the two boys till their exploratory interests have either died out or been otherwise satisfied.

Get Them Out of That Bedroom

I wonder if you have any suggestions for the problem that is troubling me. My daughter, Alice, aged seven, and a neighbor boy, Peter, aged nine, often play together in the bedroom with the door locked. I don't want to seem like a suspicious-minded mother, but I know they are "playing doctor" and the like. I realize that this is a part of normal development, and that distracting them from that sort of play is recommended without making any comment.

But my problem is how much or how long can you go on distracting? On nice days I knock on the door and tell them they have been in the house long enough. Other times I pretend the room needs cleaning or some such. I have toyed with the idea of having a talk with Alice about it but I hesitate, as I don't want to embarrass her.

If I ever ask her casually what she and Peter were doing in the bedroom, she gets very flustered and red. That is why I hesitate to speak to her about it. What do you recommend that I do about this?

I recommend that you stop pussyfooting around and get Alice and Peter out of that locked bedroom, and keep them out. Many mothers just make the rule—no playing in the bedrooms. You can, too.

It is true that some of the more broad-minded parents and child specialists feel that sex play in very young children is not harmful and should not be interfered with.

Interest in sex, and a certain amount of sex play, *is* a part of normal development, but Alice and Peter are moving on toward the age where the results could be serious. If you don't want an unmarried mother on your hands, you're going to have to step in eventually. I'd say, the sooner the better.

It does not take a "suspicious-minded" mother to figure out what a boy and girl are doing in a locked bedroom.

So, unless you and your husband prefer to have this kind of play continue, just tell Alice that she's a big girl now and too old to play with boys in the bedroom. Your daughter will know very well what you mean!

Her Grandchildren Play with the "Wrong" Kinds of Toys

Though this may be a strange admission from a grandmother, I seem to have two of the most screwed-up little grandchildren you ever heard of. Patty is five and Timmy is four and contrary to anything I ever imagined, Timmy loves dolls and Patty ignores them. Even when Timmy is putting his dollies to bed or taking them for a ride, Patty will have nothing to do with them.

Her preference is for cars and trucks and stuffed animals. Even when given a pretty little doll and carriage last Christmas, she barely glanced at them. To make matters worse, her parents do not seem at all concerned about these preferences. I feel that if they would just put their foot down, something could be accomplished. But since they seem quite content with their children as they are, I suppose this will just go on and on. Heaven knows what kinds of grownups these children will turn out to be unless somebody does something, and soon.

If Patty and Timmy's parents, too, were upset, there would be a problem. But since they, like many young parents today, are willing for their children to play with the toys they prefer and not simply with the toys that adults prefer them to play with, there really isn't much of a problem, except in your mind.

It is not at all unusual for young boys to play with dolls, if permitted. And it really is not unusual for some small girls not to care for dolls. In your grandchildren's case the whole thing is more conspicuous because both children have crossed over the traditional lines when it comes to playthings.

Either of the children, or both of them for that matter, may later be influenced by their friends' presumably more conventional choice of playthings. But whether this happens or not, you can't do too much about it.

Her Son Is a Pretty Boy

My son, Teddy, is slightly built and pretty rather than handsome. He likes to associate with girls and women and tends to act rather girlish at times. Children fight him often and call him sissy. He is not popular with boys.

He dislikes rough sports and boy games though he often gets into trouble in regular boy fashion. I was wondering if there was a doctor I could take him to who would give him hormone shots or something to make him more masculine.

Your problem is a fairly common one. We don't worry too much, as a rule, about tomboyish girls, but nearly all parents worry about less than totally masculine boys.

It seems conceivable that at some time in the future, when we know more than we now do about the human body, some kind of hormone shots can safely slow down or speed up growth (as some parents hope), or might conceivably (though I rather doubt it) alter sexual balance. Certainly so far as I know, this kind of help is not available now.

If, as I believe, not too much can be done along these lines, it will be your responsibility to help Teddy grow up thinking well of himself. Boys like this very often grow up to have perfectly good lives and to be contributing citizens. Try to figure out what he is good at and then try to help him excel at these things.

How you and his father feel about him can in the long run have quite as much effect on his own sense of self as the things his inevitably cruel playmates have to say.

Children are very cruel to anybody who is different in any way. Fortunately the adult world is becoming increasingly tolerant of those who do not fit the customary norm.

Will Jeffie Grow Up to Be Gay?

We have a beautiful almost four-year-old little boy, Jeffie. We love him dearly but worry about him dreadfully. His favorite color is pink and he doesn't play with other little boys. They are too rough and he is afraid he will get hurt. His teacher tells me that when the children play in the dress-up box he always chooses girls' clothes. I am truly concerned that I may be raising a less than masculine boy. And I wonder whether we should seek psychological help for Jeffie.

I know I am partly at fault. When he was an infant I hovered over him and trembled that he might fall and hurt himself. Now that I have realized my mistake, I'm having a hard time convincing him that it is okay to go out and play roughly.

I put some of the blame on my husband. He works hard and when he comes home, finds it hard to play with Jeff. He will hold him on his lap while he watches TV, but that's about as far as it goes. He does not initiate games with Jeff, and he never suggests that they go outside and play ball.

Jeff goes to nursery school but it is a structured school. He seems to prefer this to others we visited where the children were allowed more freedom.

I may be making a mountain out of a molehill, but I feel threatened by my son's gentleness.

Your fear is a common one and has caused many parents many sleepless nights. Though there is nothing wrong with a preference for pink, and nothing wrong with being gentle and kind and unathletic, or choosing girls' clothes from the dress-up box (usually, the girls' clothes in the box tend to be a bit more flashy and generally more appealing than the boys'), parents *do* worry that their gentle boy will grow up to be a too-gentle man. When girls are rough and tough, parents tend to be rather proud; but when boys are quiet and gentle, they worry.

It is true that it helps a boy to grow up to behave in what we consider masculine ways if there is a good father image present in the home or close by in his life. Fortunately your son does have a father who provides an image, even though your husband, like many fathers, is not too enthusiastic about playing with his son. This is not necessarily fatal.

There is no reason to suppose your son is going to grow up to be homosexual, as you fear. Even if he did, that's not the end of the world. Deviation from the more conventional ways is increasingly accepted. Not all men who prefer the company of other men grow up, as their mothers fear they will, to cruise the bars and get beaten up by roughnecks and contract AIDS. I have no reason to suppose that seeing a psychotherapist at this point is going to change his basic personality. There are some who believe that femininity in a boy is caused by something that people (presumably his parents) do or don't do and thus that a psychotherapist can straighten it out. There are many others, myself included, who believe that for the most part sexual preferences are pretty much biologically determined—and therefore should be accepted and reckoned with.

So try to enjoy your boy for what he is. Encourage physical activity and socializing with other children but *do not push*. There is much to be said for a gentle man.

Is Homosexuality Normal or Abnormal?

As the mother of a gay son I have experienced many heartaches, but have managed to accept the situation, and George and his father and I get on very amicably.

Unfortunately, there are never-ending arguments with relatives as to whether homosexuality is just one of many possible reasonable ways of adjusting to life, or a real abnormality. What do you think?

I can give you the opinion of people probably better qualified to answer your question than I—the response of 2,500 psychiatrists who answered a questionnaire distributed by the journal *Medical Aspects of Human Sexuality,* as reported in *Behavior Today.*

This is what these professionals reported. When asked if homosexuality is usually a pathological adaptation as opposed to a normal variation, 69 percent said yes, 18 percent no, 13 percent were uncertain.

When asked if homosexuals can become heterosexual by means of therapy, only 3 percent said in most cases; 37 percent said fairly often, but 58 percent said almost never.

When asked if homosexual men are generally less happy than others, 73 percent said yes; only 26 percent said no.

To the question "Can bisexuals have successful heterosexual marriages?" 21 percent said usually, 65 percent said occasionally, only 12 percent said almost never.

To the question "Are homosexuals generally more creative than heterosexuals?" 22 percent said yes, 74 percent said no.

When asked "Are homosexuals generally a greater risk than heterosexuals to hold positions of great responsibility?" 43 percent said yes, but 54 percent said no.

These answers are somewhat discouraging, but interesting in view of the fact that an American Psychiatric Association poll of its membership in 1974 agreed by a small majority that homosexuality should *not* be defined as a disorder unless the person is dissatisfied with his or her sexual orientation.

There is still a major difference of opinion between those who believe that homosexuality is a basic biological fact (that is, some people are simply born with a preference for this way of relating to others) and those who believe that something somebody has done "wrong" causes the individual to behave as he does. Probably the majority these days, we among them, believe that homosexuality is a biological fact of life. We hold this position even though there are those who feel that a strong mother and a weak father, or some other environmental situation, causes this preference. Some of the suggestions made seem to me pretty ridiculous—as when an official in the Reagan administration recently went so far as to suggest that using marijuana might cause homosexuality.

At any rate, as to your son, George, so long as you and your husband and George get along okay, I would try not to worry and would refrain from discussing your son with relatives. It is none of their business.

Are Girls and Boys Just Naturally Different or Do We Make Them Different?

I am having a severe disagreement with one of my feminist friends. She insists that most of the differences in behavior between girls and boys occur because we treat them differently. As a mother of two boys and two girls, there is no question in my mind that the main reason we treat them differently is that they are *different. There is no way I could make my sons as gentle as my daughters, no matter what I did.*

Do you think there's a chance that my friend and other ardent feminists could be right and that we as parents, and as a society, do cause sex differences?

No I don't. No way. It is true that we support and even perhaps exaggerate the differences between boys and girls by the way we treat them—but the basic differences are there to start with. If it is true that to a large extent people behave as they do because of the way their bodies are built, the answer is obvious.

For any of you interested in a fine book on the subject, I recommend *Boys and Girls at Play: The Development of Sex Roles* by Evelyn Pitcher and Lynn H. Schultz. These writers base their research on their own careful observations of nursery-school children at play. They tell us clearly:

> Boys and girls behave differently from each other at every age, not only in the roles they adopt but in the type of behavior favored by one sex or the other. Girls tend to be nurturant while boys favor rough-and-tumble play. Boys experience more conflict than girls. Girls are much less aggressive. Girls in general prefer to play with

other girls, boys with other boys, and the characteristic behavior of the two sexes is different. Assaultive and molesting behaviors are higher among boys, nurturing behavior among girls.

Whereas boys tend to use rules or reprimands for their own purposes, girls seem more interested in the larger issues of preserving social order for its own sake. Insulting behaviors are infrequent and mild among girls. Boys insult one another frequently and intensely—they engage in a wide variety of name calling at every age.

When one teacher, to discourage doll play among the girls, took away the doll corner equipment, she found that "casual housekeeping arrangements were popping up under tables, and breakfast was being served at the sand table."

These authors conclude:

Children learn narrow sex role concepts which conform in general to their culture's stereotyped belief system. Through their play behavior, children steadily incorporate the gender role initiated by their biology, demanded by their psyche, understood by their mind, and supported by their culture. Human beings have characteristics which no society has created and to which all societies must respond.

In short, Mom, I'm with you.

Researchers "Reluctantly" Admit Sex Differences

You keep saying that the big observable differences in the behavior of girls and boys are inherited and not caused by the way we treat them. Yet so many scientific articles of late, particularly those by such authorities as Dr. Eleanor Maccoby of Stanford, show that research has found that most of the differences between the sexes are man-made. How about that?

I can really answer that one. Dr. Maccoby and several other investigators have for many years been writing to the effect that we do indeed produce most of the differences that exist between boys and girls. However, just recently most of them have, "reluctantly," reported that further research does not bear out their original theories.

Now Dr. Maccoby herself, as reported in the magazine *Behavior Today*, concludes that "Popular beliefs to the effect that boys are more difficult to raise than girls *are* correct. As early as eighteen months, boys are more likely to react negatively to parental pressures, parents are more likely to react negatively to a boy's than a girl's mischief, and the boy is more likely to have a malfunctioning relationship with the parents."

She also finds that children playing with boys are more likely to experience a hurtful encounter that leads to withdrawal from the play situation. And more than that, says Maccoby, sex-based differences intensify with age, and no research has ever been able really to confirm the popular belief that boys are *encouraged* to be more aggressive than girls. According to her, parents are as likely to tell their female children to fight back in defense of their interests as they are their boys.

In other words, even those who for a while insisted that we cause boys to be aggressive, girls to be passive and dependent by the way we treat them, are beginning to admit what some of us have claimed all along —that most of the big differences between the sexes were made by God and not by man.

On Eating

Breastfeeding Was Great for Pammy and Her Mom

I am a very young mother and wanted to tell you how great I think breastfeeding is. Sure, I couldn't go out evenings with my husband for a while, but my daughter, Pammy, wasn't going to be a baby forever and I had many years of going out ahead of me.

What a success! Pammy had no trouble with spitting up, colds, or colic as some bottle-fed babies I know did. People often commented about how happy and healthy she seemed to be. Breastfeeding was not a burden to me, either. I think it has made me especially close to my daughter.

When you breastfeed, you don't have to worry about sterilizing bottles, warming a bottle in the middle of the night, or finding time to mix the formula. The time you would have spent doing those things now becomes extra time to devote to your baby.

Some of my friends say that they didn't breastfeed because they didn't have enough milk, it wasn't rich enough, they didn't want to be deprived of going out in the evenings, or they couldn't stand the discomfort. I think they were just too chicken to try. I believe that if you want to give your child the very best possible nourishment, you will at least give breastfeeding a try.

Thanks for writing. Your letter speaks for itself. I hope that other readers, to whom it applies, will take it to heart.

Mother-in-Law Says Her Milk Isn't Right for the Baby

I very successfully breastfed my first two children but am having a little trouble with this one—he spits up more than I like.

My mother-in-law insists that it is because my milk probably doesn't agree with him and she urges me to have a chemical analysis of my milk to find out what is wrong with it.

Ah me! I'm so sorry that you have run into one of those fiends in human form, a mother-in-law who, expressing what one assumes is unconscious hostility, tries to make a nursing mother feel insecure about her milk.

Pediatricians assure us that, except in the case of a few rare diseases such as beriberi, a mother's milk is *always* right for her baby. According to the American Academy of Pediatrics, "Human milk is the miracle food of nature. It not only provides nutrition, but immunizes the newborn against a variety of diseases." But some babies *are* spitters.

It sometimes helps to gently express the first streams from your breasts until the milk is just dripping. Then the baby does not have to struggle to swallow it. As Dr. T. Berry Brazelton has explained in *Doctor and Child,* "Noisy gulps contain air with each mouthful and contribute to a bubble in the stomach that will come up, bringing milk with it. A baby who continues to spit up after feedings can be propped at a thirty-degree angle for thirty minutes or so after feeding, before he is burped. This gives the milk a chance to settle by gravity, and the ingested air has time to rise to the top of the stomach. When a baby is bubbled after this period, the milk stays down; and the bubbles come up without it."

But don't forget, some babies just do spit up after some feedings, for a long time. It may be a function of eating too much or too rapidly. It may also be a symptom of an inadequate esophageal sphincter. Check with your pediatrician, but try not to worry.

And keep in mind—there are difficult babies and easy babies. Most are not easy in every respect *all the time.* The important thing so far as feeding goes is to have confidence in your milk, and to avoid your mother-in-law. If your pediatrician can't give you all the time and advice you need, call La Leche League. They have branches in most big cities and are all too glad to give you support.

We Change Our Advice About That Bedtime Bottle

Y ou recently advised a mother that a bedtime bottle was not necessarily harmful and gave two-and-a-half to three years of age as an outside limit for permitting this bottle.

As a nutritionist, I feel strongly that a bedtime bottle can be very harmful to a child's teeth. It causes a condition referred to by pedodontists as "nursing bottle syndrome" or "nursing bottle caries." This refers to destruction of the anterior teeth as the result of prolonged contact with carbohydrate-containing solutions fed by nursing bottle.

Most nutritionists would prefer that babies be offered some other comforting object at bedtime: fingers, blanket, a bottle filled with water, or even an empty bottle.

T hank you for your letter. It is true that we have always been rather permissive about late bottles. Of course, as you know, we would actually prefer no bottles at all. Those mothers who breastfeed often transfer the child from breast to cup without any intermediate bottle.

However, unfortunately, not everybody breastfeeds. And certainly there are many inconsolable or difficult children for whom that bedtime bottle makes all the difference in the world.

Nevertheless, parents as well as dentists and physicians are becoming increasingly aware of the bad side of the bedtime bottle. It isn't so much that it is babyish, as that prolonged contact of teeth with carbohydrate-containing solutions can indeed be harmful. It is true that a bedtime bottle permits this undesirable prolonged contact.

Though we would not recommend, as you suggest, that a child suck on an empty bottle, you are right that water in the bottle would be much better than milk or formula.

Therefore, for once we are going to reverse our earlier advice to parents. For those for whom it is not too late we would suggest not starting a bedtime bottle of milk. If there must be soothing sucking at bedtime, have it be on a pacifier, thumb, or bottle of water. Thank you for bringing us up short.

Should Tommy Have to Eat All His Spaghetti?

I am a loving and concerned father. I try to be reasonable with our—so far only—son Tommy, who is two and a half years old.

It seems to me that he must learn to do what I say, but sometimes it is very difficult to force him to carry out my orders. I believe that a child should finish his main course before he gets his dessert, but sometimes this is very hard to enforce!

For instance the other evening we were having spaghetti. Tommy was dawdling and dawdling and fooling around with his food. I told him, as I always do, that he must clean his plate before he could have dessert.

Well finally it got so almost half an hour had gone by. The spaghetti of course was cold and Tommy's tears, falling into it, probably didn't make it any more palatable. I may have been weak, but I just couldn't make him sit there any longer—but of course I didn't let him have his dessert. It was a very sad scene. Did I do right?

Probably not. Certainly there have to be a few rules about mealtime, but it usually works best if we give very small portions to preschoolers and then don't make too much fuss about clean plates.

Certainly one hopes they will take a few bites of the main course; but if dessert is nutritious (fruit or some such) that, too, is good for your child. Most parents today find that the less talk about and the less fuss about what and how much a child consumes, the easier all around.

As you discovered, even with the best of intentions you didn't do much good to anybody by forcing Tommy to sit there crying over his cold spaghetti. As you realize now, if you hadn't made the rule in the first place, dinner would have been much happier for all concerned.

How to Get Your Child to Eat Well

Many factors combine to cause the numerous eating problems we used to hear about. One was the strict "every-four-hour" feeding schedule that got so many babies, especially those who needed to eat every three hours or who had an uneven demand, off to such a bad start.

Another thing was that parents used to lay more stress than many do today on variety and quantity of foods, especially of vegetables, to be eaten. Many young children have very special food dislikes. They especially tend to dislike cooked vegetables, and if too much emphasis was given to their consumption, this was the start of many feeding problems.

Mostly, though, it is relaxation that does it. Most children *do* eat as much as they need to keep not only alive but reasonably healthy. And if you don't let fights about feedings start, they can hardly fight alone.

Two mothers, Antoinette Hatfield and Peggy Stanton, in a book called *How to Help Your Child Eat Right* give some good food presentation and serving ideas. I've combined them with our own points in the following list for establishing good eating habits (or at least for *not* producing troublesome ones):

Start in with breastfeeding, and with a self-regulation schedule.

Don't introduce solids too soon. Four to six months is plenty soon enough.

Respect the tremendous individual differences that exist both as to quality and quantity of food the child wants and needs.

Don't exaggerate to yourself about how little your child eats. If you feel sure that he eats "practically nothing," make a check on what he actually does eat.

Don't talk too much about it if your child isn't eating. Many mothers tell their friends, in their child's presence, "He never eats a thing. I have the hardest time getting even a bite of food into him." Children enjoy living up to this kind of billing. Make sure there is not some basic conflict between you and your child that he finds he can win by not eating—or, similarly, that he finds he can get attention from you when he doesn't eat; no attention when he does.

Be alert to the possibilities of an allergic reaction. Some foods are refused because they really do not agree with the child.

Allow finger feeding for the very young. In fact if you

stress manners too much too soon, you may have a mannerly child who is still a feeding problem.

Be (or appear to be) very relaxed, calm and relatively uninterested in how much is eaten. The less mothers fuss, the less fun it is for the child not to eat. The more you fuss, the more power it gives them to bug you by not eating. And most children are very good at judging how worried you are about what and how much they eat.

Give *small* helpings. A big eater can come back for more, but a small eater will be totally discouraged by a too big serving.

Respect preferences and refusals. Don't push disliked foods, and if your child has a run on some favored food, it probably does no harm as long as an exclusion of other foods does not go on too long. However, according to pediatrician Lendon Smith, if your child loves a food so much that he must eat it every day, chances are that it is bad for him.

Be sure the food is appetizing. A little red and green on a plate help. Try broccoli and carrots, carrots and asparagus, green beans and tomatoes.

Give your child raw vegetables if he dislikes them cooked.

Be sure that food isn't lumpy or stringy or sticky. Just a lump or two in the mashed potatoes will throw most any child off.

Appeal to your child's do-it-myself tendency. Buy him a little plastic jug or pitcher so that he can pour.

Try not only different colors but different shapes. Baked potatoes, asparagus spears, and lamb chops give you a variety of shapes. Round potatoes, meatballs, and peas are less interesting and appealing. You don't have to rely on the natural shapes of foods. Sandwiches can be cut into all kinds of shapes. Animal shapes are great favorites.

Don't expect (unrealistically) three good meals a day. Many children have only one really good meal a day.

Don't make mealtime too demanding. Some children eat best if served their dinner before the grown-ups eat. This is especially true if Father is extremely demanding about amounts and manners. Or if mealtime in your household is, as it is in many homes, a tense or unpleasant situation.

Don't be too worried about an occasional between-meal snack. If food furnished is healthful, some of your child's best eating may be between meals. Raw fruits or vegetables cut up in small shapes that have eye appeal are usually well accepted; or try a cherry tomato or a cantaloupe cube. Carrots of course can be sticks or curls, as can green peppers.

Perhaps the main thing, if your child is not a good eater, is not to act as if his not-eating is bad. Rather, it is a problem that, like any other, can usually be solved with a little brain work and much restraint on your part.

Mother Feeds Children Separately from Father

*O*ur family problem is mealtimes. My husband, who is basically a good husband and a good provider, always seems angry at meals. As a result there is a good deal of disciplining, complaining, shouting, punishing, and usually somebody ends up in tears.

I have solved this problem by having the children eat separately. I have insisted that my husband get up a little earlier than they do. I make him a good breakfast, whatever he wants, and then he leaves for work. It means getting two breakfasts but is well worth it.

For dinner, the children eat early and then I have them play quietly in some other part of the house while he and I have a nice, quiet, friendly dinner. I considered this a good solution till I, foolishly, wrote to one of the columnists about it—thinking it might help others.

She criticized me. Said my solution was no solution at all, just removed the children from the battle zone. She said that "parents and children should eat together and enjoy mealtime." She suggested family counseling.

Dr. Ames, my husband wouldn't go to a counselor. And since our whole family is well satisfied with the present arrangement, I still recommend it to others.

R ight you are! If every family in the United States that has trouble at mealtimes went to a family counselor, there wouldn't be counselors enough to go around. . . . I personally am a strong advocate of trying family counseling as a last resort, only when it is desperately needed.

But family counseling is no magic. There is no guarantee that even if you could drag your husband to a counselor, the deep reasons (whatever they are) why your husband is unhappy at family mealtimes would be revealed.

And leaving the deeper reasons out of it, there may well be ordinary superficial reasons why things go so badly. Many parents are not well satisfied with their children, and meals are one time when everyone is present and available for scolding and criticism. Mother, too, is often dissatisfied, but her role is eternally that of peacemaker. Father usually feels less obligation to keep things smooth and happy. So it may be quite natural that mealtime is the time when he scolds and criticizes.

The statement "Parents and children should eat together and enjoy mealtime" is a very loose way of speaking. One might more correctly say, "It would be nice if parents and children could always eat together in harmony." But to say that they *should* do so is a meaningless bit of optimism.

A Sneaky Approach to Improving Your Family's Diet

E verybody and his dog is writing these days about the importance of proper nutrition and the avoidance of junk food or any foods that are a step away from natural. That's all very well and I personally go along with the idea. But how to convince my family!

My husband is very set in his food preferences. Can't eat fish. He thinks it makes him sick to his stomach. Won't touch fresh vegetables. Etc., etc. And the children go right along with him. The idea of trying to feed this family a nutritious diet is laughable.

W e all know what you mean. I have wondered myself how in real life a mother could put into practice the things the nutritionists advise. Now comes help.

Barbara Richert suggests ways of tricking your junk-food junkies into preferring food that is good for them. Her recipe? Sneak nutritious food to your children by combining, masking, tricking, distracting. Though the concepts of good nutrition may seem mind-boggling to you, here are some suggestions that may work:

1. Some of the most popular foods make excellent hiding places for more nutritious elements. Hamburgers, meatballs, and meat-loaf, milkshakes, soups, all are places where you can hide almost anything.

2. Cram as much nutrition as you can into one dish. Add wheat germ where it won't be detected. Sneak honey into dessert instead of sugar. Grated cheese or grated carrot will enhance a variety of dishes. Mask vegetables your children don't take to with an au gratin topping, if they like that.

3. Introduce good things gradually. For instance combine white and whole-wheat pastas and gradually increase the proportion of whole wheat. Or if your child is addicted to a brand of peanut butter high in sugar content, try mixing more and more natural peanut butter with the favored brand until gradually the heavily sugared product can be eliminated.

4. Disguise and fancy up. If your child doesn't like spinach, disguise it as a light soufflé with a rich cheesy topping. Or, whatever it is, stick a toothpick though it. Children like almost anything with a toothpick in it.

5. Don't talk too much about what you are doing. Try teaching good nutrition as much by what you actually serve as by what you say about it.

One thing we strongly recommend to you, though probably your husband would not be interested, is for you to read some of the many good, and easily readable, books on nutrition now available for parents. I especially recommend *Feed Your Kids Right,* by Lendon Smith. He advises the avoidance of what he calls antinutrients, that is foods which when consumed not only are not in themselves nourishing but increase the body's needs for more nutrition. Among foods to be avoided, so far as you can, are any kind with sugar in them. Also try to avoid commerical ice cream, boxed cereals, white flour, and perhaps homogenized, pasteurized milk. As Smith points out, if a food has been packaged, processed, added to or stabilized, emulsified, colored or preserved, it is out of Nature's hands.

Also try to get your family to eat natural foods several times a day in frequent, small amounts. Thus try raw vegetables, eggs, white cheese, nuts, fish, chicken, peas and beans, raw fruits.

And if you have not already done so, check with your own doctor about what kind of vitamins your children should be eating. Perhaps your husband will not object to vitamins, at least for you and the children, even if he, himself, does not want to take them.

On Sleeping

Should Baby Nap in the Daytime?

*M*y *baby refuses to sleep in the daytime. He is four months old now and is quite good nights—that is, he wakes up only two or three times. But all day long he is wide awake.*

My friends say I should force him to nap since it is normal *for young babies to have daytime naps. But I don't know how to make a baby sleep unless he wants to.*

Neither do I. My guess is that your friends either are childless or they have beautifully sleepy babies. Some babies, at a very early age, sleep right through the night and also take one or two naps a day.

Others seem almost impervious to the need for sleep. Some are at least seven months of age or more before they sleep right through the night, and are also very weak in the nap department.

In general, babies' bodies seem to *know* how much sleep they need. If your own baby appears to be healthy and happy, I wouldn't worry about his not napping in the daytime. But just for your own sake, I would see to it that he spends some time, morning and afternoon, alone in his room in his crib. Supply him with a reasonable number of toys and trust that he will entertain himself.

You need this time away from him and actually he needs this time away from you. So, though he is very young for this, let him enjoy what we call, around four years of age, a "play nap." And let us hope that as he gets older, he may develop a greater need for sleep.

Baby Doesn't Sleep

*M*y problem is my eight-month-old baby, who has never been a good sleeper. I find myself exhausted after being up several times a night with her. I got into the habit of bringing her into bed to nurse. She falls asleep fine but if taken back to her crib, awakens and cries to be with me. We are not at the point where she actually does not sleep in her crib. She wakes at least once an hour and cries for me. Now even her naps are a problem.

I hate to let her cry at night because it wakes my three-year-old and also my husband doesn't like it. (He doesn't like having her in bed with us, either.) My friends think I should toughen up and let her cry. Also how important is a set routine? We are very flexible in our household, perhaps too flexible.

Sorry to hear about your problem—one of the most exasperating a parent can face. If your child doesn't eat, at least you don't go hungry. If she doesn't sleep, you don't either.

All too often, as in your case, only mother's presence will calm the child down. Erma Bombeck once commented that the reason older women don't need much sleep is that, as young mothers, they got entirely out of the habit of sleeping.

It seems that right now you have two rather clear-cut choices. Go on as you have been doing, which of course makes you a twenty-four-hour-a-day slave to this baby. Or decide to *try* the toughen-her-up method. This will certainly lead to several nights of crying, and probably total sleeplessness for the whole family. If you do try this, you probably should keep it up for at least a week. If that doesn't help, then clearly it is not your solution.

Though most of us feel that "breast milk is the best milk" it is possible that something you are eating is a substance that makes your baby uncomfortable. A good pediatric allergist should be able to help you determine this.

Another possibility—some people find that if someone other than Mother takes over at night, babies and preschoolers are less demanding. How about your husband, who doesn't like to hear the baby cry? This, if you still have night feedings, would mean that you would have to express your milk in advance, so that she could have her feeding, and that may seem to you like too much trouble. Or, if your pediatrician agrees, you could try a formula at night.

Since some children continue to wake their mother with demands right through the preschool years, it would almost seem as if you might do best to take the bull by the horns right now. Though of course this is easier for me to say than for you to do. . . . And yes, a fairly set routine often does work best. Actually we recommend what we call a self-demand and self-regulation schedule for the very young—feeding the baby pretty much when he or she is hungry. But by eight months of age, most babies are able to accept a reasonably set routine.

Must Preschoolers Be Put to Bed at a Certain Hour?

*D*o *you think that a preschooler absolutely has to have a set and early bedtime? My husband and I are very relaxed people and have an extremely relaxed household.*

We love our two preschoolers and enjoy having them around in the evening. So we let them stay up as late as they want to—it is seldom past 9 P.M. and often earlier.

All our neighbors think this is terrible. They say the children won't get enough sleep and that it's just bad anyway. Actually when the children stay up late, as they usually do, they sleep later in the morning. And this is fine with me because my husband and I like to sleep late too. (Fortunately his job is such that we can do this.)

When things are casual, most preschoolers probably get as much sleep as they need. It is the (usual) forced bedtime that so many resist. In casual households we have known of sleepy children who ask to be put to bed.

Children's sleep needs vary, and even among preschoolers some require more sleep than others. The usual early preschool bedtime is most often instituted on behalf of the adults, most of whom feel that they need some time by themselves in the evening.

If you and your husband, who must be miracles of patience, don't mind having the children around in the evening, I can't see that any harm is done. It really doesn't matter what the neighbors think. It's how you feel about it that counts.

Boy Wants to Sleep on the Floor

My husband and I are having a big argument. Our only son, Danny, almost three years of age, insists on sleeping on the floor. We put him to bed in his crib every night, but after a few minutes—in fact, as soon as we turn out the light, there he is on the floor.

His father says it is a matter of discipline to make him sleep in the proper place. I don't think it matters all that much and I feel that we should save our serious disciplining for things that really matter. Who is right?

We say you are. Not only does it do Danny no harm, so far as we know, to sleep on the floor, but floor sleeping is something that a great many children prefer around his age. Since sleeping on the floor is normal (that is, many children do it) and since it is harmless, we would allow it to continue. It seldom lasts very long.

We definitely agree with you that parents may be wise to save their serious disciplining for things that really matter. We would continue to put Danny to bed in his own bed, but would provide an alternate bed on the floor. Make very little of the whole problem and before you know it, it will go away.

Too Old for Bedtime Bottle

Our problem is keeping our little boy in bed once he gets there, and getting him there in the first place is no picnic. Jacob is now four years old, and he is a boy who seems to need almost no sleep, and also one who is very social.

So it is hard for him to leave the family group in the evening, to begin with. And then once in bed, he keeps getting up and popping out into the bedroom. He also still insists on a bottle, morning and night. How can I solve these problems, if they are problems?

They're problems all right, and they are telling you loud and clear that your son Jacob is a little immature for his age. Two and a half to three tends to be our outside limit for the bedtime bottle and even those ages are late for a morning bottle.

Some children do best, if a big change must be made, if it is made all at once. Just chop off the offending behavior. Most, however do better if given a warning and a little time. You can have a talk with Jacob and explain that as he knows, he is now a big boy of four, and four-year-olds do not drink their milk out of a bottle.

It would be fair to omit the morning bottle right now. He will surely get out of bed without its help. As to the night bottle, you might try providing a calendar, with a deadline marked big and clear. Tell him you know it is a little hard to give up his bottle, and that he can still have it for another so many days or weeks. Then, on your big calendar, let him mark off each day, till he approaches the final date.

What will actually happen on that date, I don't know for sure, but my guess is that your son may actually want some help in giving up what he knows is a babyish behavior. As to his bedtime, some children (especially boys) really do need very little sleep. But parents do need some evening hours to themselves. A little bedtime difficulty is not unusual with any preschooler, but popping out of bed and reappearing in the living room is more characteristic of the younger child than of the four-year-old.

How will you manage it I can't tell you for sure, but I would make every effort, both parents working together, to prevent his constant reappearance. You might bargain with him: in return for a later bedtime, he will stay in bed once there.

You might prolong the bedtime chatting time. You might let him have his own little radio. Father may just have to come in with a strong command, "Stay in your room."

Whatever, both the bottle and the popping up at bedtime give you the warning that your son is a little young for his age and must, to some extent, be treated accordingly.

Little Girl Worries at Bedtime

We are having a terrible time with our four-year-old daughter, Diane. She has always been a somewhat fearful child, but now, every night when I am putting her to bed, out come the fears.

Some of them are easily handled—the bugs in her bed, the lion in the closet. As you have advised I brush the bugs out of the bed, drive the lion from the closet.

Other fears are more intangible and much harder to deal with. She says she is afraid that I might die. She is afraid that she herself might get run over. Some of these fears are undoubtedly real. With others it sometimes seems that she is stretching her imagination just to keep me with her and talking. But I am not sure. She may really fear all these things and I hate to leave her alone in the dark with these unhappy thoughts.

What I am asking is, how much attention should I pay to these fears and how far should I go in sitting with her and discussing them?

It is very hard to say without knowing Diane whether she really does genuinely fear all these things, or has just found a good way of keeping you with her at bedtime.

Your best way of finding out is by trial and error. Some mothers manage to terminate the night chatting time with a timer. That is, you tell your daughter that you are glad she lets you know when she is afraid of things and that you want to help her be less fearful. And that every night, so long as the need exists, you and she will have a chatting time for, say, fifteen minutes.

Explain to her that you obviously won't have time to discuss *all* of her fears in any one evening, but that you will cover as much ground as possible. And that if there is anything special on her mind, that won't wait till the next evening, you can talk about it during the day.

Chances are this will work. If it doesn't, and you conclude that your daughter is more than "normally" anxious (whatever you think the norm may be), you may decide to seek professional help. I doubt that this will be needed, but if it is, a series of sessions of play therapy may make Diane feel more secure and less anxious. Added age should help too. Many children do go through these fearful spells and then grow out of them without anybody doing anything very special about it.

Fearful Child Sleeps in Parents' Room

O ur six-year-old daughter, Henrietta, a normally very good little girl, has suddenly become the victim of all sorts of night fears. She hears sounds, she thinks she sees things moving in her room. She really seems terrified. All that makes her feel better is to come into our room.

She makes no demand to get into bed with us and is quite content to lie on the floor at the foot of the bed, wrapped in her blanket. We don't think this is right but we really don't mind.

However, her pediatrician says it is terrible and we must stop *it at once. We tried and the result was that she cried all night long. Also, when she thinks we are mad at her at night, this seems to hold over into the daytime. She acts very insecure. She hugs me a lot and asks if I love her. What should I do?*

S orry, but I don't go along with your doctor. I believe that Henrietta's fears are very real to her and should, for the time being, be respected. Since she is willing to sleep on the floor and doesn't disturb you, I would go along with her need, for the time being. It is bad enough to be frightened, without thinking your parents are mad at you.

However, I would start planning with Henrietta that she is a big girl now and that pretty soon she won't need to come into your room every night. Make a chart and promise her a gold star for every night she manages not to come in, with some good reward promised for every five or ten gold stars.

In the meantime, ask her what you could do to make things seem not so scary in her room. Could she have a kitten or puppy? Would a night light help?

The important things now are first, to respect the fact that your daughter's fears are very real to her; second, not to make her feel that you are mad at her; and third, to try to work together with her to solve what is a total family problem. Avoid giving her the impression that it is you against her. And if your pediatrician doesn't approve of her sleeping in your room, just don't tell him.

Jerome Can't Get to Sleep

*I*t takes my eight-year-old son, Jerome, forever to get to sleep and he lies there and frets. Recently, though, I read this simple statement that has helped me in one of your books, Don't Push Your Preschooler. It said that the child with an ectomorphic physique, that is the slender child with skinny arms and legs, "has trouble with sleeping as with eating. He finds it hard to get to sleep. But once asleep finds it hard in the morning to wake up and get going. He needs a great deal of sleep but it is hard for him to fall asleep unless he is close to physical exhaustion. He sleeps lightly and dreams a great deal."

Well, I read this to my son and he said, "How could she know all that? She hasn't even seen me." I can't say that the information has actually improved his sleeping. But it certainly has improved his attitude toward his wakefulness. He seems rather proud that his behavior, as it were, makes sense.

Thanks for telling me. It is interesting to us that it is often the ectomorphic child who, though not necessarily brighter than those of other physical builds, is often the most thoughtful and finds it most interesting to know that much of his behavior is probably closely related to his actual physique. The more muscular mesomorph often really doesn't care; and the easygoing endomorph (who tends not to have trouble with eating and sleeping in the first place) is more apt to shrug off information about his or her personality.

Many parents, however, find it helpful to know what, more or less, they may expect of their child as related to his actual physical structure. The book this mother refers to will tell you something of what you can expect of boys and girls of different physical builds, in relation to eating, sleeping, reaction to other people, emotions, and behavior in general. If this kind of information interests you, you might like to look it up.

Eleven-Year-Old Elaine Won't Go to Bed

*B*edtimes in our household are a mess. We have only one child, an eleven-year-old girl named Elaine, but you would think it was twenty, for all we go through.

Elaine just won't go to bed at what we consider a proper time. She wants to stay up for a 10 P.M. television show that she likes. After that she has to eat, and dawdles and dawdles. Also she claims that she is afraid of the dark. She has insisted on a sixty-watt light being left on all night. Her father has finally cut that down to forty watts.

Once she finally gets to bed, she reads in bed. Gets very little sleep and as a result is very crabby in the morning. Yells at me and wants me to comb her hair. So mornings aren't much better than evenings. What can we do to improve matters?

Clearly this is a case of what Dr. Spock has described as weak parents and strong child. You are going to have to toughen yourselves up quite a lot. Your husband's reducing the wattage on the electric light bulb that is left burning all night is only a baby step. If Elaine dominates you now, what are things going to be like when she is a teenager? Offhand I suspect that as a threesome you need a little help from family-therapy sessions with a capable specialist.

However if you want to try it on your own, you might try a method that is labeled "behavior modification." There are three simple steps to behavior modification: (1) You identify specifically the behavior you want to change; (2) you intervene by reinforcing the desired behavior and finally rewarding it; and (3) you evaluate your success.

Now the fact that your daughter is a mess is not a single specific thing you can change. So narrow down. Decide, for instance, that you and your husband will get together and insist that Elaine be in her bed with lights turned off, except for a supportive night light, by ten o'clock. This automatically rules out her ten o'clock television programs, as it should. In fact it would mean that she would probably need to be finished with television by nine thirty in order to get herself ready for bed in time.

Then you intervene. Just see to it that this rule is followed. Keep a chart with marks to indicate those nights when this plan is followed out. Plan ahead that once Elaine has earned a certain number of success marks she will be rewarded with some reasonably substantial item of her own choosing.

Stage three, the evaluation, of course, will be included in the charting. Now, maybe all of this won't work right away. Behavior-modification specialists advise that if any such plan does *not* work, after a reasonable amount of time, you check on yourself and ask: (1) Is my goal justified? (2) Is my goal reasonable? (3) Is my goal specific?

Actually your goal *is* justified; it *is* reasonable; and it *is* specific. Also, ten o'clock is a much later bedtime than is typical for an eleven-year-old. However, it may be that you will come to the conclusion that Elaine really does not need as much sleep as many. Thus, if you cannot enforce the ten o'clock bedtime you might set the time for ten thirty. Or, the reward you selected may not be sufficiently motivating. Or perhaps you could permit a little reading in bed *if* she were in bed, all washed and brushed and whatever, at your specified hour.

There is no magic solution that will turn a household that is "a mess" into a nice, orderly household. But you might at least take the first steps. If you absolutely cannot do it on your own, you will indeed need to get professional help.

On Toilet Training

Spanking a Two-Year-Old Who Wets?

*D*aphne *is twenty-seven months old and has always been a pleasant, well-behaved child who took joy in pleasing her father and me. She seemed to react nicely to the birth of a baby brother. And since she seemed intelligent, I anticipated no training problem.*

In the beginning we were delighted to see how smoothly things went. A couple of weeks after her second birthday she was wearing training pants all the time. She had no accidents during the day and remained dry at night.

About two weeks after she had no accidents at all, she began soiling her panties. Naturally I scolded her. This first accident was followed, and still is, by others. Our pediatrician, whom we respect highly, said that she is asserting her independence and that we must spank her every time it happens.

So, I have been spanking her hard for two months but it has no effect. How much longer do I have to go on? Would it be safe to stop spanking in hopes she might begin to cooperate again? We want to do the right thing, but seem to be getting nowhere.

My heart bleeds for your little girl, and for that matter, for you, too. That you have been spanking this baby for two months because your doctor told you to is a very sad thing to contemplate.

At any rate, I can assure you that Daphne's experience is a common one. Whether the birth of your second baby has anything to do with it or not, we don't know. But many children who feel pressured to be dry and clean early, and who achieve it early, do slip back. And then you have a more difficult time than if you hadn't tried so hard or had such good and early success.

Though we hesitate to contradict your doctor—after all, he knows you and your child and I don't—it is certainly against most modern thinking to spank a child for having toilet accidents. Especially such a young child. We just wouldn't say much about the whole thing for some time to come. You don't have to put your feelings into words. Daphne knows what is expected and knows how you feel when she fails.

Put her back into diapers and rubber pants. Realize that twenty-seven months is still young. Suggest that she tell you after she has soiled or wet. Compliment her when she has told you. Then judge your next step as she becomes aware when she is functioning or maybe able to warn you ahead of time. A potty chair is often preferable to the toilet seat.

Daphne's behavior, though trying, is by no means a sign that anything is deeply wrong, or that, as you put it, she is not "cooperating" on purpose.

Susie Is Three and Still Wet

My three-year-old daughter, Susie, is not yet toilet trained. Our pediatrician says, "Just wait till she's ready," but I have waited and my patience is worn out.

I think now it has come down to a battle of wills between Susie and me. Is spanking ever justified? Perhaps we started too soon—eighteen months. We bought her a potty chair and she was very proud when we "caught" her at the right time. But then the novelty wore off.

So we let it go; and then the baby came and that seemed a poor time to work on anything as delicate as toilet training. Just recently I took off the diaper and tried training pants. I give up!

It does seem that you started too early, tried too hard, and now are giving up too soon. You might try leaving off not only the diapers but also the training pants. Even a casual girl like Susie, who doesn't mind soggy training pants, may not like to have urine running down her legs. Children do find that uncomfortable.

You might try that for a month or so—just pretend you have run out of training pants. That is, don't let her think you are trying something new—just act, if you can, as if you had forgotten about the whole thing.

Your best bet might be to enroll her in a nursery school. A few of the best ones will take wet children. By their casual attitude and by the fact that all the other children do better, they often cannot so much induce a wet child to be dry as just set up a situation where dryness comes naturally.

Don't spank. It *is* a temptation. But spanking just aggravates or exaggerates the battle that now goes on between you. A child of Susie's age should normally eat enough to keep herself alive, sleep at night, stay dry —unless it has become useful and interesting to her not to do so.

Your daughter is apparently just naturally immature in this respect. But even immaturity comes to an end some time. By waiting and remaining calm you are really not doing *nothing,* as you fear. You are doing the hardest thing of all.

Try to take a long-range view and realize that few girls or boys ever get to college or even high school (unless something is seriously wrong with them) in a state of dampness.

Is there a grandmother that Susie could visit? It isn't that grandmothers necessarily do better with toilet training than mothers do. It is just that any different person might set up a different relationship in this respect and might get better results.

Bed-Wetting at Three Is Not a Sign of Emotional Distress

I read something in a widely syndicated column that upset me very much. This column said, "Bed-wetting by anyone over three years of age is a symptom of another problem—either organic or emotional. My experts tell me it is at least 90 percent emotional."

Well, my four-year-old son still wets the bed, as did his sister at the same age and our doctor says it's nothing unusual and not to worry about it. Is our doctor out of date, or is the columnist wrong?

The columnist is wrong, and I'd suggest that she get some new "experts," at least on the subject of bed-wetting.

There are many young boys and girls who actually are dry all night even as young as the age of three. There are probably just as many who are not. This is not a topic that people should make loose talk about, since parents' worrying can do quite as much harm as a preschooler's bed-wetting.

Does Mother's Yelling Cause Bed-Wetting?

My granddaughter Kitty, just four, still wets the bed every night. Before going to bed she goes to the bathroom and her father takes her up at midnight, but by morning she is always soaked.

What we don't understand is when she stays with me she doesn't wet. I just say to her, "I don't want you to wet my bed," and she says "Okay."

Kitty is an active child, never still. Her mother is continually scolding and yelling and her father says she should be spanked for wetting. I tell them I don't think that will help. What do you say?

It is most encouraging that your granddaughter can stay dry when she is at your house. This makes us hope that complete dryness may not be too far away.

What you tell us—that Kitty's mother is continually scolding and yelling, and that her father thinks she should be spanked—makes it seem that the tense atmosphere at home may have something to do with her wetting. And that the calmer atmosphere of your home may be producing the good results of a dry bed.

However don't forget that there are many children whose mothers yell and whose fathers spank who still don't wet their beds. The possibly unfavorable home atmosphere may make things worse, but in itself we doubt that it produces wetting. And don't forget, many four-year-olds are still not dry.

One other factor to be kept in mind. Some children, under ideal circumstances, produce good behavior that they are not able to keep up on an everyday basis. Thus even if her parents were nicer to Kitty, we're not sure that your command of "I don't want you to wet my bed" would necessarily work at home.

We sometimes see this same contrast in children who are terribly difficult at home but angels at school. Some children put their best foot forward all of the time, some none of the time, most just part of the time.

Since it is unlikely that you can markedly change the mother's or father's attitude toward Kitty, the best solution might be for you quietly to arrange to have her visit you as often as possible. Time will probably do the rest.

Five-and-a-Half-Year-Old Returns to Bed-Wetting

O *ur five-and-a-half-year-old son, Steven, has us really worried. After being dry at night for well over a year, he has suddenly returned to nightly wetting. He is dry in the daytime but never at night. This has been going on for more than a month now. Our pediatrician says there is no physical reason that he can determine for this wetting and mostly advises us that if we remain calm it will eventually stop. But we are very worried, and just waiting passively seems hardly enough to do for our son.*

C hances are that if Steven had never been dry at night, you might be somewhat discouraged but not specially worried since a good many quite normal children are not entirely dry at night till six or even later. The fact that he was dry for a while naturally makes you fear that something is wrong. It may not be. Still, you obviously have to take some position.

To begin with, try to remain calm and don't make a big fuss about this. Use a rubber sheet, of course, and diapers, and if you can find some big enough, rubber pants. It was wise to check with your doctor, but since he can't help at this point you are pretty much on your own.

It may be a little consoling to know that many young children, for reasons that we often never discover, do sometimes after doing nicely for a while, revert to bed-wetting, sleep disturbances, and stomach problems. These often disappear as quickly as they appear and we do not always find out their cause.

Since your doctor remains calm, I would wait for another month or so before taking major steps. Then I would try one of the good conditioning devices. Many of the major department stores sell these or you can ask your pediatrician.

Try this for a month or so. It may work. If not, ask yourself—is there anything special about Steven's life that may be upsetting him? Over-placement in school, and thus too great a demand that the child cannot meet, sometimes brings on bed-wetting.

And if your own doctor is not particularly interested in problems of nutrition, try to find one who is. Sometimes bed-wetting is associated with the intake of some particular food or foods to which a child is allergic.

Time is on your side, though. If none of these things works, and the wetting continues, you may want a further check on your child's physical status. Sometimes real bladder problems are at the basis of wetting.

Mostly, though, we would emphasize that it is uncomfortable but not unusual for a five-and-a-half-year-old child still to be wetting his bed.

On "Bad Habits"

Eighteen-Monther Holds His Breath

My daughter and I have a difference of opinion about how to handle my eighteen-month-old grandson, Peter. Peter is a very strong-minded baby and when he doesn't get his way he holds his breath and vomits.

I told my daughter that a good way to break him of this is to smack his bottom a few times. She disagrees. We are waiting for your reply.

Clearly an eighteen-monther who not only holds his breath but even vomits if he doesn't get his way is a very strong character. (This may be a new thing for eighteen-monthers. Peter is the second boy of this kind we have heard of lately.)

If he is hard to manage now, quite certainly he isn't going to become too much easier as he grows older. Thus how you handle him right now is very important. Though we do not like the term "break his will," it is true that if you can't control your own child, chances are that *he* will control *you*.

Therefore it is important for parents of even a very young child, especially when he is as strong-willed as Peter, to help him appreciate that he cannot control every situation, no matter how far he goes in his efforts to do so.

Some parents in the past have indeed found that a few sharp spanks do get their message across. Today parents use this method less than in the past. Many prefer the principles of what is called behavior modification. The idea of this is that you help the child to see that by behaving in ways of which you approve, he gets what he wants. When he behaves in ways of which you do not approve, he not only does *not* get what he wants, but people ignore him.

Admittedly it is a bit difficult to ignore a child who is not only holding his breath but vomiting, because you would eventually have to clean him up. But you could ignore him while he is merely holding his breath.

For breath holding alone you might feel better if you checked with your own pediatrician to see what he might advise. When this is combined with vomiting, I most certainly would check. It is conceivable that something about Peter's diet is making him uncomfortable and thus causing stress, which in turn may be at the root of this unhappy behavior. However, as to breath holding alone, most authorities agree that the ordinary child will not harm himself (even though he may frighten others) by holding his breath.

In general, I feel that grandmothers do best, if they and their daughters disagree about child raising, to allow these daughters to do things their own way.

Binky Has Tantrums Everywhere

O ur two-and-a-half-year-old son, Binky, is the tantrummiest boy you ever saw. He has tantrums everywhere: in the stores, at Sunday school, at friends' houses, and of course especially at home.

Whenever something bothers him or he doesn't like the way things are going, down he throws himself onto the floor and kicks and screams and carries on. It's terribly embarrassing and even frightening and so far we have found no way really to cope with it.

One clue to Binky's problem may very likely be that he goes to too many different places. Like many children his age, he may not be ready for visits to stores, Sunday school, and people's houses. So that's the first thing to try. Simplify his life.

Second, our advice remains—the best way to handle a tantrum is to prevent it before it begins. Find out what kinds of situations bring on these tantrums. At what times of day do they occur? Is it when he is hungry? Tired? When there are too many other people present? Often by charting the times and circumstances of occurrence you can step in *before* a tantrum occurs and thus prevent it.

Once it has happened, embarrassing or not, most agree that your very best bet is to ignore a tantrum (as much as you humanly can). Just do not let Binky feel that he has anything to gain by throwing it.

It may be interesting for you to see if your son fits into the personality type that we have found most prone to tantrums. These tend to be children who are poor adjusters, slow to warm up, rigid, ritualistic. And then when things go wrong they suddenly explode. Such children tend to be highly dependent on a well-structured environment—one structured around their weaknesses, with not too many surprises and not too many things that are different. They like sameness and they like repetition. That is, they need to have things just so. They tend to be hard children to handle because they need so *much* handling.

This means, of course, that to do a really good job in preventing tantrums a mother must have a clear picture of her own child's individuality. She must have the patience and ingenuity to keep him from being too greatly thwarted, disappointed, overstimulated, fatigued. It is no small order. But if you could do away with even some of your son's tantrums, you might feel it was well worth the effort.

What to Do About Biting

I have a two-and-a-half-year-old boy, Douggie, who bites. He bites everybody—children at nursery school, me, his father, our baby. We have tried everything with no success. Help!

According to one parent of a child in our nursery school, nothing works but time. "We tried everything with our son. Finally, around three years of age, he stopped."

Other parents report varying success with varying methods, including the "time out" method: "I remove my biting daughter from the room, explain that biting is totally unacceptable, and tell her she may come back if she will stop biting. This doesn't cure the biting permanently, but it does take care of it for the time being."

Some parents cry and carry on and let the child know it hurts them to be bitten.

Others bite back. They say, "Oh, I see you want to play the biting game," and then bite back. They contend that two or three times of playing this game should do it.

This strikes us as a not very kind or effective practice. One mother told us, "I just explain that biting hurts. My son hadn't realized that before, and always looked confused when his little brother cried after being bitten."

We go along with those mothers who try vigilance. As one mother explained, "An adult must stay at the side of the biter, and I had one of the worst ever, and stop every attempt at biting until the child outgrows it. Of course this does rather cut into the time you have to spend on other things."

As to what the vigilant person does when the child starts to bite, suggestions differ. We have recommended quickly cupping your hand under the child's chin, as he or she starts to bite, and pushing upward quickly. Then the child bites his own tongue. Possibly cruel, but nevertheless effective.

Kinder is the suggestion of the mother who advises: "Hold the jaw on either side of the mouth with thumb and index finger, apply slight pressure and say, 'No biting.' It seems to work."

We recommend any of these methods that works for you. The only parental advice we do not support is "Try spanking!" If you are a parent who does spank, it may make you feel better, but it is unlikely that it will stop the biting.

Rocking May Be a Sign of Hyperactivity

E very night, my two-and-a-half-year-old son, Chad, rocks his crib. We have put a thick rug under it and this cuts down the noise and movement of the crib. But his activity seems to us excessive.

Also, he is a head banger. We try to reduce any possible hurt or damage by encouraging him to bang on a soft rug or carpet, but he seems to prefer hard surfaces.

I have read in some of your earlier books that these behaviors are not necessarily harmful, but they worry us. Will you comment?

O ur position has been that in a great many young children, both head banging and crib rocking may fairly be considered just an extreme example of what we call tensional outlets. That is, the child feels tension and relieves it in his own way. Some suck their thumbs, some pull out their hair, some bang their heads, some rock their beds. These last two may have no more serious significance than thumb sucking, which most of us nowadays take pretty calmly.

In fact, crib rocking is sometimes thought to have its distinctly positive side. It seems to occur in many children who have good rhythm and possibly even real musical ability.

However, a more serious note enters the picture. Some specialists suggest that rocking or head banging may at times be an early expression of hyperkinesis (overactivity). Hyperactivity, of course, at least in its extreme form, *is* harmful, causing child and family and, later on, classmates and teachers considerable difficulty.

Happily, hyperactivity can in many children be reduced, if need be, by a proper diet. You might try removing from your child's diet all artificial coloring and flavoring.

In any case, continue putting a soft rug under Chad's crib, and keep on encouraging him to bang his head on soft surfaces only. But also, if you choose, check with your pediatrician about the possibility of improving your son's diet.

Little Girl Pulls Out Her Hair

M y trouble is that my little girl, Jennie, pulls out her hair. All of her hair—until she is entirely bald.

She did this once before when she was eighteen months old. She had to stop when her hair was all gone. I got her a doll with cotton hair and she loved the feel of that. Now she is four years old. Her hair had grown in beautifully, but she is pulling it out again. Not all the time, but all too often. What can I do?

It seems as if your Jennie pulls out her hair not only because she is uncomfortable, but perhaps also because she is going through a period of extreme stress. At least it isn't continuous. You might try two things. Get her another doll with cotton hair *and* buy her a nice little fuzzy cap that she can wear to bed. She may then pull either on the doll's hair or the fuzz on her cap.

I don't guarantee this method, but it has worked nicely with other little girls with the same problem. It's harder to get boys to wear a cap, but fortunately not as many boys as girls pull their hair.

We have had a further suggestion from another mother who had the same problem: "Our daughter pulled her hair out till she was bald. Finally we discovered she had a hearing problem. She has been wearing a hearing aid for nearly a year now and her hair has grown out so beautifully— it is shoulder length and she no longer pulls it out. She hasn't had even one bald spot since she got the hearing aid. So in her case, at least, deafness seems to have been at the root of the problem."

Charlotte's Clothes Don't Feel Right

This may be an old problem to you but it is new to me. My seven-year-old daughter, Charlotte, is giving me a terribly hard time lately because nothing fits or feels right. All her clothes are too tight or too loose or scratch her skin or some such. Shoelaces are always tied too tight or too loose. She makes me tie them and sometimes we spend ten minutes on her shoes. Pigtails are the same. I don't do them right, she says, and just as soon as I get them fixed she pulls them out and insists that they be done over again.

I do want her to be comfortable, but this daily ordeal is getting to be too much for me. What can you advise?

There are at least two possible reasons for Charlotte's complaints. One may be that all of them are signs of a not very good relationship with you. In this case, almost anything you do for her or with her will not be satisfactory. So how about Dad? One can just bet that shoes and pigtails will be much more satisfactory, or at least acceptable, if he does the work rather than you.

But actually a seven-year-old girl should not be needing much help with tying her shoes. Perhaps you are hovering too much. As for her hair, short hair would solve the pigtail problem. This might make her very unhappy but you could give her a choice. Either accept your first attempts at pigtail braiding, or have her hair cut.

A different possibility is that Charlotte may actually be a child who has great sensitivity of scalp, skin, and so on. Check with your doctor and see what he recommends.

Charlotte doesn't sound like an easy girl to live with, but there should be things you can do to make your days with her at least a little easier.

It might also be extremely interesting to you to have a good parent-teacher conference. Find out how things *really* are going at school. Even if your daughter *is* having trouble at school, it would not be along the pigtail-and-shoelace line. But there might be other things happening at school that could give you clues as to where her basic problem really lies.

Six-Year-Old Still Sucks Thumb

Our oldest child, a boy of six, still sucks his thumb and has done so from the moment of birth. We have tried to persuade him to stop, by offering a reward and also by painting his thumb. But when we painted his thumb, he switched to his middle finger. He does this only at home, not at school.

Kevin is a popular boy with other children and he has had more love and attention in his six years from all of us than many children have in a lifetime. It is important to us that he stop this habit. Can you help?

N ot too much. Most specialists and most parents nowadays tend to look on thumb sucking as a tensional outlet—either a reaction to stress or merely a comforting behavior—rather than a bad habit. You say you show your son love and affection. The two things are not necessarily related. Many much-loved children suck their thumbs; many who may be loved less do not.

I'd like to quote from recent comments of correspondents on this subject:

"I have accepted thumb sucking as a built-in instinct, weak in some children and strong in others, and not an indication of abnormal feelings or insecurity."

"Yes, it does bother me when my children suck their thumbs, particularly at ages five-and-a-half and seven. In fact, it is sickening to me and I hate it but so far I haven't found any cure. My older two stopped of their own accord when they were ready."

"It never bothered me when one of our children sucked their thumb. They outgrow it eventually."

"Our middle child was a thumb sucker. We never made much of it, feeling that it was something that would work out by the time she started school, and it did. The hospital told me she was born sucking her thumb."

"My oldest sucked her fingers, and the only thing that bothered me about it were the sarcastic remarks from know-it-all women. In fact, if you ever had a baby that could cry for an hour at a time, you'd give almost anything if it would settle down and suck its thumb."

"My children both sucked their thumbs and it did bother me because I was told it would ruin their mouth conformation, teeth, etc. But I was also told they would feel unloved and frustrated if denied their thumbs. Also, as they got older, it looked stupid. However, they sucked on, victims of their mother's indecision and inertia. The more impassioned thumb sucker has a perfect mouth now; the other one less so."

If you son does not suck his thumb at school, it seems probable that he is well on the way to a final resolution of this behavior.

On Discipline

How to Discipline a Baby

This question may be premature, and maybe I am just worrying too soon. But our son, Dennis, our first baby, is now six months old and already he seems to be an awfully spoiled child. He wants his own way and wants it all the time.

My husband says it's time we started disciplining him, but I don't know quite what kind of discipline one would use with a six-month-old baby!

It's probably never too soon to think about disciplining, but it is sometimes hard to think of it in an effective way. Disciplining, especially with a baby, is not so much a matter of specific things you do, or of specific requirements you make of a child, as of the relationship between the two of you.

Actually as you yourself will realize if you stop to think about it, you have actually been disciplining Dennis right from the beginning. Parents teach children to set limits for themselves from their earliest days. Even if Dennis may seem a bit spoiled to your husband, it seems fairly safe to say that this baby is not ruling your household.

Discipline is of course not just a matter of punishment, though some people seem to think of it that way. Ideally discipline is made up of your total relationship with your boy or girl. With infants we discipline, if one wishes to use that term, by gently easing them into some sort of schedule or routine. We try to help them appreciate, gradually, that they will not always be picked up or fed the very minute they start to cry.

Our concept of this is the self-demand and self-regulation feeding schedule. At first we feed the baby whenever he seems hungry, but gradually as he gets older, we expect him to wait a bit. Following this method, many infants by six months of age or so work out for themselves a very reasonable and restrained daily schedule of sleeping, waking, and feeding. We used to feel that we were *disciplining* a baby by making him wait. We now feel that nothing was gained and a lot was lost.

At any rate all of this involves its own kind of discipline. You and the baby learn to live with each other, happily and comfortably. This is the best kind of discipline.

Daughter Calls Mother "Dummy Mummy"

I have what I fear you will consider a ridiculous problem. My two-year-old daughter, Florence, seems to be an early talker and she has a wonderful way with words. If she really wants you to do something she will address you as "Honey." Thus she says, "Mummy, honey," or "Daddy, honey."

That's okay. But when she is angry she calls me "Dummy." That is, she says "Dummy Mummy." I'm sorry to admit that she got the adjective from my husband, who does not think much of my intelligence and who does sometimes call me "Dummy."

But what can I do? I can't spank a two-year-old. Or can I?

It would seem rather harsh. Also kind of weak on your part to be outsmarted by a child so young. Three paths seem open to you. One is just to ignore the appellation. Just look very uninterested as if you hadn't heard her. This might not work, however.

A little more theatrical, but it might work, would be whenever she calls you that, just walk away from her. Quite quickly she will learn that the pleasure of a tantrum or a fight or just of name-calling is greatly diminished if the audience walks away.

Of course that would be harder to do if you were out in public, so till she gets over this habit, you may have to reduce the number of occasions when you take her out with you.

It is in a way a small thing, but it is not a good thing. Though you really can't blame Florence, since your husband also calls you dumb, it would be very wise to put a stop to this kind of name-calling.

A third possibility, when she calls you "Dummy Mummy," is to reply in kind. Thus you could call her "Funny Florence." We do this in nursery school sometimes—by rhyming or making a joke when we don't like the way the children talk.

The important thing is to arrange that there be no satisfactory payoff for Florence when she uses this term. Thus ignoring is possibly the best. But walking away might also do the trick. Or turning her words against her. Straight old-fashioned punishment, such as spanking, should be tried only as a very last resort, and we do not recommend it.

Getting your husband to treat you better would be the ideal solution, but somehow I have a feeling that this is not going to be easy.

Do You Spoil Your Child When You Use Preschool Techniques?

Sometimes I think you give quite bad advice, especially about preschoolers. Why all this pussyfooting around with what you label as preschool techniques?

If I want a child to do something, I tell him to do it. I do not fool around with all this, "Shall we pick up the toys?" "How about picking up the toys?" "Where do the big blocks go?"

I just tell my son, "Pick up your toys." I have the strength of character and the courage to give a direct command. And if he doesn't pick up his blocks, then no outdoor play, or no supper, or no whatever comes next.

Fine, if you see life that way and have the time and patience to hang around forcing your child to do some simple thing that really does not make all that much difference anyway.

The main idea of preschool techniques is, when things really don't matter, to give the child, and, more important, to give yourself an acceptable out.

Many mothers who prefer your methods find that long before their child has responded to some direct command, so much time and energy on their part has been spent that they wish they had never brought up whatever it was in the first place.

If you have a good understanding of preschool behavior you can usually tell which things can be offered as direct commands—and which are much safer given in such a way that you can slide out of them.

As your child grows older he obviously becomes more capable, not only intellectually and physically, but in his ability to do what you tell him to. Using techniques while the child is young and not very cooperative does not mean that you are not a good disciplinarian. It mostly means that you are respecting a young child's immaturity and inability always to do exactly as told.

Questions and Answers About Discipline

Q. If a small child who doesn't talk yet touches something he shouldn't, isn't it okay to slap his hand?

A. Probably not. Your best bet with the very young is to put breakable or otherwise valuable objects out of reach. If this isn't always possible, when the child does touch some breakable object, tell him that it is breakable but his stuffed dog isn't. So he should play with that. If you have the patience to repeat this message numerous times, usually words are better than a slap.

Q. When several children are together, and some misdeed occurs, isn't it important to find out which one did whatever it was that you don't like?

A. Not only perhaps unimportant, but often impossible. Chances are that each child involved will swear that he wasn't the one who did whatever it was. A wise mother may say something like, "I'm not interested in knowing who did it. I'm not interested in blaming anyone for what happened in the past. I am interested in seeing improvement in the future."

Q. I try not to punish my son but merely scold him or express disapproval instead. However even though he looks very penitent and says "I'm sorry," actually the very next day he will do the same thing all over again. What now?

A. Most children say "I'm sorry" simply to get you off their backs. It is important to make them realize that if they are really sorry, their feelings of remorse will be translated into action. The repeated offender could be told something like, "Sorry means behaving differently," or "Sorry means making changes."

Q. All this expressing disapproval is very fine, but isn't it just letting the child off very easily when he has done something wrong?

A. Quite right. Your best bet, after expressing disapproval of some wrongdoing, is to present some alternative way of behaving that would more or less right the wrong. Thus you come home and find that your daughter hasn't done the dishes—her task for that evening. Instead of saying, "You can forget about going out tomorrow. Maybe that will teach you to do what you promised to do," try, "It really upsets me to come home to a sink full of dirty dishes when you promised you would do them. I'd like them washed and put away before bedtime."

In short, in terms of the old song, try accentuating the positive and eliminating the negative. It might work.

Her Four-and-a-Half-Year-Old Daughter Is Impossible!

I have a daughter, four and a half years old. And she is impossible! She doesn't listen to anybody. She could be told fifty times to do something and she won't budge. But as soon as she knows we're going to really hit her, and when we show that we mean business, she jumps to it and says, "I'll be good!"

What should we do with her? Other times she's an angel.

S he's impossible but she's an angel! How many preschoolers strike their parents that very way, though admittedly sometimes the angelic side is most conspicuous when they're asleep.

You actually have given your answer to your problem in your letter. When you are just talking—"She could be told fifty times,"—she doesn't respond. *"When she knows we really mean business,"* she responds at once.

So, stop talking and start meaning business. Give fewer commands, and give them only at times when you are prepared to stop everything else and follow through.

Too many parents do as you do. They lapse too easily into the "If I have to tell you *once more,* I'll do so and so," and you *do* tell once more and they *don't* do so and so.

It really isn't all that difficult, but it does take time and it does take follow-through. The child has to know that you *do* mean business, or he or she is *not* going to pay attention to what you say.

Reward or Bribe?

I have found both praising and rewarding almost foolproof when it comes to getting along with my children. But when I reward them, my mother-in-law claims that I am bribing. She argues that they should just be good naturally. Can you help me convince her that a reasonable reward is not a bribe?

I can identify the difference for you. Whether or not this will convince your mother-in-law I have no idea.

I consider that it is *bribery* if a mother says to a child who is objecting to some task or responsibility, "I'll give you ten cents if you'll finish your meal," or "I'll give you a quarter if you'll do your practicing right now."

A *reward* is usually thought of more in the nature of a contract that you make with a child, and is usually given *after* the task or duty has been performed. Thus if you tell your son that if he keeps his room reasonably neat all week, you'll give him a certain amount of money or a certain privilege, we don't consider that bribing but rather rewarding.

A bribe is given to stop misbehavior (a child is given twenty-five cents to stop fighting), or to prevent misbehavior from occurring ("I'll give you a cookie now if you promise not to throw a tantrum in the supermarket").

Here are a few suggestions for successful rewarding.

Be specific. Pick only one or two very specific and observable behaviors to reward. Don't reward for some vague, global trait such as "being good."

Make the reward depend on the desired behavior: "After you finish your homework you can watch TV."

Give rewards somewhat sparingly. Don't reward a child for everything he does or he'll expect to be rewarded for everything and anything.

Rewards might best, for the most part, be reserved for situations in which you need to give your child a boost to perform a difficult or new behavior.

If concrete rewards are at first given in conjunction with social reinforcers (praise, affection, appreciation, individual attention), then gradually the concrete rewards can be phased out.

One of the best ways to tell the difference between a reward and a bribe is this. If *you* feel that you are in control of the situation, and can give or withhold the present or pleasure, chances are that you are rewarding. If the child is in control and you have to give whatever it is in order to get him to behave, chances are you are bribing.

To Spank or Not to Spank

I am a mother who occasionally spanks. Well, actually it is more of a slap than a spank, but I do now and then lay a hand on one of my children. I have four under six years of age and things sometimes get pretty hectic around here. If I stopped to argue and explain and discuss every time things went wrong, I would never come to the end of it.

A quick, sharp slap seems to me to do more good than anything else. Am

I so wrong? Everyone acts as if I am a monster or child beater, except my husband, who goes along with my kind of discipline. I love my children, but sometimes the whole thing is just too much.

Spanking, which used to be a very common form of punishment, is, admittedly, in considerable disrepute today. Dr. Gesell used to say that if you plan never to spank your child, chances are you may end up by spanking just the right amount. That is, most people *do* spank, even though they don't admit it. But certainly it is not the best kind of discipline. It punishes but it does not correct. We don't recommend it, but certainly do not condemn any parent who now and then resorts to it. And it's fair to say that if you occasionally do spank one of your children, you are no exception and should by no means feel guilty. Spanking is not a good technique for enforcing discipline because it is not particularly constructive. You can punish in this way for bad behavior, but it doesn't teach your child much of anything except that you are displeased with him. It doesn't point him toward a more constructive kind of behavior.

It does teach the child that he will be whacked if he is bad. But it doesn't really improve the relationship between the two of you. It does not put him on the right track. And if and when the child gets to be bigger than you are, it becomes impractical.

It is important to remember that good discipline consists of teaching the child to behave well and helping him to do so.

A special warning against the use of physical punishment comes from Professor Murray Straus of the University of New Hampshire. After an intensive study of violence in the American family, he comes out rather strongly against spanking. His point of view is interesting.

According to Straus, physical punishment is the foundation on which the edifice of family violence rests. It is the way most people experience violence, and it establishes the emotional context of associating love with violence. The child learns early that those who love him or her are also those who hit, and that bigger people hit smaller people.

And, when physical punishment is used to train the child or to teach him about dangerous things to be avoided, it establishes the moral rightness of hitting other family members. A further unintended consequence of spanking is the lesson that when something is really important it justifies the use of physical force.

Unfortunately early experience with physical punishment lays the groundwork for the legitimacy of all types of violence, but especially intrafamily violence.

Rules For Disciplining

Here are some of the latest and, I think, some of the best suggestions about disciplining, provided by Saf Lerman, a well-known leader of parenting groups.

1. Keep in mind that discipline doesn't mean punishment. It means helping children to make parental standards their own.

2. Children need to have their parents set definite limits. They cannot do this for themselves.

3. Remember that there is no one "ideal" way to approach a discipline situation. What one parent may handle with humor another may approach by offering a choice, while another may express anger.

4. Parents are human. They won't always be able to make a positive approach but they can and should make a commitment to discard definitely hurtful methods such as hitting and name calling.

5. Each discipline situation that occurs in our homes is not a battle in a war. As parents we should not be out to win and prove who is stronger, but rather to guide our children and build their consciences over a period of time.

6. We do not have to "face" every situation. When things are relatively unimportant we can sometimes just ignore them.

7. Do not waste energy blaming children. Use your energy, and whenever possible your child's energy, to find a creative solution for problems.

8. Sometimes children misbehave just to get our attention. Try to make this unnecessary by giving them lots of good, positive attention.

9. Don't always deal with things at a surface level. If

misbehavior seems serious and continues, try to get at the root of it.

10. Do your very best to eliminate negative methods of discipline such as sarcasm, hurtful teasing, verbal abuse, humiliation, and physical punishment.

11. It is helpful when parents let children know exactly what they expect. Too often we assume that a child is aware of what we want when he or she really doesn't know.

12. Tell children what they may do as well as what they may not. Thus if you have told them not to jump on the chair or bed, point out that they may jump on the floor.

13. Give instructions positively. Instead of saying, "Why can't you ever put your toys away," say, "I expect you to put your toys away when you are through with them."

14. Keep instructions simple. Don't go on and on. "Cut it out" may do just as well as something more complicated.

15. Warn your children if their behavior is having a negative effect on you: "Right now I'm still feeling pleasant but if this keeps up, in a few minutes you will have a very angry mother to deal with."

16. Humor is a wonderful aid in solving conflicts, if you feel up to it.

17. Sometimes, with older children, writing a brief note works better than giving instructions verbally, especially if it is a matter you have been arguing about in the past.

18. Allow children to air their feelings about a situation before expecting them to resolve an issue or accept your decision.

19. "Time out" works well for both parent and child. Sometimes you can send a child to his or her room; sometimes you can remove yourself from the situation.

20. As children grow older, a certain amount of flexibility is useful: "Come home from your hockey game around nine thirty or ten."

21. Avoid threats. Offer choices.

22. Try not to rub things in. Once a child already feels unhappy for something he or she has done, don't go on and on about it.
23. Try to be sure that your requirements meet the age and stage capabilities of your child.
24. With the very young, distraction is an indispensible technique. You don't have to solve every situation head-on. If you can distract, they very often forget.
25. Let your children know that you notice and appreciate any efforts they may make to improve. Praise whenever you possibly can.
26. Try to avoid physical punishment, which mostly teaches children that those who are bigger can hit.
27. Try taking away a relevant privilege when house rules are abused. Of course this means you will have to set up house rules to begin with.

Discipline Has Gone to Pieces in This Family

Discipline, which I know is crucial, is rather going to pieces in our family. My husband and I have four children, age two years to twelve, and none of them can be said to really mind.

I realize that without knowing our family you can't tell us specifically what to do, but any suggestions would be gladly accepted. And please don't recommend some book that we can read as neither my husband nor I are readers and we don't have time, anyway.

Well, since you don't want a book, of which there are many quite good ones, here are a few basic, general rules about disciplining.

To begin with, your discipline of any child is strongly connected to your relationship with that child. If you like and respect the child, and he or she likes and respects you, things should go fairly smoothly.

Next, are you and your husband well-disciplined people yourselves? If a mother and father yell and scream around a lot, at the children or at each other, obviously they don't set a very good example.

Are you trying too hard? Sometimes if you will let some of the smaller things go and concentrate on the important ones, you'll get farther.

Carry out the things you say. That is, don't threaten that "If you do that once more, I'll punish you in such and such a way." If the rule is "Don't do something," skip the threats and give the consequences immediately.

A basic rule is for mother and father either to back each other up, or at least, if they do differ, not to undermine each other.

Also, any discipline should fit your own temperament and that of the child. If it embarrasses you to yell, don't yell. If you are going to have a guilty conscience if now and then you use physical punishment, don't hit. But also consider the child. Some children are much impressed by a frown or look of displeasure. With others, the house could fall down on them and they wouldn't care. Some can be reasoned with. With others you're wasting your time talking, and you really do need to act.

It is very important to appreciate that if you are managing your family in an ideal way, relatively little actual punishment should be necessary. But it is also important to appreciate that in almost any family a certain amount of punishment will be necessary. Some children actually need it to keep them in line and to make them feel secure.

If it is true as you say that none of your children are well disciplined, I personally would start on just one at a time. I'd start with the "best" one, the one who most nearly fits your standards, so that you will be encouraged with your results. This may not seem fair but it might work out best.

And keep in mind that it is unusual for all the children in any family to be satisfactory. As one mother reported, "Two of my five turned out well. I think that's fairly good, don't you?"

No More Psychological Games with His Son

M y husband just said such a marvelous thing that I would like to share it with other parents. For a long time we've tried to be very correct and psychological with our three children. Tonight my husband was having his usual hassle with our now thirteen-year-old and all of a sudden he exploded: "I'm tired of playing psychological games with you, Kenneth. From now on I'll tell you the way I want things and that's the way they're going to be."

Kenneth looked as if he were about to become the victim of child abuse, but I was delighted. I don't mean to be hostile, but sometimes I think you child specialists make life even harder for us parents than it would be without so much advice.

You are so very right. True, like other child specialists, I hope that much we have to say is helpful to parents. But I personally have never much favored what your husband so correctly calls "psychological games." A bright and verbal boy or girl is likely to run circles around his parent once these games do start. It is not that the child is smarter than you. It is just that he or she is more interested in keeping the argument going.

Particularly questionable to me has always been the Haim Ginott–type of "mirroring back the child's feelings." Say he tells you that the coach never puts him on the team. Instead of suggesting things he might do to improve the situation, you're supposed to say, "It really bothers you that the coach doesn't put you on the team." Supposedly this makes him feel better.

Or say he or she blows up at some parental rule or regulation. Tells you that it makes him good and mad. You're supposed to say, "It really makes you angry that we have this rule." If I were that boy or girl I'd be even angrier. Having just told you that I'm good and mad, I don't want you to tell me that I'm good and mad. I already know it.

All very well and good to be sympathetic. But your husband is right that parents can go too far with all this understanding. Sympathy when it's called for, yes. But you are the parents and you really do not have to explain or justify everything you say or do. Nor do you have to understand all the reasons behind every bit of misbehavior on the part of your child. He will be unreasonable often. You have the right to your own periods of unreason now and then.

On Mothers

Bonding May Not Make Much Difference

*A*s a mother who had one baby according to regular hospital routine, and a second under circumstances that used so-called bonding—my baby was placed on my chest immediately after birth so that an immediate bond could be formed between us—may I report that both my children seem to relate to me equally well.

As a breastfeeding mother, I do definitely believe in warm and strong contact between mother and child. But I think all the recent talk about the importance of bonding has led to considerable anxiety on the part of mothers who didn't "bond."

*B*onding is a notion about which many child specialists seem to have gone overboard. It's nice work if you can get it, but in my opinion not necessary. For decades we got along without bonding. Common sense tells us that many parents established fine relationships with their children before the world ever heard of bonding.

Current research supports your own discovery that it really may not make all that much difference. A 1980 study reported in the journal *Child Development* compares the behavior of a group of children who were bonded—that is, had immediate contact with their mothers right after birth and for ninety minutes at each feeding, and a group who received the regular hospital routine and thus were not bonded. No differences in behavior were obtained on twenty-eight separate measures.

A further report in the same journal, dated December 1983, summarizes as follows: "Most of those who have reviewed the matter conclude that the evidence does *not* support the existence of a sensitive period for parent-infant bonding." That is, you can relate to your infant at any reasonable time and not necessarily immediately after birth. "There is only minimal support for the view that the first hours after birth are critical for the establishment of parent-infant bonding and that parents who miss such opportunities will be impaired in their ability to care for their infants or to relate to them."

So, bond if you wish, but don't worry if you didn't.

In fact, whenever you read about a new notion that somebody or other claims to be essential for good parenting, check with your doctor if you like. But if common sense tells you it may not be necessary, don't worry too much about it.

Never Mind What Other People Think

My problem is my seventeen-month-old son, Robin. He is an extremely active little boy and he gets into everything. That isn't so bad at home —we do use gates and have other ways of keeping him out of real danger spots.

But when we go visiting, he also is into everything and I'm afraid people will think I am not a good mother. Can you give me some rules or ideas of what to do so that he will behave better and not be an embarrassment to me when we are out?

One of the most crippling things that can happen to a young mother is to worry about what other people will think. If Robin seems reasonably good and healthy, and if your own husband is reasonably satisfied with your methods of dealing with your son, that is what matters most.

People who understand about babies and small children will not be too quick to blame you if your son is less than perfect when in other people's homes. I would avoid the others. If it is absolutely necessary to take Robin visiting, as for instance to your in-laws, then just face the fact that, if he is an into-everything little boy, much of somebody's time and attention will need to be devoted to him, rather than to the other adults present.

She Can't Stop Screaming at Her Daughter

I am a rather nervous and also rather new mother. The whole business of parenting is hard for me and I find myself constantly screaming at my daughter and making terrible threats. Then she cries, and I calm down and I am terribly ashamed of what I have done. My husband is not sympathetic with my problem. He says I could stop all this screaming if I really tried. But I have tried and am getting nowhere.

Yours is not an unusual problem and actually you may be harming your daughter less than you and your husband fear. So long as your basic, underlying treatment is kind, a child can and does forgive quite awful threats. *If you are basically fond of your daughter,* chances are she knows it.

Keep in mind that screaming is a lot like spanking. An occasional scream, an occasional spank, is nothing to criticize yourself for. But if your only response to any trying situation is spanking or screaming, clearly things are out of hand and you will want to change. Here's how:

First of all, take the task seriously. Swearing off screaming is in some ways not too different from swearing off smoking. Plan for it. Don't just tell yourself you'll do better. Undertake a campaign to improve your way of communicating with your daughter.

You might try the tape-recorder method. Many mothers know they *do* yell, but they have no idea of how awful they sound. The shock experience of hearing yourself on tape often reduces both the quantity and volume of screaming.

Or you might, as with children, try the chart-and-reward method. Keep an honest record of how many times you yell during any one day. When the number of yells per day has been reduced to some small, arbitrary number, give yourself a reward.

Check to see what times of day and in what situations your screaming occurs. Once you have identified these situations you may be able to change or avoid them.

Next, you might ask yourself what other kinds of discipline are available to you. Could you whisper instead of yell? Could you leave the scene (provided your daughter is not doing something really dangerous) till you calm down? Are you trying to discipline too much? Are your standards for your child's behavior too high?

If none of the common-sense things you try seem to work, then it is possible that you may, indeed, need a little professional help so that you can improve your mothering and your relationship with your little girl. But the fact that you are looking for help is, obviously, a very good first step toward finding it.

Mother-in-Law Thinks It's All Mother's Fault

O ur eight-year-old son and first child has been a source of difficulty almost from the moment of his birth. And as the years go by he gets worse, not better. Not that we don't love him. He has many endearing qualities. But he is a very difficult little boy, to say the least.

A recent psychological examination showed him to be performing at about a five-and-a-half-year-old level with an intelligence to match. School was murder till we finally got him into a learning-disability class.

All these things have presented problems, but problems that my husband and I have been able to cope with. What I cannot cope with is that so many people seem to blame me for the fact that Eric is babyish, rude, and rebellious.

Most criticism I try to shrug off but I cannot shrug off my mother-in-law's constant nagging. She is certain that it is my lack of discipline that causes Eric to behave as he does and she says so almost daily. Fortunately she doesn't live with us but she does live in our same town so we cannot escape her. The fact that she is so critical of Eric seems to bring out his very worst behaviors. I have to admit that he is terrible with her.

I can see that he is a disappointment to her, he being her only grandson. But I feel that I have enough to cope with in trying to keep life on an even keel with my admittedly difficult son, without having to take so much criticism.

Y ou are not alone. Many parents of difficult children find that one of their biggest burdens is the criticism handed out so freely by their nearest relatives. In your case, hard as this may be to do, you and your husband will have to make Grandma face the fact that your house must be out-of-bounds to her unless she can manage not to comment on Eric's behavior or your handling of it.

Your husband would be the best person to make this rule and convey it to his mother. Of course you two can visit your mother-in-law, but ideally these visits would not include Eric. At least not for the time being.

It is totally unfair for people to criticize mothers (especially to their faces) for the behavior of atypical boys and girls.

Sally Never Lets Her Mother Alone

My problem is that my five-year-old daughter, Sally, never lets me alone. She demands my constant and total attention. Even my facial expressions draw her questions—"What are you thinking, Mommy? Why do you look like that?"

If even for a moment I seem to be absorbed in my own thoughts, she demands that I pay attention to her. It makes me frantic—especially when I'm driving. If I merely slow down to see which way to go, she has a stream of questions as to why I stopped, why I slowed down, and which way we are going, until I yell at her to be still.

Sally is our adopted daughter. She knows this and so far as I can tell, it doesn't bother her. But how can I get her to let me alone? How can I get some privacy for myself? Or how can I learn patience?

Can you believe it that the opposite extreme is almost as bad? Most of us feel that one of the best preventatives of future delinquency is good communication between mother and child. You have that—even though in excess. So try to feel, even when you are your most impatient, that there is a good side to Sally's insistence on constant communication.

Also her sensitivity to your facial expressions has its good side. Some children, and some adults, have no idea of and no interest in other people's reactions. Sally will one day undoubtedly be a highly responsive friend to someone.

Though Sally may seem not to worry about being adopted, it's altogether possible that the fact that she is not your biological child may add to her basic insecurity and increase her demand for constant and intense rapport. Whatever the reason, she seems to need this intensity.

I doubt that you can change Sally very much, but you may find that by setting aside certain periods of the day during which you give your total attention you may reduce the vigor of her demands at other times. While you are driving is perhaps not only the most aggravating but also potentially the most dangerous time. It is obviously bad for a driver to have her attention distracted and her emotions stirred up, as in your case. Try having Sally sit in the back seat with rather strict rules about her not talking. If she can't live up to these you may need—even at considerable inconvenience to yourself—not to take her with you when you drive.

School will soon cut down the amount of time you spend together. Also, try to plan substantial periods of time when the two of you will be apart. Have her happily occupied during these times, but away from you.

If Sally's overdependence continues, or increases, you may eventually need to get some special help for her, though ideally you will be able to make it without.

Boy Takes Everything Out on Mother

*I*s it natural for a child to take everything out on his mother?
I am the mother of four boys, and my middle son, Henry, age ten, is just awful to me. He is disrespectful and arrogant, often in the presence of others, and actually seems to resent me.

He joined the Cub Scouts awhile ago and I became a den mother just to ensure his getting in. But he complained that I "had to be in on everything." Recently I went on a long motor trip with him and some friends (again I went so that they could have the trip) and he snarled, "Why do you always have to come along? You always spoil everything."

He is very jealous of his brothers and resents any privileges I give them. Fortunately he is wonderful at school, and we never have a single com-

plaint. I am trying to turn him over to his father more and more, as they get on quite well.

It is, unfortunately, very natural for any child to take everything out on his mother. That is probably the reason that in the preschool years, many children get on better with a baby-sitter than with their mother.

It is also one of the reasons some women find that their children treat them better when they (the mothers) work outside the home. A home mother tends to be a victim for everybody.

However in your case it sounds as if you are trying to do a little too much for Henry. Often it does *not* work out when a child's own mother runs the Cub Scouts or the Brownies group. As for the long motor trip, surely you have learned your lesson on that one.

You might do best to explain to Henry that while he still feels that you "spoil everything," he is going to be on his own. If he finds that he can have your help and company only if and when he treats you nicely, it is possible though by no means certain that he may improve.

Are the Roles of Mother and Father Really Interchangeable?

Recently I heard psychologist Lee Salk say, on the air, that the roles of mother and father are nowadays interchangeable, that there really need be no difference between mothering and fathering. Do you agree with that? As a mother of four I don't. My husband is a very good father, but I feel he would have a very hard time in the mother role.

I agree with you 100 percent. The roles of mother and father are by no means interchangeable, biologically or emotionally.

So far, only a mother can produce children. In a single-parent family where a father has the sole care of child or children, he can and often does, admirably, take on many of the aspects of the mother role.

But in an ordinary two-parent family, it is almost inevitably the mother with whom the child makes the closest relationship. It is "Mummy" he calls, a dozen times a day, whenever he is in difficulty. It is "Mummy" he takes things out on when he is at a difficult age. In the early years of adolescence, when boy or girl is having such a struggle to be free of family and to be an independent person, it is, especially at eleven when the struggle is so intense, "Mummy" he struggles against the hardest.

Though it is popular nowadays to speak as if the two roles were interchangeable, experience tells us that they are not.

Quiz For Parents

How well do you, as parents, agree with the Gesell Institute's feelings and findings about child behavior? Here are some multiple-choice questions you might like to answer. Give yourself a score of one for each "correct" answer. A score of fourteen means that you are really on your toes. Ten or more is good. Below that, perhaps you'd like to brush up on your reading.

1. Relative speed of movement in individual infants and children:
    A. Is usually slow at first and increases as the child matures.
    B. Is largely determined by the amount of training you give.
    C. Is an index of intelligence—the faster the brighter.
    D. Is to a large extent a consistent, constitutionally determined factor and cannot be appreciably hurried by either training or practice.
2. Thumb sucking is currently considered by most child specialists to be:
    A. A normal tensional outlet, occurring in many though not all children.
    B. A bad habit that should be prevented at all costs.
    C. A habit for which the child should be punished.
3. The average age of first walking, in children in this country, is:
    A. Twelve to Fifteen months.
    B. Ten Months.

    C. Eighteen Months.

    D. Two Years.

4. The amount of sleep a child needs:

    A. Should be determined only by the child's own wishes.

    B. Can be determined from available charts. The amount of time indicated in the charts should be strictly adhered to.

    C. Varies from age to age and from child to child.

5. Going-to-bed "rituals," such as demands for certain specific objects and activities during presleep period, are generally considered to be:

    A. A fair indication of neurosis or emotional disturbance.

    B. Nearly always caused by loneliness and/or jealousy of siblings

    C. A sign that the child has been "spoiled" and is just trying to get his own way.

    D. A common characteristic of the two-and-a-half-year-old age level.

6. Infant intelligence tests are generally considered to be:

    A. Not predictive of later behavior.

    B. Moderately predictive of later behavior.

    C. Highly predictive of later behavior.

    D. Still in an exploratory stage and not yet adequately refined for definite use in predicting later behavior.

7. If your two-and-a-half- to three-and-a-half-year-old boy or girl suddenly starts to stutter, you would be justified in believing that:

    A. Your child is in serious psychological trouble and in need of special help.

    B. He has likely merely reached the stuttering stage frequently exhibited by quite normal children in this age range.

    C. Your child is showing early signs of a serious speech defect.

8. The child who plays with an imaginary playmate or companion:

A. Is expressing a behavior quite normal around three to four years, occurring in rather superior children.

B. Is expressing a sign of emotional disturbance.

C. Does this because he is lonely and has nobody to play with.

9. If your six-year-old consistently objects to going to school and even says he feels sick to his stomach in the morning, you will be wise to:

A. Force him to go to school in order to teach him that he can't get away with his complaints.

B. Respect his complaints and try to find out what about school is bothering him.

10. When brothers and sisters fight, you should:

A. Punish both, every time.

B. Try to get to the bottom of every quarrel and find out who is "right."

C. Try to change the daily routine so they won't fight so much.

D. Ignore it as much as you can, appreciating that most siblings fight and probably enjoy it no matter how they holler.

11. The I.Q. is considered by many psychologists to be:

A. The most effective single measure of intelligence that we have so far.

B. A complete and guaranteed measure of intelligence.

C. An absolute, fixed figure that does not ever vary.

12. If your seven-year-old complains that you are not his parents and that he is adopted, you will be wise to conclude that:

A. He is expressing the normal foster-child fantasy, common at this age.

B. He is not receiving as much love as you should give him.

C. He is probably emotionally disturbed.

13. If your eight-year-old repeatedly runs away from home and you cannot, by discussing the behavior with him, find out what is the matter, you should:

A. Punish him severely.

B. Prevent him from running away by keeping him under constant supervision.
C. Ignore the behavior as characteristic of his age.
D. Seek professional help for his problem.
14. The ability to tell the truth consistently:
A. Should be insisted on as soon as the child can talk.
B. Should be trained into the child and insisted on, on every occasion.
C. Is not arrived at by most children before eight years of age or even later.

Correct Answers:
1-D, 2-A, 3-A, 4-C, 5-D, 6-D, 7-B,
8-A, 9-B, 10-D, 11-A, 12-A, 13-D, 14-C

On Balancing Family and Career

How Long Need Mother Stay at Home?

I am a professional woman, married and six months pregnant. There is no question that I shall continue to lead a professional life. My question is, How long need I plan to stay at home after my baby is born?

There seems to be such a variety of advice on this subject that I am rather confused. Some say that a new mother should stay at home for at least a year with her baby. (Some imply that she should never go back to work so long as any of her children are small.) Others seem to think it okay to start working again almost immediately.

I want to do what is right for the baby, though I prefer not to stay away from my job any longer than is absolutely necessary.

The answer to a question like yours depends on many factors— chiefly your own personality and your family's financial situation. If a second income (that provided by you) is essential you will probably need to go back to work fairly soon.

However, you apparently work because you enjoy it, enjoy it more than staying at home, and chances are you have more choice.

Some psychologists insist that you are harming your children unless you stay at home till all are at least three years of age. Any child is fortunate whose mother can manage to do that but no one is certain that children are harmed if Mother goes back to work sooner.

I personally would find it difficult to leave a baby much under six months of age unless I were absolutely *certain* that I had made excellent provision for his or her care. I, a real workaholic, and a person not interested in housework and in staying at home, was fortunate that my baby was born in April. It wasn't necessary for me to go back to graduate school till September. So without making any painful decision, I was able to be at home with her for the first five months. I was then doubly blessed to find a middle-aged neighbor who was willing to take care of my baby during the hours I was at school and at work.

The answer to your question to some extent would seem to me to depend on how you feed your baby. Even if he is to be bottle fed you may very probably want to stay at home for the first month, just to be sure things get off to a good start. After that, provided you have trustworthy and competent help, most think it okay to go back to work whenever you wish.

If you breastfeed, as one hopes you will, there are still two possibilities. If you prefer that your baby conform to some set schedule (say with a feeding every three hours or every four hours regardless of his or her wishes), you do not actually need to remain at home for more than the first few weeks. You can arrange, if you wish, to be at home for part of the feedings and can express your milk and leave it bottled for those times you can't be there.

But the best kind of feeding there is, breastfeeding on a self-demand and self-regulation schedule (though it can be arranged as above) does best with a bit more sacrifice of time on your part.

If you follow a self-demand schedule, in the early weeks you feed the baby whenever he or she is hungry and makes a demand. Gradually, self-regulation comes in and the baby learns to wait a little, and the daily schedule takes on more shape and regularity.

All of this works out best if you are right there at home with the baby, ideally for at least the first two or three months. Getting to know your baby and helping him adapt to the world around him is close to a full-time job in these very early months.

You get to know what he wants and needs, and how he feels, and what his different sighs and sounds and cries mean. He gets to know you and comes to feel that the world around him is safe and secure because you are there and he can count on you.

There is a wonderful synchronization that, under ideal circumstances, takes place between a mother and her new infant, and many think it quite worth the sacrifice of other activities for at least the first few months.

Work Without Guilt

*U*p *till now things have gone remarkably well with my life. But last year we had a child. I tood six months' leave of absence, because I am a strong advocate of breastfeeding and also believe that if possible a mother should be with her baby in the early months.*

But when Sandra was six months old I went back to work. And though I have a very good housekeeper who also takes care of Sandy, every now and then I am assailed with feelings of guilt, especially when I read things that say a mother owes it to her child not to work when the child is young.

I guess what I want is reassurance that I am not harming my daughter.

I can give you reassurance that you are *not* harming your daughter. Only the most diehard conservatives, nowadays, criticize the mother who works when her children are very young.

It is now generally believed by the many mothers who work, and by the professionals who support their doing so, that a normally endowed child, if his or her care is reasonably well provided for during the daytime, will not suffer from the fact that mother works. Children can make multiple attachments. Mother does not need to be the only one to give out love.

The conclusion being drawn today is that if the baby can successfully become attached to a number of people, he will receive comfort from all of them. If there is consistency of care, the child will develop a number of emotional investments, and will be able to build the trust necessary for healthy emotional growth.

Mother's continued absence may interfere with the normal development of the infant unless very good arrangements are made for his care. And the young preschooler *may* show symptoms of separation anxiety, but these can usually be alleviated if a stable substitute is provided.

Many investigators find that by kindergarten little difference in dependent and independent behavioral patterns exist between children of working mothers and home mothers. There is even evidence that school achievement may be higher in children of working mothers.

Day-Care Okay

O *ur only child, a boy named Richard, is now eighteen months old and I am most anxious to go back to work. Since no other arrangements seem feasible, I would have to put Richard in a day-care center.*

My husband is willing for me to do this, but my own mother and my mother-in-law, for once united on something, both think this would be a terrible thing to do. Nothing I say will allay their fears. Can you help?

Admittedly the quality of care offered by different day-care centers varies tremendously. Certainly you would want to visit the center where you plan to place your son and assure *yourself* that it is the kind of situation in which you could comfortably leave him.

However, the whole idea of day-care, especially for middle-class families, is so new that many grandmothers do view the notion with anxiety. It might help if you could assure these ladies that as noted an authority as Dr. Jerome Kagan of Harvard has admitted that *he had to change his earlier opinion that day-care may be harmful.* In an issue of *Behavior Today* he reported a five-year experiment with children aged three-and-a-half months to twenty-nine months. According to his findings, day-care had no notably adverse effect on a child's cognitive functioning, language, social behavior, or even his attachment to his mother.

A recent report given by psychologist Jay Belsky to Congress tends to support this conclusion. According to Dr. Belsky, the research evidence is compelling in demonstrating that out-of-home day-care, be it in centers or in families, has absolutely no adverse effect on children's intellectual functioning. In fact, some research indicates that day-care is beneficial, particularly in the case of children from economically disadvantaged families. Belsky did note, however, that "when we examine the effects of day-care on preschool children's social development the picture is complex. Preschool children reared in day-care tend to be more cooperative and empathic, but at the same time tend to engage in more aggressive and disobedient behavior. They seem more skilled at getting along in the social world, using both positive and negative strategies."

If the prospect of day-care suits you and your husband, you are really all set. And let us hope the grandmothers come around to your way of thinking when they see, as I anticipate they will, that day-care is not having an adverse effect on their grandson.

Some recent figures predict that by 1990 the majority of preschool children will have mothers who work. So if you do work outside your home, you will certainly by no means be the exception.

However, the fact that most of us agree that a working mother should not feel guilty about a career outside the home does not mean we should ignore or denigrate those many mothers—whom the media largely ignore—who stay at home and bring up their children themselves *because they choose to do so.* Such mothers will find support as well as entertainment and good reading in a new book called *What's a Smart Woman Like You Doing at Home?* by Linda Burton, Janet Dittmer, and Cheri Loveless.

Mothers should not be upset by what other people do or by what other people think. Many of them work because they want to—it's their nature and life-style. Others work because they need to help support their family. In contrast, others stay at home and bring up their children because it's what *they* want to do, choose to do, or feel that, at least for some years, this is the thing that benefits their children most.

It isn't a contest. One way of living is not "better" than the other. In the old days it was very simple. Mothers stayed at home. Now that there is a choice it is harder. It's important for every mother to make the choice that fits in best with her own way of being, her children's and her family's needs, emotional and economic. And not to feel guilty or inadequate because she cannot be everything to everybody for twenty-four hours of every day.

The essential thing for any mother today is *not to feel guilty.* If you are a working mother, whether from choice or necessity, do the best you can to arrange good day-care for your child or children. Nobody knows for sure the ultimate result of day-care. But certainly good day-care can be as effective for children as reluctant mother care. Some women are most comfortable at home, some at work outside the home. Your children tend to be happier if you, yourself, are happy with the way you have chosen to live.

Mother's Home—Everybody Cry

*I enjoy my work and I also enjoy my family. But one thing drives me
bats. Every day, the moment I enter the house everybody starts crying,
fussing, fighting, demanding.*

*Well, that's bad enough, but even worse is that the lady who takes care
of them says, most every day, "I can't imagine what's gotten into them.
They were so good till you got here." The implication seems to be that I am
at fault, that there is something about me that upsets my children. Help!*

Your experience is duplicated in many homes where the mother
works. This phenomenon has been called "The Reentry Frenzies.
Mommy's Home—Everybody Cry."

Husbands have been experiencing this phenomenon for years—the
minute they get into the house everybody rushes at them, each with his
or her particular triumph or tale of woe. Everybody wants to communicate. Now wives are getting it, too.

Two quite opposite solutions have been suggested by mothers who
have been there. Some find if they spend their first half hour at home
responding, as best they can, to all the multiple demands, then the rest
of the evening will go more smoothly.

Others, with quite an opposite approach, plan with their children (this
works best with older children) that the children will give their mother
half an hour to pull herself together, relax, or get dinner—the choice to
be hers—and then they can have as much of her as they want.

But whatever you do, be available to your children, if possible, in a
way that is comfortable and fun for you. If you are merely doing things
with them from a sense of duty, and are not enjoying it, they'll probably
know it. Also it is important, however you manage it, that your children
feel they are important to you, that they matter to you quite as much as
your work or other outside activities.

Men Say Women Can Work— If They Keep on Cleaning House

Fewer than one-third of married men in this country approve of changes resulting from the new roles of women in our society, according to a survey released by Doyle Dane Bernbach Inc., a New York advertising firm.

"One of the major concerns of the men in this survey is how these changes might impinge on their personal comfort and well-being. It's easier for men to accept the possibility of women as brain surgeons than to release their own wives from the drudgery of laundry and cleaning the bathroom. When one's own wife does not fulfill her traditional laundry obligations, the husband may find himself filling the gap. This is a role he only reluctantly accepts."

The study concludes, "Man's reluctance to do housework occurs at a time when women increasingly are investing numbers of hours in outside-the-home employment equal to their husbands'. And these women are more likely to expect the sharing of household tasks as a right and obligation, not as a favor on the part of their mates."

Are You Letting Your Work Interfere with Your Family?

According to Earl Grollman and Gerri Sweder in *The Working Parent Dilemma: How to Balance the Responsibilities of Children and Career,* it is not their parents' working that children object to, but that sometimes parents give the impression of preferring work to family life. Here are four questions from Grollman and Sweder that can help you check to see if you are keeping a proper balance between job and children.

1. Do you devote what seems to the children like too much time to work? As one boy put it: "The only person she has no time for is me." Children are not impressed with how famous or competent their parents are on the job if these parents do not spend time with them at home. Another remarks, "My dad works late almost every night. He acts as if his work is the most important thing in the world."

2. Do you come home from work in a bad mood and take it out on the family? If you do it is clearly a sign that your work is overflowing into your home life. All too many children don't know exactly what to do when their parents come home from work in a bad mood. Some are afraid that whatever they say may make an uncomfortable situation worse.

In many homes youngsters become the target of their parents' wrath when parents are upset by a situation on the job. Normal child behavior unexpectedly becomes unacceptable, and parents lash out verbally or mete out swift punishment. True, children can't be sheltered from all your problems at work, but some problems are for adults only.

3. Do you monopolize family conversation with long stories about the people at work? Most children are reasonably interested in their parents' jobs. But most do not really want to listen to long stories about their parents' coworkers. Especially not when they have their own failures and successes, their own adventures or disasters, that they need to talk about. If you spend every dinner hour talking about the people at work, interesting as they may be to you, you are sending your child the message that you are more interested in the people at work than in your own family.

4. And lastly, do you go out too often at night? Not only when you really have to work but also to classes, evening meetings, or exercise groups. Most certainly grownups need some recreation for themselves. But most children feel rejected when their parents continually place their personal needs for relaxation or entertainment above the children's needs.

According to Grollman and Sweder, if you have answered yes to any one of these questions, or if your children complain that you never have time for them, chances are you have let your work invade your home and displace your family.

On Fathers

Fathers Vary

I am a new father—well, actually not all that new, the baby is a year old now. My wife is always bringing home books that tell her how to be a good mother but I find very little advice for fathers. Can you help? Also, do you believe what some people say—that sex roles today are blurring? That the roles of fathers and mothers are becoming increasingly identical?

Perhaps you haven't been looking in the right places for advice for fathers. Actually there are numerous good books now available. (See the bibliography at the end of this book.)

Also, I have some advice of my own to offer. To begin with, many fathers, like many mothers, find that they may do best at parenting if they know a little something about the way babies and children develop. Some of your wife's books will certainly tell you that.

You will also do best if you accept the fact that you cannot make any child into anything if only you do the right thing. Accept your unathletic as well as your athletic children; your not-so-bright as well as your very bright.

Our suggestion has always been that any father, when he comes home from work, be given a few minutes to pull himself together before he is inundated with family problems.

Remember that fathers vary. Be the kind that is comfortable for you. Some really like to take part fully—diapers and all. Others just aren't comfortable in a co-mother role. And if you are not, by nature, a pal type, don't try to be. Those father-son banquets may not be for you.

Also, remember that fathers, like mothers, vary as to the age child they relate to best. Some are best with babies, many prefer preschoolers, some do best with teenagers. However, if it is older children that you prefer, you can't ignore a child until he becomes what you consider an interesting age. You need to relate, at least to some extent, right from the beginning.

The ideal father is reasonably effective all along the way. He knows that his children will grow and change. He realizes that if the relationship is to be a good one it must start in infancy and early childhood. He accepts the fact that rebellion is part of growing up and that a successful relationship with any teenager requires much effort, tolerance, and patience on the part of a parent.

Advice for Fathers of Girls

Here are some specific suggestions from a book *Daughters,* by Stella Chess and Jane Whitbread.

• DO get into the act from the start. Feeding, bathing, dressing, changing a baby is the best way to get to know her. Taking care makes you care.

• DON'T say things like, "Here's your daughter!" and hand her to her mother when she's cross and tired and you want to watch TV.

• DO give your daughter experiences that will stimulate her imagination, satisfy her curiosity. Play with her and teach her. It's never too soon to start.

• DO treat her as an individual. If you think of your daughter as a person with a future, rather than a picture-book child, you will enjoy her vim, vigor, daring, and inquisitiveness as much as her sweetness and charm.

• DON'T teach her to use guile and wiles to get her way.

• DO teach her to be responsible.

• DON'T spoil her.

• DO set standards to suit her, according to her age and individual capacity.

• DON'T exchange the old "sugar and spice" stereotype for the "I have to be the first woman president" one. Bring up your daughter to realize herself, according to her individual capacities and interests, and to accept herself as fully as possible.

• DO teach your daughter to value herself by paying attention to her needs, questions, interests. Enjoy her and her friends, and DO let her choose her friends by herself.

• DON'T keep her from being responsible by protecting her from responsibility.

And finally, DO support her expectations of her future self by supporting her mother as wife, mother, and woman, now. If you can't bring her up in harmony together, bring her up in harmony apart.

The point is, if you have a good *attitude* toward your little daughter, your *actions* will in all likelihood take care of themselves.

Father Feels Rejected

Our problem is that my husband feels rejected when our twenty-one-month-old daughter insists that "Mommy do." He thinks that Sheila likes me better than she does him and it hurts his feelings terribly. I tell him it's just a stage she's going through and that it has no deeply significant meaning. Which of us is correct?

Your daughter's behavior is quite, quite normal. Not all, but probably the majority of very young children, when in trouble or even when it's a matter of daily routines, do insist that "Mommy do." Gradually they spread out to Dad and other members of the family.

I saw a little boy the other day who had just broken his collarbone. Dad was taking him to the emergency room. That poor little fellow cried and howled for Mommy as if the end of the world had come. Father was firm and carried him out to the car. Within a block, sobs (in fact, screams and yells) stopped and the little fellow asked his dad, "Did your daddy ever have to carry you to the hospital when you were hurt?"

Around twenty-one months of age, many do stick to Mommy like glue. Somewhat later, around two and a half, many insist that whoever is *not* doing for them do it. Thus, Mommy starts to feed them, they cry, "Daddy do." Daddy starts and they shift over to, "Mommy do." It is part of the natural contrariness of the age. Here again, a certain amount of giving-in, if convenient, is okay. But when it isn't, whoever is handy must harden his or her heart and "do" for the child, no matter how vehement that child's demand for some other person.

None of this means that the child does not like the person currently being rejected.

Boy Prefers Father; Mother Upset

I have an extremely heartbreaking problem. No one of my friends has ever had this happen to her. It is that my two-year-old son, Brian, prefers his daddy to me.

I can't carry him to bed at night or naptime; I cannot comfort him when he is unhappy. If I ask him, "Do you want to go to the store with me or stay home with Daddy?" he always chooses Daddy. If I leave the room, fine; if Daddy does he screams bloody murder.

Now I am pregnant again. Will my second child treat me as callously as Brian does, as if I were no more than a glorified baby-sitter?

Do you have any recommendations as to how I should behave? I have tried ignoring, waiting, being superaffectionate, and finally letting me know how much his cool attitude hurts me. Nothing works.

Your son's preference for his dad is rather unusual, but it really doesn't need to be a problem unless you let it be. Certainly we all like to be first, even with babies and small children. And it is true that the majority of infants and preschoolers do prefer Mom, especially when they are in difficulty.

Actually, this is not always comfortable for Mother. Many young mothers feel that they are virtually prisoners of their children. Many young children will not let Mother out of their sight. Should she go to the bathroom and lock the door, they will huddle on the floor just outside, like orphans of the storm.

Many a mother would give anything for the emotional freedom you have, especially since your husband appears to be warm and responsive to your son's demands. You can reduce the tension you feel by not giving him choices when it is not necessary. Just tell him how things are going to be.

There is no reason to assume that your second child will prefer Dad. Chances are ninety-nine in a hundred, more or less, that *you* will be the preferred parent.

By all means, don't let Brian know it hurts you that he prefers his Daddy to you. Children can become real emotional tyrants if you beg for their love and attention. Just be calm. Be casual. And try to appreciate that your value as a person does not depend on you being the preferred parent. Fathers put up with this constantly and do not feel downgraded when a child cries for Mommy. Though in your household things seem to be reversed from what we usually expect, I do not consider it harmful or abnormal.

If you cannot accept the fact that Brian prefers his dad to you, at this time, indeed you may eventually need to get psychological help to find out why this is such a big hurt to you. My guess is that as your new baby matures he or she will prefer you. Then it will no longer matter to you so much about Brian. And as Brian sees it doesn't matter, he may distribute his affections more evenly.

However, nowadays there are a few infants and preschoolers who actually do prefer Father to Mother. In those still somewhat rare instances in which Father is the one who stays home and keeps house and brings up the baby (as described in the lively book, *The Nurturing Father* by Kyle Pruett), it appears to be not too unusual for the child to prefer Dad over Mom. In such cases it seems to be the care-giving parent who is preferred rather than mother or father as such.

What's a Father For?

Like many of my friends, I am pretty much of a feminist. Needless to say, my husband and I have a marked difference of opinion about a father's role in the household. I don't need to tell you which of us thinks what, as it is all rather predictable.

Will you please comment?

What seems to be happening in some households is not so much the blurring or reversal of roles that some have anticipated as role sharing. There are unusual situations where the man stays at home and does the housework and raises the children, but, more commonly, in certain households, women and men are establishing increasingly mutual roles in the upbringing of children. However, roles are definitely not reversing or even blurring. Rather, husbands seem still to be the bosses. Even in a family in which Mother works outside the home, it tends to be she who does the most housework and parenting.

Some writers, like Dr. Benjamin Spock and Dr. Robert Coles, feel that men should share fully in child care; Dr. Coles is even reported to believe that the function of the father is the same as that of the mother. On the other hand, New York educator Eda LeShan is *adamant* about the difference between parents. Dr. LeShan and I (among others) question whether most fathers ever will or even should share fully in child care.

My own feeling is that a father's role should not be that of co-mother. In fact, perhaps the most "liberated" woman is she who can live her own personal and professional life with a fair degree of freedom, but who can accept the fact that men's and women's responsibilities toward their children and toward their family, as a rule, differ greatly.

When Dad Speaks, Rob Is Expected to Jump

I have a nice family and, I think, a very special husband, but he does one thing that hurts me so. He is very harsh and directive with our three little boys. He almost never praises them and he expects them to jump when he speaks. The other evening the oldest, who is in first grade and very proud of his newly acquired abilities, asked his dad if he would like to hear him count to one hundred by tens.

"No," said my husband. "I'd like to see you print your name. And do it decently for once." Robbie did print his name and my husband was very critical about the way the letters were formed.

Well, I can stand the hurt for myself, but do you think my husband's attitude is really harming the children?

How many mothers like you are out there, loving their husbands but wishing they would be a little kinder to the children!

On the other hand, there are a lot of other mothers whose husbands leave all the disciplining up to *them,* and these mothers wish their husbands would be a little firmer and do a little more of the disciplining.

It's fair to say that, in general, mothers being with their children all day, at least those who do not work outside the home, are more aware of their children's sensitivities, abilities, and limits, than are the fathers. Ideally, your kindness and gentleness will balance your husband's firmness and harshness. If your husband basically loves the children we can only hope they sense it.

However, it is true that there are many grown men in therapy today because they, as children, never managed to live up to their fathers' expectations. About the best I can say in your case is that too firm is probably better than too wishy-washy. Your husband is showing his concern for Robbie in, presumably, the only way he knows how. You are not alone with your problem.

In Robbie's case you can let him count for *you;* show off any newly acquired abilities to *you.* You can also tell him, as many mothers tell children, that Daddy is tired when he comes home from work and just because he's sometimes cross doesn't mean that he doesn't love them.

His Sons Are Bored by His Stories

You may say that I waited too long, but I am a man who is not very good with small children. Now that my boys are older, in their early teens, I find them extremely interesting. And I would like them to be interested in me. But stories of my youth seem to fill them with yawns. It is very disappointing. How can I get them to be interested in the things I have to tell them about what, I realize, they consider the "old days"?

I'm afraid you waited too long. Timing is everything in relating to one's children. You can't suddenly, after twelve years or so of indifference, turn on to them and expect them to be turned on to you.

In fact, even if you had been companionable with them earlier, there are some years in the teens when some of the most devoted father-son couples split up. By thirteen years of age many of those boys who have earlier been much interested in their fathers, lose interest. (Girls as a rule continue their admiration longer than do boys.) And even if your boys were still willing to relate to you with enthusiasm, chances are it might be with regard to some shared interest, as sports, but *not* with regard to listening to stories about your boyhood.

So I'm afraid I really can't help you. But for other parents who are just beginning, I strongly urge—take advantage of the fact that children between the ages of five and ten are as a rule very much interested in their parents and in anything you may have to tell them. Make the most of those years.

From personal experience I can assure you, your stories mean much when a boy or girl is young. I even remember people I never met, whom my parents told me about—a firm and rather mean principal my mother worked with when she was teaching school; a Colonel Cobb in whose office my father studied law. Those people are very real to me.

So take advantage of the enthusiasm of the young, not only to have a good time yourself but to fill their minds with memories they won't forget.

On Brothers and Sisters

Jealousy of Baby All Too Normal

I know that this is a problem that has been written to death. But since my husband and I planned to have only one child, we never thought much about it. Now that our Timmy is just three, we discover that we are to be blessed with a new baby. Any suggestions would be welcome. We don't want Timmy to go through all the jealousy pains that so many children are reported to have.

As you say, the subject *has* been done to death. So may I answer you with another mother's description of her own experiences? She tells us:

"When our Donny was three his baby sister was born. He was miserable that Baby took over his top spot in our family. He was so furious that he wouldn't have anything to do with me for ages. In fact it wasn't till his sister was two that he began to realize that she could be on his side and a real asset as a companion.

"So then the next baby came along, a year after our little girl. He didn't mind this baby quite as much as the first one, but he did show a certain amount of hostility. I realized that if he showed a little, he must be feeling a lot.

"So instead of punishing him when he lost control I went out of my way to sympathize with his problem and his feelings. Closer supervision of the baby is helpful (at least it protects the baby). But more time alone with the older child, and real sympathy with the way his life is being disrupted, work wonders.

"When a preschooler harms a little baby in any way, even the slightest, it is natural for a mother to fly to the rescue of the baby and to be quite harsh with the culprit. Without a planned alternative, this is an impulse that is hard to control.

"A mother can point out that even though baby *is* a bother now, that later on he will grow bigger. That if the older child is nice to the baby now, later on baby will grow up and be his friend. Donny seemed able to grasp this concept and we had many happy, intimate moments discussing it.

"Then, of course, I did the usual things. Talked about 'his' baby. Spent as much time as possible alone with *him*. Planned special excursions and outings while somebody else took care of the baby. I tried to make him feel important by 'baby-sitting' his little sister while I was involved in household chores, though in such cases I tried to stay right in sight. He was not really baby-sitting but he thought he was.

"I hug and kiss him a lot and tell him how special he is. I praise him a lot. But I also try to make his life lively on the outside by encouraging friendships with children in the neighborhood or school. (Even though nowadays encouraging friendships with children at school may involve quite a lot of transporting.)

"And I especially try to help Donny see that being an older brother involves certain privileges to balance the increased responsibilities. And I try *not* to make him feel that just because he is older he *ought* to 'do better' or 'know better.' He's still just a little boy.

"Sometimes he will say, 'She's almost ready to play big with me, isn't she, Mommy?' ('Yes, just a few years more,' I say, though I try to phrase it a little more hopefully than that.)

"Now he plays what he calls 'easy' with her and though I don't leave them alone, I do see an increasingly good relationship and attitude. In short, I think it helps to be understanding, sympathetic, and nonpunitive while at the same time pointing out the advantages of being nice to a new baby so that she will like him and trust him later on."

I hope this mother's experience helps the many of you who have this very common problem of an older—though still often very young—child when faced with the common problem of an unwanted, unasked for, and unappreciated baby sibling.

Jealous Brother Pesters Baby

*M*y problem is how to keep my three-and-a-half-year-old son, Buzz, from teasing and even hurting his nine-month-old baby sister. We thought we had spaced them quite well, but Buzz is apparently extremely jealous.

You have said that babies and preschoolers should be kept apart as much as possible, even if it requires a locked door. But now Baby is creeping all over the house and it is difficult to keep them apart.

Buzz loves to play with her, but play takes the form of, for instance, covering her up with a blanket as fast as she can get out of it, thus upsetting her and making it difficult for her to breathe. I spend half my time saying "Leave Baby alone." I have tried hard to ignore this behavior as attention-getting, but I am afraid that it could result in her getting really hurt.

I t could indeed! Even though his attentions may seem primarily somewhat playful, Buzz could hurt his baby sister, perhaps fatally, if allowed to play with her unwatched.

I urge you, don't leave them alone together. This will take quite a lot of planning on your part and will be time consuming, but obviously it will be worth it. To begin with, if Buzz is three and a half, perhaps some of the day he will be in nursery school. When he is at home, see if you can't get a baby-sitter for him for at least part of the time. Stagger naps if possible. When Buzz is asleep (if he still naps) have Baby awake, and vice versa.

If your baby is only nine months old, she should accept a playpen. This may help protect her from her dangerous brother. But it is not just a matter of protecting Baby when it is convenient. It is a matter of protecting Baby *all day long, every day,* until your son matures to the point that teasing, and possibly harming, the baby no longer is so fascinating.

It is hard for most parents to appreciate the real hostility and even hatred that many small children feel for this creature who has, unasked, come into their lives and usurped so much of their parents' attention. No fun from their point of view, a baby is pretty much all to the bad.

Such directives as "Leave Baby alone," or "You ought to be ashamed of yourself, hurting your little baby sister," are virtually valueless. You need to *protect* the baby.

But in the meantime, try to work things out so that Buzz will feel better about the baby and about himself. Try to plan for him to help you with her at times—running little errands, getting things she needs. Of course stall visitors who may still tend to pay immediate attention to the baby. Let him be the center of attention for at least a few minutes and then let him help you show off the baby.

Also, talk to him about when he was a baby. Show him his baby pictures and tell him how cute he was. Give him some new privileges: a slightly later bedtime, special things to do with you on the grounds that he is now such a big boy. (He may, or may not, get the message that *big* boys behave nicely toward those younger than they.)

New Baby Arrives—Preschooler Returns to Baby Ways

We have just had a new baby in our family, and our older son, Jimmy, who is almost three and who has always seemed quite mature for his age, is acting in the strangest way. Really weird. Now, much of the time, he creeps instead of walking and even insists on having back his bottle, which he gave up almost a year ago.

My mother-in-law says there is surely something very wrong with this boy and that we should see a psychologist. But I wonder.

You are right not to be too alarmed by Jimmy's behavior. Nor would I blame it all on the new baby. True, when there is a new baby in the family, preschoolers often regress. But children around your son's age, especially when fatigued, often slip back into babyhood even when there is not a new baby. Some not only make babyish demands but say things like, "I'm a little baby. I can't talk. I have no teeth and I have no hair." Others, more practically, tell us, "I'm a little baby. I have to have a bottle. I sleep out in a carriage. But I *can* talk."

In most cases there's nothing wrong with this behavior and we advise going along with it. However, there's another demand for attention that most often *is* connected with a new baby, and this is comments to the effect that "I don't love you," or "You don't love me," or "You love the baby more than you do me." The variations on this theme are endless, bounded only by the child's imagination. And though probably he should be allowed to make such remarks (how are you going to stop him?), you should not give him the satisfaction of paying attention to them.

If your preschooler says, after the new baby arrives, "I don't love you," it is very important to say merely, "That's too bad. I'm sorry," and then go on to other things. It is *always* dangerous to give a small child power over you by seeming to *care* when he claims that he doesn't love you (or loves Mom—or Dad—more than he loves you). Any child can learn to play the emotional-blackmail game very quickly, if given encouragement.

Life Isn't Fair

My husband and I have three children and try as we do to keep things fair, somebody is always dissatisfied. Susie has a bigger piece of cake. Johnny got new shoes and Billy didn't. Susie got to go somewhere with Dad and the boys didn't. Anybody would have to be Solomon to keep these kids satisfied. Help!

We have always felt that many parents try too hard to make things fair, to keep things even. We point out that life isn't fair and that children might as well find it out early as late. Now family specialists Andrew and Carole Calladine join us in this chorus, recounting their own family experiences.

They point out that when they tried, in their own household, to keep things fair, as in cutting a specially delicious cake, they were met with cries of "How come he has more frosting?" "His piece is bigger than mine." "Why do we always have chocolate cake? I like strawberry short-cake better."

Children have a way of keeping close tabs in a family that plays the fairness game. They know when you're guilty of the slightest unevenness. You know it, too. They play on this guilt until you squash it by duplicating whatever you gave to, or did for, another child. So don't play their game.

Since life definitely is not fair, why try to teach our children that it is? If Jimmy needs a new pair of shoes or a special tennis racket, get it for him. You don't then buy a substitute for each of your other children. You don't buy them *anything* till the time comes when *they* need something. And then you get it for them.

Instead of trying to keep things even, try to teach your children that there is a difference between measured fairness for all, and being fair to each child based on what is needed and what is available to give. If each child gets what he needs when he needs it, all children in a family should feel secure about their specialness.

Children Jealous of Each Others' Birthdays

We have four children in our family, so inevitably birthdays come around rather often. When they grow older we hope the children will understand that only the birthday person gets presents, but now that they are still rather young—the oldest is only seven—there is great disappointment, unhappiness, and bitterness whenever a birthday comes around.

"How come he gets all the presents?" "How come I don't get anything?" "He always get the best!" (not true). We try to explain that everybody has a birthday and that everybody gets a turn. But this doesn't seem to mean much to them. We have tried giving everybody (birthday or not) at least one present just to make up, but this isn't enough to prevent unhappiness. As a result our birthdays in this house are not as pleasant as they should be.

Many parents, like you, try to give at least one present to everybody, birthday or not. As a rule this doesn't work out. Instead why not try involving the nonbirthday siblings in the planning for the big day? Young as yours may be, each could contribute something.

A birthday is a special day for the person having that birthday. Parents who play the fairness game tend to lose out. Complaints, no matter how sincerely felt, are likely to dry up if the complainer sees that he or she has no audience. Your best bet is to make a simple rule—birthdays are for the birthday boy or girl. You may have especially grabby children but chances are your difficulty lies in your own ambivalent attitude. Make it clear to your children that you have the courage of your convictions and chances are they will accept this fact.

Other suggestions for maintaining family harmony have to do with the matter of handing down clothes from the oldest to the youngest. This is a natural and necessary procedure in many families, but it can be rendered less unhappy for the younger ones if even the youngest can have at least some chance to buy one or two garments that are brand new to him. Even if there are plenty of hand-me-downs available, every child deserves the privilege of a few new things now and then.

And how about in a sports-minded family if some one child doesn't enjoy sports? Here again, does everybody have to behave the same? Almost any child, even the least athletic, can do something well in the physical-activity line. It may not be and doesn't have to be what the rest of the family is doing. So don't push skiing (or whatever) if your child absolutely has no interest or talent in that direction.

Everybody in a family does not have to be just like all the rest all of the time.

My Children Fight All the Time

My three children fight all the time. It's driving me crazy. I've tried everything I can think of—punishing for fighting, rewarding for not fighting, long talks, short talks—nothing really changes things much. You'd think they hated each other the way they treat each other. Will you advise?

There is no real magic remedy for all this fighting, but I suggest that a parent might try what someone has called the six S's of harmonious family living:

Separation: Keep them apart as much as possible.

Space: Even if your house is small and your family large, sometimes you can arrange for them to play in separate areas.

Scheduling: This of course is a sort of separation. When they are young, staggering naps can help.

Something else to do: This takes effort on your part, but if their time is filled with interesting activities there will be less opportunity for fighting.

Supervision: This, too, takes time on your part, but most children fight less if their parents are right there.

And, though you shouldn't overdo this, sometimes one parent can plan with the children that they treat each other nicely as a *Surprise* for the other parent.

I repeat, there is no way to stop jealousy and fighting. It's a normal and inevitable part of life.

What's the Best Discipline When Children Fight?

My children fight all the time. I sometimes feel that if my discipline were better they might not fight quite so much. Will you give me some general ideas about discipline in relation to children fighting?

I will. First, with young children, try setting the kitchen timer for a calming time when siblings must sit apart from each other. The timer successfully takes your nagging voice out of things.

Try taking away a relevant privilege whenever house rules are abused.

Remove any fought-over object for a realistic period of time.

Securely hold from behind any physically attacking sibling.

Give suitable work assignments to all angry siblings to channel their aggression and to get some constructive use from this powerful drive.

Learn to ignore and stay out of sibling power plays for parental attention.

If problems arise about turns, have the children pick a number from one to ten to see who is closest to a chosen number and thus gets the first turn.

If at all possible, stop a growing struggle before it snowballs completely out of control.

If quarreling is vigorous, isolate the children until they are ready to play well together.

On the other hand, isolate yourself if you find you are becoming irritable. Disciplining children works best when you are in control and can use a calm voice.

Praise, and praise, and praise whenever you suitably can. Also be sure you communicate with your children as fully and freely when things go well as when they are going badly. Don't make them feel they have to behave badly to get your full attention.

Change the activity that is causing a sibling dispute. Give them something better to do.

And last of all try to teach your children the power of words to work out any disagreement.

How to Deal with Your Children's Fights

"My kids fight all the time and I can't stand it." This complaint is the one we hear from parents probably more than any other.

What can you do about it? Not as much as you might hope. It's very hard to keep siblings from fighting with each other, because they enjoy it so much. "What do you like more than anything else?" I recently asked an eight-year-old. "Fighting with my brothers," he replied gleefully.

Partly, of course, siblings fight because there are so many things to fight about—their parents' love and attention, privileges, objects, to be first, to come out ahead, to get revenge, to get even, to get a sibling into trouble.

But the main reason for fighting is often not the surface reason. It lies much deeper than this. Fighting is fun because it involves direct, emotional contact. It is a wonderful way to relate to other people. It *makes* them notice you.

And so, children will probably always continue to fight, till each grows old enough to find other and more attractive sources of emotional gratification. Since this seems to be the case, the trick for parents is first of all to stop thinking that their children ought *not* to fight, or that something must be wrong for them to fight so much. If it really bothers you, do your best to stay in a part of the house where you can't see them or hear them.

If one sibling or the other is actually getting physically harmed, separate them. In fact, you'd be wise to make a rule that no sibling is allowed to harm another physically. (You may not be able to enforce this rule, but it's a good one to establish).

And here are a few dos and don'ts:

• DON'T allow yourself to be habitually dragged into things as judge and jury.

• DO try to take a long-range view of things. Remember that sibling relationships in most families get better as time goes by.

• DO keep in mind that when you are called on to step in, an overcharged situation may sometimes be defused by relatively simple techniques. Make a joke. Suggest a different activity. Read to them.

• DO remember that the more the fighting bugs you, the more attention it calls to themselves, the more they will fight.

• DON'T try to get to the bottom of every single struggle, but in a long-range kind of way try to identify the reason for any single pattern of fighting that is repeated.

• DO try to make each child feel special in some special way, so that each can get your attention in positive rather than in negative ways.

• DON'T allow yourself to get trapped in any demand for total fairness.

• DO try to avoid situations that by their very nature are going to cause trouble. If two boys under four each have a box of pennies, each is bound to believe that the other has some of *his* pennies.

• DO, especially with young children, use the concept of *rules.* Many children, especially preschoolers, tend to be absolutely snowed if you tell them that something you want them to do is "the rule."

• DO try to help your children find good outlets for their energy, so that fighting with siblings need not be their primary pleasure.

• DO help (older) children not to let others get a rise out of them. Teach them that if they ignore misbehavior, it may not be repeated. Teach them that age-old bit of doggerel, "Sticks and stones can break my bones, but words will never hurt me." (It may not be true, but it often works).

• DO all you can to encourage siblings, unless they are vastly ill matched, to work out their own solutions to problems.

• DO try using behavior-modification techniques. That is, reward behavior that you wish to have repeated. So far as you can stand it, ignore the bad.

• DO all you can to reduce tattling by making it unrewarding. Unless the behavior reported sounds definitely serious, say, "Oh, is that so?" and show by your indifference that tattling isn't going to get anybody very far.

• DO on occasion try role playing or role reversal. That is, let a younger child play the role of an older child and vice versa. This can on occasion be both entertaining and effective.

• DO take advantage of that extremely useful device—time out. The child is sent to his room and told that he cannot come out till the timer rings.

• DON'T allow your children to draw you into a pattern of spending a vast amount of time and energy discussing and trying to straighten out disagreements.

• DON'T allow yourself to favor one child or the other conspicuously, even though your heart may urge you to do so. You very likely will have a favorite, but try not to make this grossly obvious. And don't encourage hostile competition by forcing the children to compete for your attention.

• DON'T, at least not in their presence, compare your children to each other. Don't hold one up as an example to the others: "Why can't you mind me the way your sister does?" Don't compare them with relatives or children in other families who, according to you, behave perfectly.

• DON'T go on and on about some misbehavior that is now safely in the past.

• DON'T push sex differences, as by telling your daughter she can't do this or that because she is "only" a girl.

• DON'T allow children to play you against your spouse. In all likelihood one of you will be a little more lenient, one a little more strict, than the other. This is natural and not necessarily harmful. But do your best not to let the children capitalize on it or use it to gain favors. Do your best to back each other up.

• DON'T set unrealistic goals with regard to the degree of family harmony that you expect. Start where you actually are and then try, little by little, to improve matters. *Don't* start out with some inaccessible goal and then berate your children and criticize yourself because that goal is not reached.

• DON'T allow yourself to overidentify. For instance, try to avoid overidentifying with your poor darling daughter who is always being picked on by her mean big brother. If anything can cloud a clear evaluation of a present situation, it can be an overidentification with your own past.

• DO try to see that each child in the family has activities separate from those of siblings. The more you separate them, the more harmonious your household will be.

Alex Blossoms Away from His Brothers

I have just had the biggest eye-opener of my life as a mother. I have four children, nine and under, so our household is pretty active. My first three children are boys. My biggest problem is my second son, Alex. Admittedly he is rather squashed in between his two high-powered brothers, but he certainly does give us the most difficulty.

He is a handsome little fellow and we think quite bright but he is so moody and mopey. Nothing is ever right. The frown on his face would curdle your blood and he is always complaining. He really has been the least fun of any of my children.

Well, this summer we had a wonderful experience. His grandparents invited us to bring Alex to visit with them at a summer hotel on the coast. The other grandparents, who live near us, agreed to take the other three children, so Alex and I set out all by ourselves for the coast of Maine.

You would not have believed the change in Alex. Smiling, friendly, he just went around beaming from morning till night. Seems as if he made friends with almost everybody at the hotel, old and young. I could not believe that this was my sulky little son. Now I see him in quite a different light. And the fact that my expectations of him are different has carried over even back into our rather crowded home situation. I just wanted to share this wonderful news with other parents who like me may have one child who sometimes seems to get left out.

You've said it all. Not everyone will be lucky enough to find the specific solution that you came up with. But as most seasoned parents know, that child who often gets lost in the shuffle of a big family can be quite a different person if he or she has a chance to be the only one.

Many grandparents appreciate this when they say they will be happy to have a visit from any one of their grandchildren but only one at a time.

This isn't laziness on their part, as some seem to think. It is more that while some children are safest and most secure and most comfortable in the bosom of their families, many others indeed blossom when they are out of the crowd.

Not everyone has available grandparents. But most anyone has somebody—friend or other relative—who can give one of your children that breathing space that so many need to show themselves at their very best. And congratulations on your own success.

On Grandparents

Her Grandson Is Fresh

I spent this past Christmas vacation with my daughter's family. It was a delightful experience except for one thing. My grandchildren are so fresh, especially the four-year-old. He says things that I am sure my own children never said. And I certainly know that my brothers and I would have been killed if we had ever talked that way.

There is a great deal of "I'll punch you out," a lot of very silly talk about "poopy" and many threats to throw people into the garbage. My daughter and her husband seem to take all this very calmly, but I think it is disgraceful. Has discipline been forgotten?

You are quite right that in the old days a child who spoke rudely to his or her grandmother or anybody else would have really gotten it. However, as people understand more and more about young children and how they normally behave, many parents have become extremely relaxed about the out-of-bounds behavior of four-year-olds.

Your four-year-old grandson is right on target in the things he says. (He could have read the book.) Most parents find that since children of this age do say wild things, at least in part, in order to shock, that the less fuss you make about the whole thing, the less rewarding it is for the child.

I was at a neighborhood party recently when a four-year-old came up to one of the mothers present and said, "Hi, Poopy." The mother replied calmly, "Poopy to you." Well, that wasn't much fun for the child.

Closer to home, not too long ago my own four-year-old great-grandson, as he kissed me goodnight, said, "Goodnight, weirdo cutie." I just said, "Goodnight." Another six months and he will in all probability be talking like a perfectly normal person. Nearly all four-year-olds calm down as they turn five. So, Grandma, relax and let Nature take its course.

Her Grandchildren Don't Thank

I am a loving and very proud grandmother of three fine grandchildren. My problem is that they never thank me for gifts. And to write to me out of the blue, as it were, would be unheard of. I do a lot for these children. I do it because I want to. But a little response from them would be appreciated. They are fine with me when we visit back and forth, but to put a letter into the mail or to make a spontaneous phone call—forget it.

Your feelings seem to be shared by many grandmothers these days. Certainly, we all like to be thanked for gifts we give. But, as a grandmother quite a few times over, I believe that we give to our grandchildren mostly because we enjoy doing so. Being thanked is an extra bonus.

A parent can—and many do—force children to write their thank yous, after birthdays and after Christmas. Others try, without much luck and, admittedly, some do not try. I was well brought up and I did thank, but I certainly did not write spontaneous letters to my grandmother, in spite of her urging.

I suspect that the grandmothers who complain about their ungrateful grandchildren are partly unhappy about not being thanked. But they may also be unhappy about not being loved.

Actually, many grandchildren do love their grandparents, but perhaps in a rather casual way, which does not always extend to thank yous and the writing of letters. For any discouraged grandparent, I personally would suggest that just because a grandchild is not responsive today doesn't mean that he or she may not be tomorrow.

Unfortunately, our grandchildren seem to love us best, and to be most demonstrative, when they are so young and small that letter-writing would not be possible. As they grow into their teens, grandparents as well as parents admittedly are not always appreciated. But, when adults themselves, grandchildren are often extremely thoughtful, friendly, and caring.

Time brings many changes. Hang in there.

Grandma Pushes Sweets

I have a serious problem with my mother-in-law. My husband and I are very conscious of the importance of a proper diet. We try to omit all artificial colorings and flavorings from the children's (and our own) food, to cut down on all so-called junk foods, and especially to omit sweets from our menus.

My mother-in-law thinks that is terrible. She is a person to whom food means a great deal. When we go there she is always trying to force us to eat more than we want to. And she thinks we are positively cruel to the children, not allowing them to have sweets. At her house she is always providing them, and even when she comes to see us she brings candy or cookies and talks about the whole thing a lot in front of the children.

How should I handle this?

I have always been on the side of letting grandparents do a little spoiling if they want to. Children do not, as a rule, carry over the privileges that they permit to their own homes. Most can appreciate that their grandparents are more lenient than their mother and father.

But food is one thing about which parents have not only a right but a responsibility to be firm. It would be best if your husband would speak to his mother about this. But if he won't, you'll have to. Just explain, kindly but firmly, that you and your husband take diet very seriously. You can add, if you feel it will bolster your argument, that the diet has been prescribed by your doctor and you intend to stick to it.

If your mother-in-law is a literary lady, you could suggest that she read some one of the several good books now available that stress the importance of a proper diet. I recommend either *Why Your Child Is*

Hyperactive, by Dr. Ben Feingold, or *Improving Your Child's Behavior Chemistry,* by Dr. Lendon Smith.

Chances are, though, that books won't help. You'll just have to be firm. This should be possible in your own house. Obviously it will be harder to control things at her house, but if she won't go along with your wishes, you may have to reduce the number of the children's visits to Grandma. The children's eating is one area where firmness on your part may have to take precedence over smooth relationships.

Teenage Grandchildren Ignore Grandmother

Judy and Billy are my only grandchildren and, perhaps since I am a widow, they have been the absolute joy of my life. So dear and friendly and appreciative. I remember once when Judy was six years old, I overheard her saying to Billy, "What wonderful person do you think it is coming down the stairs?" And then, disappointedly, "Oh, it's only Daddy."

Our conversations were always so much fun. They were constantly begging me to tell them another story.

Now all that has changed. They hardly pay any attention to me when I come to visit and worse than that they sometimes say quite unfriendly things, such as, "Oh, you're always telling the same old story." Where have things gone wrong and what can I do to get back my formerly delightful grandchildren?

It *is* disappointing, but actually nothing has really gone wrong. That is just the way of life. There can be exceptions, of course, but in general teenagers who have adored their parents and their grandparents begin to find nearly all grownups, especially those in the immediate family, almost impossible. Just as they criticize and run down their parents, so do they also belittle their grandparents.

So for a few years now you will do best to lie low. Be friendly but not overfriendly. Don't try too hard to have a satisfactory relationship. Most, given a few years growing time, will come back to a good relationship with their elders—not perhaps the adoring one they maintained when they were very young, but at least most of them do become friends again. Have patience.

How to Be a Welcome Guest in Your Children's House

Many grandparents find that their long-awaited visits with children and grandchildren often go sour. Here are some general suggestions for trying to make visits more successful.

To begin with, keep your stay short. A happy week is much better than a month of friction.

Second, keep your opinions to yourself unless somebody consults you or asks your advice. True, it's hard to see your child or in-law making what you consider to be a mistake, but it is not up to you to set them straight.

Third, even though you are visiting your own family, try to be a good guest. This doesn't mean you have to be on pins and needles all the time. But do try to be as thoughtful as if you were visiting a mere friend.

Try to travel light. Unless your child's home is large and has a separate guest room, chances are you'll have to share a room with one of your grandchildren, or perhaps sleep in a study or family room.

In all likelihood there won't be too much closet space. Nobody will mind if you wear the same outfit on more than one occasion. Be prepared to fit in with as little displacement of others as possible.

And make sure your clothes are comfortable, especially your shoes. As Dr. Fitzhugh Dodson comments, in his remarkably comprehensive and helpful book, *How to Grandparent*, "Nobody wants to hear Grandma complain about her blisters because her new shoes don't fit right. Nobody wants to have to cut short an outing because Grandpa's feet hurt."

And beware of surprises. If you are on a special diet, let your family know in advance.

Be resourceful. Don't expect to be entertained every minute.

And don't boss your grown child around.

Live-in Grandmother in Trouble

I am a recently widowed grandmother and for financial reasons it has been necessary for me to sell my home and move in with my daughter, her husband, and their three children.

I hesitated to make this move, but was forced into it. Even though I was reluctant, I rather looked forward to this opportunity to get to know my grandchildren better and I optimistically thought that things might not be too bad.

Now I know that I made a terrible mistake. My daughter and I, admittedly, never got on terribly well and now things are worse than ever. It is fight, fight, fight wherever the children are concerned. My suggestions about ways in which she could do things differently and more effectively are scorned. And she is constantly accusing me of spoiling the children and of taking their side.

Her husband stays out of this pretty much, but in spite of that, things are so bad that I wonder how long this can go on. If I possibly had the means, I would move out.

I'm glad that it is you and not your daughter who is writing to me, because the burden of adjustment falls chiefly on you. It is your daughter's house. The children are *her* children. So whether you like the way she handles them or not, it is *her* privilege to make her own decisions.

Any grandmother living with either her own daughter or her daughter-in-law must make this a primary rule: decisions about discipline, toilet training, feeding, bedtime, whatever, should be in the hands of the children's parents. If you wish to make suggestions make them very gently and tentatively.

In situations like your own, which are not all that unusual, whenever there is trouble it is almost always grandmother-mother trouble—not grandmother-child trouble. You say that you and your daughter never got on very well. Now, chances are, you are reworking old antagonisms, reviving old discords.

Though it is quite possible that you (or somebody) may need counseling before this tangled situation is resolved, it is conceivable that you can make the change yourself.

Just tell yourself firmly that you had *your* chance to bring up *your* child or children, and that it is your daughter's privilege to do things her own way.

Your best bet is to be there as a source of love and comfort for the children. But ideally you should be this source without acting as though you were taking *their* side against *their* parents, or protecting them from cruelty.

A grandmother in a household *can* be a great addition and benefit. But it is *her* problem more than the family's to make this the case.

Her Son-in-Law is Rude to Her

I have what seems to me a serious problem. I am a widow with one daughter who has always been not only my daughter but my close friend. Now she has two adorable little preschool sons. I love my daughter and I love my grandsons.

My problem is my son-in-law. He is domineering and unfriendly with my daughter—like telling her to "shut up"—and he is rough with the children. He is also quite rude to me. My own father and my husband were gentle men and I have never had anybody talk to me the way this young man does.

However, since he won't allow them to visit me, the opportunity to be with these three people who mean the most to me of anything in the world is to visit in their home. It is very uncomfortable. I have to keep biting my tongue for fear of saying something that will set my son-in-law off.

What to do?

I don't think you have a choice. For you, a widow, no matter how self-reliant, to sever all connections with your only child and only grandchildren would be cutting off your nose to spite your face.

I would make sure visits are infrequent and short. Try not to be there weekends, when we assume your son-in-law might be at home all day.

Do your very best to think kind thoughts about him and to focus on his good traits (he must have some).

Keep up contact with your daughter and the children, by phone and letters. Remember that some people mellow with age or with success.

When the children are older, if you can maintain a surface calm till then, it's quite possible that they will be able to visit you.

One hopes that your daughter's husband will not forbid you to visit. That would be extreme for even a bad-dispositioned man.

And though this may be cold comfort, try to keep in mind that relations with in-laws are quite customarily less than perfect except in unusual cases.

I do urge you, don't estrange yourself from your daughter and the children even if you have to swallow your pride and your sense of dignity.

Who Does the Disciplining? Parents or Grandparents?

Since I have rather a number of grandchildren, this question arises fairly often. When people bring their children to anyone's house, who should provide the discipline? The parents? Or the host and/or hostess? My son and his wife, who had been childless, recently adopted a little boy (he is almost three). He seems like a nice little fellow, but they carry him around on their hands and really spoil him. Sometimes he is very rude and fresh when he is visiting us. My husband and I are terribly tempted to step in and comment, but my son is so sensitive that we hesitate to do so. So we just sit there and more or less grind our teeth.

Whether you are grandparents or other relatives or just plain unrelated hosts, this would be what I would advise. In general things go most smoothly if for the most part any child's parents are allowed to do the disciplining. Thus, say it is an overnight visit and you think that young children should go to bed early, but the parents permit a bedtime later than you think correct, I would be inclined to go along with them. After all, it is their child. And so for table manners, or the question of how quickly and adequately they mind what is said to them. However, since it *is* your house, if things get really out of hand, as with your son's little boy, it seems quite fair for you to step in and point out that "in this house" we do so and so, or don't do so and so.

Step in only if you feel it is really needed, but do feel free when hard-pressed to point out that "in this house" we do things in such and such a way. . . . If the relationship is *not* good, you may need to watch your step and let some things go by that you really don't entirely approve of.

For larger matters, it often works well, if you have some rule you want to put across, to tell the parents in a friendly way and then let them tell the children. Thus it is perfectly fair, and reasonable, to tell parents, "I prefer that the children don't bring food into the living room."

For small things, which are not necessarily repetitive, it is certainly normal and reasonable for you to speak up, especially if the parents aren't around. "Don't climb on the piano," "Don't tease the cat," "Don't hit the baby," are realistic things for you to say.

But the heart of the whole matter is your relationship with your own son, or daughter. If the two of you get on well, problems of discipline become just a natural part of daily living and do not, and should not, become a big issue.

Grandparents Can't Face Child's Illness

O ur daughter, Janie, is a victim of cystic fibrosis. Needless to say, after we received this diagnosis our whole family, as well as Janie, went through an extremely difficult period of adjustment.

I am glad to say that my husband and I are standing together very effectively in this crisis. When one of us despairs, the other always seems to find the necessary extra strength.

Our children, too, seem to me unexpectedly strong. And helpful. Janie herself is remarkable.

Our biggest problem may seem a strange one to you. It is my parents. They are not all that old—only in their early seventies—but they carry on in such a dreadful way that whenever they come over here they just go to pieces.

Instead of being a source of strength, as one might expect, they add substantially to our burden.

Though I don't have a specific solution for your problem, I can assure you that, unfortunately, your parents' response is not unusual. Audrey T. McCollum, in her book titled *Coping with Prolonged Health Impairment in Your Child,* which I recommend highly to any parent of a seriously ill child, comments as follows:

> Grandparents may steadfastly deny that their grandchild could possibly have a medical disorder. They may express stronger doubts and more lasting disbelief than you, the child's own parents. They may repeatedly stir up your own uncertainty about whether you have done the best thing for the child. They may stir up or intensify your own secret doubts about whether the doctor is right. The disbelief of your parents can interfere badly with your own struggle to come to terms with the truth.
>
> Grandparents may seem unable to understand what you tell them about your child's condition. They may become confused, forget significant facts. They may then besiege you with questions so that you must go over the painful story again.
>
> Grandparents may become so upset, even distraught, that there is a reversal of roles. They do not comfort you. You find yourself trying to comfort them. At a time when you are struggling to muster every shred of courage and hope, your parents' displays of distress may weaken your own controls and drain your emotional resources.
>
> Grandparents, also, may expect from you certain kinds of behavior that you do not find helpful. They may expect you to appear constantly grief stricken. They may expect you to give up all outside activities during the time when recreation and contact with your friends is essential in relieving your worry and sadness for brief moments.

So, though I do not have a good solution for your problem, at least you know that you are not alone.

___

Grandma Doesn't Want to Baby-Sit for Her Grandchildren

I am really quite put out with my daughter-in-law. This girl has three preschoolers under five and would like me, now and then, to take at least one of these children for, say, a Saturday. She says it would make her life so much easier and more bearable.

Well, I raised my family and I tell her she can raise hers. I enjoy my grandchildren—in small doses. I like visiting them and am quite willing for my son and his wife to bring the children here on occasion. But I don't intend to baby-sit and I think it is quite unreasonable for her to expect me to. Do you agree?

Well, actually I don't, though admittedly each of us has to grand-mother in her own way. Also it's true that nobody likes to be taken for granted or to be taken advantage of.

But for the mother of three preschoolers to ask for an occasional hand is not unreasonable. I personally consider your attitude very selfish. To me, grandchildren are one of the treasures that Nature arranges for us. You could get a great deal out of getting to know your grandchildren better and you would be doing a kindness for an inevitably overworked young woman if you would, now and then, as she requests, take one of the children for a day.

Should Grandparents Help with College Costs?

My husband and I have four children. Two are in college and two more coming right along. With the best we can do, we still cannot see our way clear to paying what are nowadays the astronomical college costs for all four.

Very reluctantly and with extreme caution we finally brought ourselves to ask my parents if they would consider helping a bit with this expense. By any standards my parents would be considered comfortably off.

They froze. Their disapproval was all too evident. They made it very clear that their money was their own, to take care of their old age. And that if there should be any left over, they looked forward to leaving me a substantial and respectable bequest. It is almost as if they were measuring their worth by the amount of money they would leave behind. Do you think I was unreasonable to make my request?

On behalf of your parents I must say that just till recently theirs was the prevailing attitude. Parents supported and educated their own children to the best of their abilities and, once that was done, they turned their anxieties and efforts to setting by enough money to cover their own old age. It was not too customary for them to help with their grandchildren's schooling.

Now things are changing in many families. College is costing more, and conversely, what with Social Security and other benefits, old age can be somewhat more secure.

And as inflation continues, some grandparents seem to prefer to spend their money on their grandchildren's schooling and other expenses while that money is still worth something. We at Gesell have long suggested that grandparents in today's world might reasonably contribute to college costs.

At any rate your expectation and request were not unreasonable, and I'm sure it was hard for you to ask. Just possibly, however, you came on too strong. Most people prefer that their gifts be made voluntarily and not on demand.

Some grandparents like to arrange support through educational insurance policies, which can be relatively inexpensive, if taken out early enough, to make the kind of contribution you had in mind.

I wouldn't give up. Hope that perhaps you have at least sown a seed. And if it doesn't work out, at least don't make matters worse by being angry at your parents. Keep in mind that it is their money to spend or not spend as they may choose.

On Divorce

How to Tell a Four-Year-Old About Divorce

I am very much concerned about something that is happening in our family, and I don't know how to handle it. My husband and I are getting a divorce and so far we haven't broken this news to our four-year-old son, Timmy. How can I tell him? How will he take it? Do you think the effects of divorce are always disastrous to a young child?

My husband and I have known for some time that our marriage was not working out. At first we hoped we could manage to stay together for our son's sake. Now we know that isn't possible. Our question now is, how can we tell our son?

We think you are right *not* to stay together "for the sake of your son." Child specialists have long felt that it may be the emotional divorce preceding the legal divorce that harms the child more than the legal divorce itself.

Timmy, obviously, will not welcome this news. Even a young child generally would prefer that his family, even though unhappy, remain intact. However a very young child often recovers from divorce and adapts to a new way of living more easily than an older one.

Timmy will be perhaps most influenced by the way you and your husband conduct yourselves. If both of you remain calm, and at least superficially friendly, and you yourself don't act as if the end of the world has come, chances are that your son, like thousands of other children of divorce, will survive emotionally.

Thus, make every effort to convey to him that this is by no means the end of life as we know it. Assure him that his father is not leaving because of anything that he, Timmy, has done or not done. Tell him specifically that he will continue to see his father.

Do your very best to refrain from saying hostile or ugly things about your husband. Try to give the explanation of why he is leaving in as calm, matter-of-fact a way as you can, explaining that when people marry they hope it will be forever but sometimes it just doesn't work out that way and that does not mean that either person is bad, or that either does not love the child.

Be sure to emphasize to Timmy that though his father will no longer be your husband, he will still be Timmy's father, and will not be lost to him.

And from a practical point of view, because even a four-year-old does have practical questions, tell him what is going to happen to him. Thus tell him, if this be the case, that he will go right on living in his own house, and that he will have a chance to visit his father on weekends.

Be aware, too, that you may need to give the same information over and over again. Don't dream that one telling, or one conversation, will suffice.

What Is the Best Age for a Child if There Must Be Divorce?

My husband and I have reluctantly come to the conclusion that there is no other course for us but to divorce. However, of course we worry about the children. I have read somewhere that divorce at some ages is more difficult and dangerous for the children in the family than other ages. Our two children are now four and six years old. Is this a bad age? Would some other time be better? We could wait a year or two, I guess, if it would make a great deal of difference.

There was a time when some psychiatrists felt that the age of the child at the time of divorce *did* matter. It was sometimes advised that the child between three and six definitely needed both parents; that from six to twelve there was less need for both. And that from twelve to eighteen the child would do best to live with the parent of the same sex.

However, current thinking tends to be, and I agree, that parents should not consider the age of their child to be the most critical issue. Also if there is more than one child in the family, one of them might always be at a critical period. If you had a large family, you might have to wait many years till *all* were past this period, and that might be extremely impractical.

Since we really do not know for sure if there *is* a critical period, or what that period might be if it does exist, and also since we cannot guarantee how much any individual child may or may not suffer, our advice to any divorcing couple would be to do your very best to help your child or children live through this difficult time, and not to worry too much about getting your divorce at what might be just the *right* time for him or them.

Children Are Taking Their Parents' Divorce Very Hard

My husband and I have been divorced for almost nine months now. I think that he and I are making a reasonably good adjustment to a difficult situation. But our two children, Betty, aged nine, and David, aged seven, are taking it very hard.

To begin with, Betty seems to think it may have been her fault that we got divorced. She continually goes over things she did that perhaps her father didn't like. I can't seem to convince her that the divorce had nothing to do with her.

David's chief problem seems to be that he keeps hoping that Daddy will come back home and we will be a family again. I hate to disillusion him and take away all his hopes. But it is totally unlikely that we'll get together again.

David also seems to feel that his father has divorced him. His father has weekly visiting privileges and is very responsible about times. But David keeps feeling that since his father left us to begin with, maybe he won't keep on visiting. I just don't seem to be making any progress with either of these problems.

Emotional problems are certain to arise following a divorce. Though there are several things still bothering your children, you have a big plus going for you—you can speak of your ex-husband in such a calm and reasonable way.

Betty's reaction is an extremely common one. Children, after all, are self-centered, so it is reasonable for them to see themselves as central in any family disaster. Your best help here may be to let Betty read a wonderful book about divorce called *The Boys' and Girls' Book About Divorce,* by Dr. Richard A. Gardner. Sometimes a child will believe something in a book even when she doesn't believe her own mother.

Dr. Gardner assures young people that sometimes a child *thinks* that his parents have gotten a divorce because *he* was bad. This is *not* the reason parents get divorced. They get divorced because they are unhappy with one another and no longer want to live together. It is *not* because of something the child has done.

As to David's hopes that his father will come back home—even though you hesitate to disillusion him, it is probably wise to gently discourage this notion. But since his father *is* reliable about his weekly visits and does show by his reliability that he is concerned about the children, you can point this out and emphasize it. As David becomes used to the notion of your divorce, chances are he will become more reconciled to the entire situation, and his fears and anxieties will in all likelihood diminish.

How Fathers Can Take the Hassles Out of Pick-up Time

Many a divorced father complains of difficulties with his former wife when it comes to having the children visit him. Pickup time can be a disaster. Sometimes the children's things aren't ready, the children themselves are not ready, or their mother has made other plans for them—and visits can start with an unhappy hassle. Here are some suggestions from a man who has been there. Frank Ferrara in his practical book *On Being Father: A Divorced Man Talks About Sharing the Responsibilities of Parenthood* gives what I consider to be excellent advice about the pickup problem.

   Have a definite schedule. Let it be understood that you'll pick up the kids every Friday afternoon at four, for example. And then stick to it. This avoids complications. It is also reassuring to the children, especially the younger ones.

If you're going to be late, phone the children's mother to let her (and them) know. This not only prevents friction with her. It also lets the kids know that you will be there and that you care enough about them to call. (If possible, talk to them as well as to their mother.)

If the kids aren't ready when you arrive, don't complain or make a scene. Help them get ready, if you can do so without making it seem as though you're indirectly criticizing their mom. Save your objections for a later private phone call to her. If it's the kids' fault that they're not ready —if they're just plain lazy or slow—deal with them yourself, later.

Don't insist on being "boss" the minute you arrive at their mother's place even if the kids are "legally" yours as of four o'clock. You're on her territory, and it's only common politeness to defer to her. If you feel she's stalling intentionally, later call her privately to complain, and if necessary make some other arrangement so it doesn't happen again.

Don't hang around. As soon as the children have their coats on, leave.

See that the children pack neatly for their return. They should check to make sure they're not leaving any clothes behind. And don't let them mix up the clean clothes with the dirty ones in their suitcases. Sometimes it can be arranged that a fairly complete set of basic needs can be left at your house, so that the number of things that have to be taken back and forth can be reduced.

If the children are nervous about getting back on time and want you to rush to leave, don't get peeved and snap at them. Be neutral and calm. If you can arrange a later return time for the next visit, then do so privately with their mother. Otherwise get them back *early*—they'll be less likely to press you another time if they've seen that the return to Mom's isn't a race against the clock.

How About Joint Custody?

*M*y husband and I are in the process of getting a divorce. We have three children, ranging in age from four to ten. My question is, what do you think about joint custody, which my husband favors and about which I have very mixed feelings?

The answer to this question varies markedly from family to family. Joint custody does work out for some people, though I have always had grave doubts about it.

Nowadays we work very hard at making everybody feel comfortable with the way they are living. Thus in an effort to make the many single parents, stepparents, living-together couples who have children though they are not married, feel good about themselves, we tend to speak as if children can benefit from any old arrangement as much as from being a part of a stable, undivorced family.

In most cases they are *not* as well off. Most children do benefit from being part of a stable family, even if it may not be the happiest or jolliest family imaginable. Most children do suffer, at least to some extent, from divorce. It is probably in an effort to minimize the shock of divorce, as well of course as to insist on their own "rights," that some couples prefer joint custody.

Sonja Goldstein and Albert Solnit in *Divorce and Your Child,* one of the most helpful books about divorce that I have read so far, suggest important questions that you and your husband should ask yourselves in making up your minds as to whether joint custody might work for you.

To begin with, can the two of you put aside your animosity and bitterness toward each other sufficiently to join in making decisions for your children? If you cannot, the children will suffer under the intolerable stress of trying to be loyal to two adults who are in conflict with each other.

Did your quarrels as husband and wife frequently center on matters connected with your children's upbringing, or was that not one of the areas of dispute? If you could not agree about such matters before your separation, do you nevertheless believe that you will be able to agree afterward?

Are you fairly certain that once you are separated and your children are the only contact between the two of you, the same inability to get along with each other (even if not centered on the child) that led to your separation will not persist or reappear in your efforts to cooperate in planning and caring for them? Do both of you have the same, or at least not conflicting, moral and ethical standards to convey to the children? Do you have similar attitudes toward school, homework, money, health-care, watching television, bedtimes, and sex?

If your children are to divide their time between the two of you, will they move from one house to the other or will they stay in the same house or apartment while the two of you rotate in and out?

If the two of you are to do the moving, are you prepared to put up with the inconvenience without resentment toward the children for causing it? If the children are to do the moving will they tolerate this well? If the children are of school age, are you both prepared to live in the same school district? If not, what school will they attend?

What will be your attitude toward joint custody if one of you remarries or moves in with another person of the opposite sex? Or of the same sex?

Unless you genuinely feel that the two of you can work out joint custody arrangements peacefully and successfully, it may be best not to undertake them. But whatever arrangement you would like to have, most specialists would urge you, if at all possible, to work it out between yourselves and not to leave it up to a court to decide.

And whatever the custody arrangement you decide on, try to end conspicuous conflict between the two of you as quickly as possible. If you both continue arguing and fighting, this can harm your children quite as much as the actual divorce itself. And don't forget, there will probably be more things to argue about if you *do* decide on joint custody.

Should Mother Face Her Children with the Fact that She Is Living with Her Boyfriend?

I don't know as you are exactly the one to ask, but, anyway, here goes. I have been divorced for three years and for reasons I won't go into did not get custody of my two boys. However they visit me for school vacations and two weeks in the summer.

Since being divorced I have had several men friends but it hasn't been necessary for the boys to know that. They are at that impressionable early teen age when they tend to be very critical of me and my actions.

Now I am living with a man whom I met recently and love very much. We're taking a cottage together this summer, or at least would like to. Jim thinks there is no reason my boys should not visit with us at the cottage. He says we should be perfectly frank about the whole arrangement. How do you feel about this?

I 'm not sure there is any "right" answer and I'm quite sure that readers will be divided in their opinions. Certainly most people nowadays don't expect divorced people to be celibate. If your children lived with you, obviously they would have to know about your dating and living arrangements.

If it were I—and I am obviously a good deal older than you—and if it were just a matter of two weeks this summer, I would make some other arrangement. Certainly introduce the boys to Jim. And if your relationship with him continues, you'll have to be frank about it.

But as you yourself say, young teenage boys are very critical of their mothers. I know two who were faced with the situation you suggest and their reaction was, "Disgusting." Whether they were right or wrong, that's how they felt. For any noncustodial parent, keeping up the relationship with the children is not an easy matter. Why throw in this clinker?

On Stepfamilies

The Wicked Stepmother

I know that the myth of the wicked stepmother has to some extent been exploded. But still most people speak very dubiously about stepfamilies. They even warn other people about marrying anyone with children. Or if one has children of one's own, they are warned not to marry.

There are so many different home situations today, more than there used to be, that things do seem complicated. There are many children of divorce who divide their time between two parental homes. There are many couples whose children are adopted, not their own natural children.

So why all this skepticism about the stepfamily? Is it all that different from any of the other not-entirely-conventional, two-parent-with-their-own-self-produced-children homes?

The stepfamily situation is markedly different from that of the divorced family or the adopted family. Divorce, obviously, starts out in most cases from disappointment and difficulty and is not a happy situation. However, in many instances, if the adults involved remain calm and strong, things *do* get better as time goes on.

Adoption, too, though the need for it usually starts in failure to produce one's own children, and though it often involves much frustration and delay before an available infant or child is found, tends to be a happy and rewarding situation. Bringing up any child, whether you have produced him or adopted him, is no picnic. But an adopted child can give much pleasure and satisfaction.

The stepfamily situation is altogether different in many ways. It often starts out badly and goes downhill from there, at least until things may stabilize. If you take the customary parent-child and child-child problems that you run into in any ordinary family and multiply them tenfold, this is what you may get.

A big part of the problem is that people tend to expect too much. When two people, one or both of whom has been married before, meet and fall in love and decide to marry, one or both of them may unrealistically assume that if they love each other, they will love the other's children, too. And that those children will love them. Nothing could be further from the truth in all too many cases.

Perhaps the majority of children whose parents remarry after a death or divorce have hoped that this would not happen. Many, at least to begin with, are openly hostile. They purposely do what they can to make things uncomfortable for the unwanted stepparent.

The hazards and traps and pitfalls to harmony are uncountable. One's best bet is to show vast patience, not just for weeks but for months and even years. Most important, both adults involved should swear to themselves not to fight over or about the children. If the new marriage is really solid, and the children see that they cannot drive a wedge between their own parent and the stepparent, most will eventually stop trying.

Her Dowry Is a Spoiled Son

I am engaged to a girl of whom I think a very great deal. The only drawback in our situation is that she has been married before and has a six-year-old son, Herbert.

I don't object to Herbert except that he was terribly ill as a baby, and because he was so fragile to begin with, Marlene has spoiled him dreadfully. He really behaves very badly most of the time. Not being a father myself, I am awfully embarrassed, for instance, when he has temper tantrums in a grocery store or in the movies.

I hate to break up my engagement over this little boy, but I do not think I would be happy looking forward to years of Herbert's company.

If Herbert, even when he is good, is personally distasteful to you, you should probably be very cautious about getting into a permanent relationship with him. Both for his sake and for your own.

If his main drawback is simply that he is a very spoiled, six years of age is not necessarily too late to correct former errors of discipline. Sick or well—and I conclude that Herbert's health is reasonably good at present—Herbert should be made to appreciate that he must behave in a way not entirely unacceptable to others.

You cannot do all the needed disciplining yourself. Marlene would have to agree to help—and mean it. But in the meantime your best bet is to keep Herbert out of grocery stores and movie theaters. Possibly a little help from a child specialist (perhaps all three of you together could try some family therapy) might give your fiancée the perspective as well as the information she needs to help her son become a more likable little boy.

Not Easy to Be a Stepparent

Is there any book that will advise stepparents how to do a better job? My problem is that my husband and I have custody of his two sons, aged four and five. Before we were married, the boys lived with their mother, without their father's supervision, for two years.

During this time their mother underwent a personality change. She began sleeping around with different men. As a result of this we have our problems with the boys. We are not going to have any children of our own, but I do so want to be a happy, comfortable family.

It is important not to dwell on the past, and especially not to dwell on the alleged immorality of the children's natural mother. Certainly her behavior, if your facts are correct, cannot have helped the children, but it may not have harmed them as much as you believe. A kind, immoral person may be as good to a child as a cruel, moral one.

Fortunately, you say both boys are under six. Thus they may not express as much rebellion against you, their stepmother, as they would if they were older. Preschoolers can be naughty, and bratty, but their basic hostility to a stepparent is often not as strong and intense as is that of older children.

And keep in mind that if the relationship between you and your husband is solid, the probability is that it will withstand the many emotional
problems that inevitably accompany stepparenthood. In fact, if it is solid,
the children will sense this and it may hasten their acceptance of you.

No book will solve your problems, but a book can help. I especially
recommend *How to Win as a Stepparent,* by John and Emily Vishner, or
Living in Step, by Ruth Roosevelt and Jeanette Lofas. Another good, and
rather amusing one (though it is hard to be amusing about stepfamilies)
is Claire Berman's *What Am I Doing in a Step-Family?* The illustrations
show what a monster a little boy thinks his perfectly nice stepfather is,
and what a monster the stepfather thinks the perfectly nice little boy is.
Or you may like to subscribe to a newsletter called *Stepfamily Bulletin*
(twelve dollars a year, order from Human Sciences Press, 72 Fifth Avenue, New York, New York 10011).

As the first issue of this helpful newsletter comments, "Compare it to
a chess game—challenging and complex. To a spider's web—delicate
and intricate. Or to a toddler's birthday party—chaotic and confusing.
Each analogy describes the stepfamily, a blended family unit that has
evolved from the rising remarriage rate."

If you are part of a new stepfamily that is experiencing growing pains,
we hold out the hope that in the long run, for most, things do eventually
work out. And, easy or not, some people believe that the stepfamily may
become the traditional American family. Certainly the rising divorce rate
and the high incidence of remarriage have resulted in the stepfamily
becoming an increasingly common phenomenon.

Nationally there are said to be more than thirty-five million stepparents, and perhaps one in six children in this country lives within a stepfamily. So be assured, you have lots of company.

Her Stepchildren Very Hostile

*Three years ago I married a man who had two children, age twelve and
fourteen. The boy is now fifteen and the girl seventeen. Even in the
beginning there were many problems of adjustment. But there didn't seem
to be the undercurrent of resentment and hostility that exists now.*

When their father is not around there is a polite coldness and sniping that is hard to put your finger on. I must say, my husband backs me completely whenever there is an argument, but I hate to run to him with every little incident.

I have sincerely tried to give above and beyond the call of duty, but this continued resentment and hostility is getting to me. I must find a way to tolerate these two until they leave for college.

Should I ignore them and speak only when necessary or should I speak out frankly about their behavior? I dislike them and they dislike me, and it makes for very unhappy living. The thing is that any discipline coming from their father they blame on me, so I really cannot win.

My advice to you is just hang on, somehow, for the few years needed. It won't be easy and it won't be pleasant. But you have already come a long way. It's hardest for a stepmother during the period while she is trying to have things go nicely. When you come to the place where you say frankly that you don't like the children and they don't like you, at least you are living in reality.

I personally would stop trying quite so hard for a nice relationship and use my efforts to keep things as smooth as possible on the surface. The really important thing now is not to let the children spoil your relationship with your husband.

At the same time, try to realize that even if these two were your own, things might not be entirely smooth. Some teenagers are fun to live with. Others are extremely trying. Growing up is not easy these days. Perhaps it never was.

I would avoid the confrontation that they so obviously seem to be seeking unless you and they are prepared to obtain outside counseling. If no real solution is likely, a confrontation probably won't help at this point.

Try to arrange for any and all vacations from each other that can be managed. Do your best to serve out your sentence successfully. Hope for very little, use your ingenuity, and get through from day to day. Stay out of things emotionally as much as you can.

Rules for Stepparenting

Each year close to a half million children are involved in a remarriage in the United States, to add to the seven million stepchildren under eighteen (as some figures estimate) who are already on hand.

According to Ruth Roosevelt and Jeanette Lofas, one of the biggest mistakes that someone who is about to form a stepfamily can make is believing that just because you get on nicely with your about-to-be stepchildren before the marriage takes place, you will get along with them afterward. A family friend who visits now and then, bringing good presents and arranging treats, is quite different to a child from a person who actually moves right in and expects to take the place of an absent mother or father.

Another big mistake is to assume that just because you, an adult, intend to show good will and friendliness and to make this new marriage a success, your spouse's children will be doing the same. Far from it! They may not only *not* cooperate—they may actually do everything possible to see that the marriage is a failure.

Here is a list of "Steps for Steps" provided by Jeanette Lofas, head of the Stepfamily Foundation of New York City.

1. Recognize that the stepfamily will not and cannot function as does a natural family. It has its own special state of dynamics and behaviors.

2. Super stepparenting doesn't work. Go slow. Don't come on too strong.

3. Discipline styles must be sorted out by the couple. They need to work out what the children's duties and responsibilities are. What is acceptable behavior and what are the consequences when children misbehave?

4. Establish clear job descriptions between parent and stepparent and the respective children. What specifically is the job of each person in the household?

5. It is vital to the survival of the parent to understand expectations for each member, especially the primary issues that produce discord, such as money, discipline, the prior spouse, visitation, authority, emotional support, and territory and custody.

6. There are no ex-parents, only ex-spouses. Learn how to best handle the prior spouse.

7. Be prepared for the conflicting pulls of sexual and biological energies within the step relationship. In the intact family the couple comes together to have a child. The child is part of both parents. In stepfamilies, blood and sexual ties can polarize the family in opposite energies and directions.

8. The conflict of loyalties must be recognized as normal right from the beginning and be dealt with. Often, just as the child begins to have warm feelings toward the new stepparent, he will pull away and negatively act out. He may feel something like this: If I love you, that means I do not love my real parent.

9. Guard your sense of humor and use it. The step situation is filled with the unexpected. Sometimes we won't know whether to laugh or cry. Try humor.

10. Remember that your spouse's children are not yours. They never will be. In fact in the traditonal sense of marriage, the partner with prior children is not totally yours— and never will be. One of the hardest things to accept is that somebody else always has a prior claim.

Should You Adopt Your Stepchildren?

About a year ago I remarried. Our new family gets along fine. The question that arises is that my husband would like to adopt Eric, my six-year-old son by my earlier marriage. Eric's natural father is willing but not enthusiastic. My own feelings are mixed. What do specialists usually advise about the adoption of stepchildren?

With nearly half a million new stepfamilies being created in this country every year, the question you ask is a customary one. There is much to be said on both sides, but many people seriously question the advisability of adopting one's stepchild.

In some instances, adoption works out well, but adoption of a stepchild is an extremely complicated emotional issue that needs to be given very careful consideration.

Adoption can settle some legal questions but it does not always provide a good solution to emotional problems within the family. It creates rights and responsibilities but it does *not* create relationships. It represents an attempt to set up a nuclear family but in reality it does not entirely do so.

Also, blood ties are very strong, particularly when the natural parent is still alive and still in the picture.

Back when divorce and remarriage were not as common as they are now, people often adopted their stepchildren so that everybody in the family would have the same name, and to avoid embarrassment. This kind of precaution is no longer necessary.

Most family specialists now advise that you explore the whole matter with a counselor before you make such a big decision.

———————————————————————————————

On Adoption

Must One Adopt a Newborn?

My husband and I are looking forward to adopting a baby. This seems to be taking quite a while but at least we are making plans. Recently we read something to the effect that if you are going to adopt a baby, it is important to do so just as soon as possible after the baby is born. Otherwise, proper mother/child relations cannot be established.

The agency we are working with tells us that it is not too likely that they will have a newborn for us. Do you think an adoption can be successful if the baby or child adopted is older when the adoption takes place?

It not only can be successful if the child is older, but it is more likely to be successful if you do *not* jump in too soon. Former students of Dr. Gesell's, Drs. Benjamin Pasamanick and Hilda Knoblock in *Gesell and Amatruda's Developmental Diagnosis* explain this matter very clearly. They also give a good concise history of adoption practices in this country.

During and right after the Depression, there were more infants available than there were families wishing to adopt. Thus emphasis was placed on getting "perfect" babies who would fit nicely into the family that was adopting. After World War II the number of families wanting to adopt outstripped even the boom in babies. Then agency emphasis shifted to being sure that the *parents* were suitable.

Now improved contraceptive information, liberalized abortion possibilities, and the fact that an increasing number of unmarried women keep their illegitimate babies, mean that today there are still fewer healthy infants available than there are people who wish to adopt them. In 1970 adoption was completed for about three-fourths of the available children.

The greatest percentage of children not adopted were nonwhite, over six years of age, and mentally or physically handicapped—that is, "hard to place."

Would-be parents are nowadays encouraged by the agencies to adopt mentally or physically handicapped children. Such adoptions do sometimes turn out favorably *if* the parents are told in advance that the child they are adopting has serious problems. What is not fair to anybody is for people, without being informed in advance, to be encouraged to adopt infants or children who are handicapped in any serious way. At least in some states, a school learning-disability checklist of possible danger signs includes the item "Adopted?" Certainly in our own clinical service we do seem to see a disproportionate number of adopted children.

This is why we have always urged that parents wait to adopt until an infant is old enough—several months old—to be given a careful physical and behavioral examination to determine, in advance of adoption, whether the child in question is of normal potential.

We assure you, it does no harm to wait. Babies do not have to be adopted in their first few weeks.

Do Adopting Parents Have a Right to Know What They're Getting Into?

S ome time ago I heard a speaker at a meeting at Yale University, Joseph Reid of the Child Welfare League of New York, make a very strong statement about adoption. He said that Dr. Gesell and his colleagues had taken the foolish position that people should adopt children whose intellectual level and potentialities were somewhat at the same level as the parents' own.

But, he said, thanks to his League and to the psychoanalysts, all that nonsense had been done away with, because how the child turned out depended on the way the adopting parents treated him.

I had always gathered from your columns that it was important for parents to insist on both a physical and a behavior examination of any child they were adopting, so that if the child did have problems they would be warned in advance. Then they could make their decision to adopt, or not adopt, accordingly.

I heard the statement, too. Mr. Reid represents a position that came in in the 1940s and has in some quarters persisted to date. The idea results from a combination of Freudian and environmental thinking.

The Freudian position appears to be that the child cannot relate, or at least will have difficulty relating, to an adopting parent unless he is with that parent from the first few weeks or preferably from the first few hours after birth. I don't know where they got the idea but that is what they seemed to think.

The environmental position is that it is not the child's basic inheritance that decides how bright he will be as he grows up, but rather the kind of home he grows up in. This is not a particularly reasonable notion, and research has not borne it out. But many still cling to it.

Our own position is that a child's potentials tend to show up very early, and that a careful behavior examination can usually tell you whether a child will grow up to be dull, average, or superior in intelligence. You can't pinpoint the exact eventual I.Q., certainly, but you can usually get a good notion of what the general level of performance is likely to be.

If you don't care about all this, that's up to you. But it can be vastly disappointing to parents who wish to give academic and other advantages to an adopted child to find out, too late, that he isn't going to make it even through high school.

Personality problems are even more important to know about than problems of intelligence, and these, too, in many cases, can be predicted. The more you know about a child you are adopting, chances are the happier the adoption will turn out to be.

When Do You Tell About Adoption?

I have put this off as long as I can. Our adopted son, Timmy, is now almost four years old and I haven't told him yet that he is adopted. Is he too young to receive this kind of information, and if not, how should I tell him?

He is *not* too young to receive this kind of information, and the way to tell him is as simply and straightforwardly as you can.

Two of the things parents seem to find it hardest to tell about are sex and adoption. The difficulty, I suppose, comes from their own emotional feelings about both subjects, since actually almost any parent knows the facts to be told and is intellectually able to tell them.

Embarrassment or hesitancy in talking about adoption probably comes from two sources. First, the parent may actually wish that the child was her (or his) own and that the story didn't have to be told. Second, she (or he) worries that the information will upset the child.

At any rate, most specialists agree that the time to tell about adoption is whenever it comes up. And if the subject doesn't comes about naturally, then make the opportunity as early in the preschool years as possible. If you absolutely cannot think of what to say, you can get help from any of several good books on the subject.

The basic facts you wish to convey are, of course, that you *chose* this child even though you did not produce him; that you love him very much and are happy to have him in your family; and that his biological mother and father, also, undoubtedly loved him too but that there were good reasons why they could not make a home for him.

Remember that as in telling about sex, you do not have to tell everything you know or think about the subject all at once. And also remember that the more casual and calm you appear to be as you tell about adoption, the calmer and more secure the child will feel. He will be influenced by your attitude quite as much as by your actual words.

So, be early, be frank, be truthful, and be calm. But my advice is not to go overboard about the whole thing. Some people keep little scrapbooks labeled "Our Own Adopted Child." Some introduce their child as "Our little adopted son (or daughter)." Some even join groups of adoptive parents. In general, this kind of emphasis seems excessive and might suggest to the child that there is something very different about being adopted—and that is not the message you really wish to get across.

Should You Adopt a Child the Same Age as Your Own?

We took Jackie from an orphanage at the age of twelve and adopted him. He is a fine boy though still quite insecure. Then a few months later we took Patrick, also twelve.

At first Jackie seemed anxious to have a brother. But after a few weeks and quite a lot of quarreling, he grew resentful of him. Talking to him availed nothing, and finally he admitted that he was afraid we would love Patrick best, and that Patrick would get to sit in my lap more than he would, and so on.

Patrick didn't help matters any. Having moved from home to home he had learned to live by his wits and was very clever at getting his own way.

So we did let Patrick go back to the orphanage without completing the adoption. Now Patrick feels a complete failure.

I know I am tackling a big job but I feel that Jackie needs a brother just as much as Patrick needs a home. I would like to have Patrick back. I want Jackie to realize that I have the capacity to love two sons.

You showed very bad judgment. Many, if not most, children resent the arrival of a baby brother or sister. With most it is only if there is a substantial age difference that some jealousy does not occur. If the older of any two is at least three years older or more when the new one arrives, chances that the baby will be accepted are better than if the age difference is less.

And, with the biological family, or with a child adopted in infancy, we are talking about an older child who has had the security of one single family from the beginning. You did not adopt Jackie until he was twelve. This means that in all likelihood he had already lived in several homes or institutions, and may quite normally have developed many insecurities.

Adapting to your home at the rather advanced age of twelve, with much behind him, and just as he was on the verge of those difficult adolescent years, might have been expected to be somewhat difficult. Ideally you should have waited until he seemed at least fairly secure before introducing another boy into your home.

Unfortunately you harbored this entirely unrealistic notion that Jackie would enjoy another boy his same age and that he *needed* such a boy and that it would be *good* for him. (Why twelve-year-old boys were sitting on your lap I don't quite know; it seems late.)

As to Patrick, you can't keep bringing him in and out of your house to satisfy your own wishes. It almost seems that you are putting yourself ahead of the boys. You say, "I want Jackie to realize that I have the capacity to love two sons."

Your best bet is to counsel with the social agency in charge of Patrick. I doubt that things would work out well with him and Jackie even if you did take him back. Now the question is how can you and/or the agency handle things with the least harm to Patrick.

How Does It Work Out When Adopted Children Meet Their Natural Parents?

As an adopting mother I am much concerned about all the current push toward having adoption records unsealed, so that adopted children can find out about and even get in touch with their biological parents.

Don't you feel that this is asking for trouble not only for the child and natural parents but also for those of us who have adopted the boy or girl? I can understand a certain amount of curiosity, but it seems to me that the possible harm that might be done outweighs the good.

I understand your concern. But experience seems to be showing that these meetings, and revelations, work out favorably more often than not.

Evidence of this recently appeared in the magazine *Behavior Today Newsletter,* which reports the findings of a four-year study by UCLA psychiatrist Arthur Sorotsky and two experienced adoption social workers, Annette Baran and Reuben Pannor. They have just examined, through questionnaires and interviews, fifty cases in which adoptees met with one or more of their natural parents and in some cases with brothers, sisters, or other relatives.

The adoptees ranged in age from eighteen to fifty at the time of the reunion. According to their reports, the meetings were a great success. Ninety percent of the adoptees and 82 percent of the natural parents were happy about the outcome. Most of the adoptees, the researchers said, reported "a sense of closure, resolution of concerns, and diminished identity conflicts."

After the first meeting, half the adoptees developed meaningful relationships with the natural parents; another 34 percent were satisfied with occasional contacts.

Admittedly the adoptive parents were less happy. While 36 percent were cooperative and understanding, 20 percent were mildly upset and another 10 percent were quite hurt. The rest were either dead or were not told of the meetings.

It is understandable that the adopting parents should feel some hesitancy about this kind of revelation. But don't forget, the information is not as a rule given, or even sought, till the young person is at least in the late teens or early twenties. And this is a time when he will in the natural course of things be beginning to move away from his family, whether biological or adoptive.

Also, adopting parents may be reassured by the warm and sympathetic comments of the birth parents about them: "They are the real parents." "I do not want to take the child away from them. I have the greatest respect for what they have done for my child." "I will always be grateful to these people who raised my child."

Moreover, most of the birth parents seemed truly grateful that someone was finally interested in them and their feelings. Most felt that they had been deceived by the public agencies who assured them that they would quickly forget the whole thing once they had given up their child for adoption.

Psychiatrist Sorotsky found that adopted people tend to be more vulnerable than nonadopted to the development of identity conflicts in late adolescence and young adulthood. Many are preoccupied with concerns about who they "really" are. They tend to feel isolated and alienated due to a break in the continuity of life through the generations, which their adoption represents. Apparently information about biological parents and/ or a meeting with these parents (even if not followed up intensively) does a great deal to resolve anxieties. So chances are it really is worthwhile. It seems that, at least in many cases, a reunion between adopted child and birth parent, if so desired, benefits all three members of the adoption triangle—the child, the adoptive parents, and the birth parent.

On Starting School

Should Terry Be Forced to Go to Kindergarten?

*M*y son, Terry, will be four in December. He is very bright—knew his alphabet at sixteen months for instance. But even now he is not completely toilet-trained and plays best with three-year-olds.

When, against my judgment, but because my family, friends, and the school insisted, I tried him in kindergarten, he hated it. Cried and fussed and carried on and clung to me. The principal said I must persist. My mother says he will lose his brightness and regress if he is put in with younger children.

The principal says that youngness and immaturity don't matter—just bribe him and force him, or he will become bored and begin to have problems in school. My neighbors say when he gets older, people will ask him why he is "only" in this grade or that. They say he will hate me, later on, if I keep him back now.

Only my pediatrician sticks with me. Plus the teacher in the school's resource room who was called in. She said that youngness and immaturity do *count.*

I really don't know what to do. Terry is out of school right now and we have a grand time going to the library, the zoo, museums, Sunday school. We also go on long walks and at home work with books, paper, arts and crafts. Will I feel guilty all my life if I don't force my son, right now, to go to kindergarten?

*Y*our mother is wrong that being with younger children will diminish your son's intelligence. If he has it, he'll show it. The principal is entirely misguided about boredom. Boredom does not come just because a child has been going to school for a long time. Boredom, if any, comes when the teacher is teaching in a boring way (regardless of what grade she is teaching) or more often it is reported if the child is not suited to the grade he is in, and thus its demands don't suit him and he cannot respond effectively. Your neighbor's dire predictions about the future are exaggerated. At one time people made rude and nosy remarks to the effect of "Why would that ten-year-old only be in fourth grade?" Nowadays, people are much less rigid, and most of them much less nosy.

We have yet to hear of a parent who did keep his or her child back when immaturity was present who later felt guilt at what he or she had done. Nor do we know of a child who hated parents because he or she was allowed to take a slower course in school. Stick to your guns!

The Importance of an Early Cut-off Date

We parents in our community are aware of your oft-repeated theory that children should be developmentally ready before they begin school. Unfortunately our schools do not go along with this. They follow the principle of admitting everybody, and then supposedly "individualizing" teaching. Since our schools at this time give no help in evaluating any child's readiness, might we not accomplish more or less the same thing by seeing to it that our children are on the old side before they enter school?

Right you are! It is our position that perhaps 50 percent of school problems might be prevented or remedied simply by having children in the grade for which their maturity level suits them. We recommend that every child be started in school, and subsequently promoted, on the basis of his behavior age (which can be quite easily determined by proper testing) rather than by his age in years. We call this policy *developmental placement.*

Perhaps the most important single thing a parent can do for a child is to see that he or she does not start school too soon, before he or she is ready, simply because that child has reached some certain age at which the law permits school entrance. Of course there is a lot more to succeeding in school than merely being in the right grade; but being in the right grade is one of the most important single factors.

We hold that age should not be the chief criterion for determining readiness, but it is indeed true that the older the child, the more likely that he or she will be ready for the work that the school requires. That is the reason why we, and many others, are pushing for an early cut-off date.

Probably the most common cut-off date now is September 1. That means that the child has to have had his or her fifth birthday before starting kindergarten. There are, admittedly, some states that are backward in this respect. In Connecticut, for instance, the date is January 1. This means that a child who in September is only four years and eight months of age can start kindergarten. A few states are advanced enough to have June 1 as their date.

For many years, teachers, especially, have referred to what they call fall babies, that is children who have their fifth birthday in the fall after starting kindergarten. Such children are notorious for not doing well in school. Dr. Ilg, our former director, supported the notion that June 1 would be a desirable cut-off date. This would protect not only fall babies but those born in the summer as well. Supporting this idea is an encouraging new book titled *Summer Children*.

There is a reasonable amount of literature that upholds our own position that older children tend to do better in school. Research in the *Journal of Learning Disabilities* for May 1980 checked on the birthdates of 552 children referred to one psychological clinic because they were having either emotional or academic difficulties in school. There turned out to be a direct relationship between birthday month and amount of difficulty. For the older children (born January and February) there were only 70 referrals out of the 552. This number increased dramatically till there were 110 referrals for those born in September/October, and 110 for the very youngest, born November/December.

So, if it must be birthday age that one goes by, we definitely favor having this date September 1 or earlier. However, the problem may eventually become merely academic. One pioneer state, Oklahoma, in the summer of 1985 passed a bill requiring that it should be behavior age, not birthday age, that determines the time when a child shall be considered ready to begin kindergarten. Other states are currently considering similar bills.

Early Reading No Sign of Genius

As the old saying goes, "If I knew then what I know now . . . " I'd like to give you the picture of an above-average child—my own daughter, Lucy, now thirteen and in the eighth grade—and what happened to her.

Lucy began to talk when she was eight months old and at one year was using simple sentences. By fourteen months she began reading words on all the cereal boxes. She would ask questions such as "Mommy, what does the K say?"

At a year and a half she was reading stories from Golden Books out loud, and had memorized the Lord's prayer and about forty nursery rhymes. By two, she knew all the verses to "The Night Before Christmas" and had a library of at least fifty books that she could read easily. By four she was doing newspaper crossword puzzles with adults.

By five she was in kindergarten, the youngest in her class by two weeks. At midyear the teacher found that she had sixth-grade comprehension in reading and tried her out in first grade. Fortunately we agreed that she was not emotionally ready for first grade. At home she was constantly whining.

In spite of her amazingly early reading, I think her school problems began when she started kindergarten so young. In first grade, though reading was of course a snap, she didn't know how to study and never bothered to learn her basic arithmetic facts. Tension increased at home, but nobody could figure out why.

At seven, in second grade, her arithmetic was still poor and the tension increased. Nightmares were frequent. Since then she has become progressively poorer with her schoolwork. She hit a low point in sixth grade and now is barely average in her marks. Emotionally she seems more like eleven than thirteen. Still shouts and talks in her sleep. Can be unbelievably pouty and unpleasant at home. She and I end up in a fury at each other at least twice a day.

I have found out the hard way that a child may be an early reader without being a genius or even ready for school. Now I feel that instead of suggesting first grade for her when she was barely five, the school should have questioned her readiness even for kindergarten. A lot more than the child's reading ability goes to school.

Y ou are so right that a child may be an early reader without necessarily being a genius. Also, a child can be an early reader without necessarily being ready for kindergarten, if he or she is on the young side, either in behavior or in age. In fact your Lucy may well be one who might be classified as gifted/learning disabled—tremendously gifted in one area but poor in others.

Often only a careful diagnosis can determine—with behavior as with health—what the story really is and what the child really needs.

Is Your Child Ready for School?

Many parents have asked us for clues to help them know when their child is ready for school. John Austin and J. Clayton Lafferty, in *Ready or Not? The School Readiness Checklist,* offer forty-three indicators to consider when deciding whether a child is ready for kindergarten. Listed below are the nine points the authors consider the most important. If first grade is the concern, following is a nineteen-point list we use at the Gesell Institute.

For Kindergarten

1. Will your child be five years and six months or older when he begins kindergarten?
2. Can he tell you the names of three or four colors that you point out?
3. Can he draw or copy a square?
4. Can he name drawings of a cross, square, circle?
5. Can he repeat a series of four numbers without practice?
6. Can he tell his left hand from his right?
7. Can he draw and color beyond a simple scribble?
8. Can he tell what things are made of, such as cars, chairs, and shoes?
9. Can he travel alone in the neighborhood (two blocks) to store, school, playground, or the homes of friends?

For First Grade

1. Does the child's kindergarten teacher recommend that he go on to first grade? If she does not, be guided by her advice. Kindergarten teachers do not, as some parents suspect, advise that a child stay back just because they are prejudiced against him, or don't like him. They advise that he stay back, when they do, because they have good reason to believe that he can't make it in first grade.
2. Will the child be fully six years old or older before the September date when first grade starts?
3. Does he seem to you as mature as other children of his same age, or as mature as his older siblings were at his age?
4. Has the ordinarily "good" behavior of the typical five-year-old broken up a bit and does your child show some of the signs of being or becoming a rebellious, argumentative *six?*
5. Can he copy a circle, counterclockwise and starting at the top? (This behavior is expected by five and a half years.)
6. Can he copy a triangle?
7. Can he copy a divided rectangle, angled lines crossing center line?
8. Does he hold a pencil in a good two- or three-finger grasp?
9. Can he print at least his first name?
10. Does he know his upper- and lowercase letters, out of context?
11. Can he count to thirty?
12. Can he write numbers up to twenty?
13. Does he know right from left?
14. Does he know his age and the month of his birthday?
15. Can he stand on one foot while you count to eight?
16. Can he throw a ball overhand?
17. Can he tie his shoelaces?
18. Can he repeat four numbers after hearing them once?
19. Can he calculate (add and subtract) within twenty?

Single-Sex Classes?

*I*n our community, some of the parents are raising the question of single-sex classes in the primary grades. They feel it would be fairer to those many boys who are less mature than girls of the same age and who find it more difficult than girls do to sit still and perform successfully at such tasks as reading and writing. What do you think of all this?

Certainly in all likelihood this would not be a popular idea with those feminists who cringe at the mere notion that there are any "real" differences between girls and boys—who even feel that girls should be allowed to play on boys' football teams.

But there are positive findings in support of single-sex classes, as Sheila Moore and Roon Frost point out in *The Little Boy Book*. Not only do single-sex classes protect immature and not very verbal little boys who find it hard to keep up with girls, they also allow classrooms and curriculums to be structured to help children learn as much as possible.

Although there isn't a great deal of research available on single-sex classrooms, what there is indicates that they are beneficial for both boys and girls. Moore and Frost report interesting conclusions from their studies.

• Boys in single-sex classes do better in some subject areas than boys in coed classes.

• In one school that experimented with single-sex classes, the repeat rate dropped from 10 percent to 3 percent.

• High-school girls gifted in mathematics did better in advanced math courses that were taught by a woman teacher and that were all-girls or largely so.

Moore and Frost also point out that the benefits of single-sex classes aren't only for the students. According to one study, teachers didn't mind the loud behavior of their all-male classes as much as they would have had the same behavior been exhibited in a coed class. Also, it has been put forth that teachers might have preferences about teaching either boys or girls and actually perform better when allowed to instruct the group they prefer.

The results of the studies are not conclusive, but I feel they indicate that making everything equal for boys and girls may not give both the greatest possible opportunities.

How About All-Day Kindergarten?

Our school is currently investigating the possibility of an all-day kindergarten program. We, as kindergarten teachers, are not in favor of this move. However, as the committee given the task of compiling data on this issue, we feel the need of maintaining an open mind. Thank you in advance for any help you can give on this matter.

The problem that faces you is, in my opinion, one of the most widespread, undesirable, and dangerous currently threatening our schools. This notion of all-day kindergarten seems, alas, to be sweeping the country.

The main arguments proposed in its favor are that mothers need somewhere to park their five-year-olds in the afternoon; and that a half day does not provide enough time to get through the academic work that is now being introduced into many kindergartens. Those who propose an all-day, every-other-day, kindergarten say that it also saves money on buses, regardless of what it may do to the children.

Our reasons for opposing all-day kindergarten are multiple. The first and main reason is that most five-year-olds are not, in our opinion, strong enough either physically or emotionally to stand up to all-day school. In fact, before this attack on the kindergarten began, we were pushing for half-day first grades, since many six-year-olds wilt by noontime.

Also *five* is a close-to-home and close-to-mother age. Admittedly, not all mothers *are* at home, but the wish for closeness still exists.

Second, it is generally admitted that kindergartens today are rather much like what first grades used to be. Even in a half-day session, there tends to be more academic (or as they now call it, cognitive) work than we would like to see. It would be an unusual teacher who had the children all day who would not increase the amount of academic teaching (for which many *fives* are not ready).

Third, there is the matter of expense. Though some schools claim that if children stayed in school all day they would get more money from the state, the fact remains that if kindergarten sessions are extended in length, somebody is going to have to pay. Professor Edward Zigler of Yale put it very aptly when he noted that in education, perhaps more than in any other field, we tend to promise a great deal more than we can pay for.

Also, as we point out elsewhere, there are a good many children placed in kindergarten because they are five years old even though their behavior age may be below that level. Quite obviously if they don't belong in kindergarten to begin with, keeping them there all day is adding insult to injury.

We suspect that there are many children in kindergarten like the little boy who, when asked by his grandmother how he liked school, said he hated it. "But," he added, "it's okay, Grammy, because I'm quittin'." Grandma asked him if, assuming that everybody would allow it, he would like to go back to nursery school, which he had enjoyed. The little boy replied, "No chance, Grammy. Once the kindergarten gets hold of you there's no going back."

At any rate we can report that in some of the towns and cities where all-day kindergarten has been tried or proposed it has later been given up. For instance in Buffalo, New York, where all-day kindergarten was proposed in three districts, parental opposition was so strong that the idea was given up in each of the three districts. Among the comments from Buffalo parents were the following.

"We think a half-day program is adequate for a five-year-old. A full-day program is too long and too tiring."

"I feel strongly that my children should not suffer just to provide day-care or a head start on an aggressive, must-succeed-at-all costs type of life-style for others."

"I don't feel that the school is the only place where my child's development takes place. The increase in cost may not justify the limited educational benefits, if any."

"How about some time outside (daylight time) for kids to be just kids? Nothing like starting a kid off hating school by making him stay all day."

"A full day will do more to disrupt the children than to educate them. Most five-year-olds are emotionally as well as physically too immature for a full day of school five days a week."

"I have a strong feeling that an all-day program would be for the parents' convenience and not the child's best interests. If parents are unwilling or unable to assume responsibility for their children, they should seek out a day-care program. Public education was not intended to replace parenting."

"I do not feel that five-year-old children are emotionally ready for a full-day program, nor do I wish my school tax money to be used for what would actually be half kindergarten and half day-care."

These are also the opinions that we ourselves hear, day in and day out, as all-day kindergarten is threatened in more and more communities. Let's hope for the best even while we face the fact that this move toward all-day schooling for five-year-olds continues to be very strong.

Questions About Developmental Placement

Here are common questions about the school readiness program that many schools are starting or have started. I'll answer them one by one.

Q. How can you determine in a thirty-minute (Gesell) test how mature (or ready) any child is for the work of the grade in question?

A. It does not take a full thirty minutes to get a reasonable idea of how heavy or tall a child is, or where his or her behavior is rating. Almost everything a child does speaks for itself—and one or two significant tests speak very loudly as to where a child is functioning.

Q. How can a child who rated youngest in the class in the fall, be ahead of some of the others in the spring?

A. A child who tested youngest in the group at the beginning of the school year would quite normally also test relatively young at the end of the year. However, there are exceptions. As a rule growth proceeds evenly, but in some children it goes by fits and starts. That is why we recommend testing both at the beginning and at the end of any school year.

Q. How long does it take for an examiner to be trained and qualified to give your behavior tests?

A. In giving any psychological test, a person clearly becomes more expert the longer he or she works with the test. One of our training courses tells a person where to begin. Expertness obviously comes with practice.

Q. Since you say that children who have not had their fifth birthday by September are usually not ready to start kindergarten, does not the child's birth date influence the examiner? And wouldn't it be fairer if the examiner didn't know how old the child was?

A. Knowing a child's birthdate is at least a clue, since on the average, the so-called fall babies often are not "ready." However, the tests speak for themselves and an examiner should not be strongly influenced by the birthdate. That is why we test. If the birthdate alone were totally adequate, tests would not be needed.

Q. Wouldn't it be better to give readiness tests in first grade, by which time the child will have learned something, rather than before kindergarten when he has not yet been in school?

A. Testing the child in first grade would *not* be more beneficial than testing in or before kindergarten. If the child were not ready when five, waiting till first grade to test could mean a whole year in a grade where the child might not belong. The fact that the child might have "learned" more by first grade is beside the point, since the development tests tells how far a child's body and behavior have matured, not how much he or she has learned.

Q. If a child wants to learn to read but the teacher says he is not ready, what should you do?

A. If a child wants to learn to read, he or she should be permitted to do so. Grade placement should not, ideally,

depend on reading ability or even on high intelligence. A
child could be highly intelligent and an adequate reader and
still young, in general, for his age.

When Do You Take Their Complaints About School Seriously?

My son, Denny, just five years old, started kindergarten this fall, and he complains every day. I don't know whether to take these complaints seriously or not. To hear him tell it, he hates school, yet the teacher says he does okay. What do most parents do about these complaints?

It is important to avoid either the extreme of taking a child's complaints too seriously and not taking them seriously enough. If you really can't be sure what to do, the school should be able to help you.

For many children, saying that they don't like school is no more than a ritual complaint. It's like a grownup saying, "I hate to get up in the morning." It often means no more than that "Life is just kind of much." On the other hand, it can be a sign of something really wrong.

Here are some of the things that may help you judge:

How *intense* are Denny's complaints? If his complaints seem half-hearted and can be easily brushed aside, you probably don't need to take them too seriously. If they persist and you can't turn them off, pay attention.

If verbal complaints are accompanied by other manifestations of upset, you may wish to take them seriously. Mere stalling in the morning is not unusual. But if you're like the mother who told us, "Every morning I have to drag my son out of bed, struggle to get him dressed, throw him into the family car, and finally drag him screaming over the threshold of the schoolroom," it is fair to say that school is too much for him.

"I hate school" may or may not be a truly significant complaint, but if your child tells you that he can't see the board, he needs help.

Any *physical complaint,* such as being sick to one's stomach on school mornings, should be taken seriously, as should complaints about headache, or eyes hurting.

Any regression to earlier and more babyish ways in any of the usual routines—eating, sleeping, elimination—can be a clue to real difficulty. Returning to bed-wetting may seem a strange way to say that school is too much, but it is a very good clue.

Your child's complaints should be taken especially seriously if they are accompanied by complaints from the teacher.

So, it may take a little detective work to determine whether or not school is really too much for Denny. Checking with the teacher may be your best place to begin.

Has Your Child Started School Too Soon?

And now, if you haven't checked on readiness, or have ignored any warnings that you may have felt, here are clues to the fact (if it be a fact) that your boy or girl may not be properly placed in school. In most such instances it will be that he or she has started too soon.

1. Does he dislike school?
2. Does he complain a great deal that "it's too hard"?
3. Does he have great difficulty in completing the written work assigned in class?
4. Does he seem unduly fatigued when gets home from school?
5. Is he a "different" child during the summer when school responsibilities have been removed?
6. Does he have terrible trouble, almost every day, in getting ready for school?
7. Does he complain of stomach aches, or is he actually sick to his stomach before he goes to school in the morning?
8. Has any marked changed for the worse in his health taken place since he started school? Does a normally healthy child suddenly begin to have a series of colds, one after another?
9. Have any of his home routines taken a marked turn for

the worse since he started school? For instance, does he eat less well, have trouble in sleeping, exhibit a return to bed-wetting after having been dry at night?

10. Has a normally "good" child suddenly become rebellious, difficult, quarrelsome, cranky at home once school has started?

11. Does your child get much poorer school marks than you and the teacher think he is capable of getting?

12. Does his teacher assure you that he "could do better" if only he would try harder?

13. Does he have trouble socially, either in class or on the playground?

14. Are most or many of his friends chosen from children in a lower grade?

15. Is his teething considerably behind that of other boys and girls in his class?

16. Does a normally "good" child find it terribly difficult to behave in class? Are there constant complaints from the school that he has had to be reprimanded, was made to sit out in the hall, or had to be sent to the principal's office?

17. Does he do desperate things at school as, for instance, not finishing his paper and then scribbling all over it?

18. Does he find it unduly difficult in class to wait his turn, speak only when he's supposed to, refrain from "bothering" his classmates?

19. Does he daydream in class or fail to pay attention, to an extent the teacher considers unreasonable?

20. Has the teacher or anyone at school suggested to you that your child really is not up to the work of his present grade and would be better off in a lower grade?

21. Last, and perhaps most important, does he seem to you babyish as compared to other children his same age, or compared to the way his brothers and sisters (if any) behaved when they were his age?

Does Teacher's Expectation Determine
Child's School Performance?

*A*s a school principal, formerly a teacher, I was trained to believe that the one single thing that makes the most difference as to whether a child succeeds in school or not is the teacher's expectation. Thus I believe that when you people at Gesell say that perhaps a third of children, if started in school on the basis of birthday age rather than behavior age, may fail, you are contributing to their failure by lowering the teacher's expectations.

Certainly a teacher's expectation can be a factor in determining a child's school success, but it is by no means *the most important* factor. Chances are you went to teacher's college at the time when the work of Robert Rosenthal was being given excessive prominence.

Dr. Rosenthal, a perfectly respectable psychologist, did have the notion that childen succeeded if teachers were told that these children were bright; failed if teachers were told they were dumb. Though his research received wide publicity, it did not stand up very well. (In this research, teachers were often given incorrect information but were, allegedly, swayed by it.)

Not only must these teachers have been awfully gullible to believe that bright students were dumb just because Rosenthal told them so, but the whole notion ignores individual differences. Some children, no matter what their teachers expect, are immature or perhaps not very gifted academically.

Many adults expect too much of children, but it doesn't necessarily improve the children's behavior. In fact, the world is full of grownups who go around saying of children, "He could do better if he would . . ." Our own version of this statement is just the opposite. We say, "He would do better if he could." That is, we think it is the child's basic endowment, not what somebody expects of him, that for the most part determines how well he does, in school and in life.

Thus, contrary to what you were taught, we do not believe that a child can be made "ready" for any grade just by having his teacher *think* he is ready. It seems best all around if the teacher's expectation is based on reality. Some reasonable behavior test can help a teacher base her expectations on what the child is really like. It is the child's behavior that might best determine the teacher's expectation. Not the other way around.

On Repeating

How to Tell Patty She's Going to Have to Repeat Kindergarten

I realize that this is an old story to you but I am new at it. My almost six-year-old daughter, Patty, is now in kindergarten and the teacher says she is not going to be ready for first grade this coming year.

An example of her immaturity is that in reading readiness, a Dalmatian was shown to illustrate D. Patty put him with F for firetruck. I like the teacher, as does Patty, but the teacher says though Patty is doing better now, as late as December while the teacher was talking to the group, my daughter would just wander off.

My husband and I agree that probably Patty should repeat kindergarten but we don't know how to tell her. Her best friend will be going into first grade. The teacher had no suggestions about telling Patty.

Should we ease into this gradually, mention the possibility of going to kindergarten again, or just tell her right out? Whatever we do, should it be now or should we wait till September?

I'm glad that you and your husband are willing to go along with the teacher who advises that Patty repeat kindergarten. Teachers are usually right when they give this kind of advice and kindergarten teachers are often the most perceptive of all.

How to break the news? That is of course something each parent really has to figure out for himself or herself. You have to speak in a way that comes natural to you. Some parents just tell the child, in as cheerful and positive a way as possible, that they've been talking to the teacher and that the teacher would like to have the child with her another year, to help out with the new children and also to give her a little more chance to grow and be ready for first grade.

Some say that they and the school made a mistake and started the child too soon, and wasn't it lucky they found out in time.

More than what you *say* is your attitude. If both you and your husband remain calm and cheerful as if this is just the most natural thing in the world, and thus Patty sees that nobody is mad at her, chances are that even though she may object a little, she will accept your decision calmly. If she doesn't you'll just have to bring in more ammunition such as that first grade will be a lot more fun and a lot easier if she is a little older when she starts.

The main thing is to avoid any implication that she has *failed* in anything. If need be you can tell her that people know more about children than they used to (way back last year) and realize now that some children need to be a little older before they start first grade.

If her best friend is a wee bit older than Patty, you can use age as an explanation. If not, you will just have to use your own ingenuity when the time comes.

Her Son Is Happier, More Confident, Since He Repeated a Grade

L ast year on your advice our twelve-year-old son repeated a grade. We obviously were very slow to make what was a clearly necessary adjustment. We suffered from the fears all parents experience—that he would be harmed emotionally by this "failure." But finally his schoolwork and in fact his whole life was so bad that there was clearly nothing else to do.

The results have been miraculous. On this last quarter's work he made the Honor Roll (the first time in his life). And the only score he made lower than ninety-three was an eighty-five.

His grades, of course, are wonderful, but our greatest pleasure comes from observing the change in our son. He is happier, more confident, more outgoing, more eager to try new things, and just more at ease with himself. And it is a joy to see him developing meaningful relationships with his peers. Thanks a million.

Y ou are welcome. We're sorry that your son's salvation came so late. But we hope that your experience, and your son's, may encourage other hesitant parents to make this same move when it seems indicated. Best of all not to start children in school till they are developmentally ready. But if the mistake has been made, next best thing is to allow them to repeat when your own instinct, or the school, informs you that this is the necessary move.

Grandma Is Against Repeating

My husband and I went along with the kindergarten teacher's recommendation that my son, Peter, needed to repeat kindergarten this coming fall, and all was going well till my mother-in-law came to visit. She insists that the whole thing is ridiculous. Peter is clearly a good, bright little boy and she asks, how could anybody flunk kindergarten?

Now my husband is weakening and I am afraid we are in real trouble. What can I do now?

P erhaps you might try pointing out to your husband that times change. Explain to him that when his mother was, herself, a mother of young children, boys and girls indeed started school depending on their birthday age, or if a child was not quite as old as the law required but was very bright or could read well, a policy called Early Entrance allowed that he or she start school.

Today people have given up Early Entrance, and many enlightened schools appreciate that more than the I.Q. alone goes to school. They believe that it is the age at which a child is behaving, rather than just his birthdate that determines readiness. If your own arguments do not convince him, suggest that he read our own book—*Is Your Child in the Wrong Grade?* This might do the trick.

If not, you'll just have to come on strong and explain that it must be the parents and not the grandparents who will make these important decisions.

How Far Do We Go with Repeating?

You are so big on having children repeat a grade, how far do you go with this?

I can go along with the idea that if a five- or six-year-old, or even a seven-year-old, is not mature enough for the grade his age would put him in, he or she should repeat. I agree that at these very early ages even one year can make a big difference in a child's readiness for the work of a certain grade.

But how far do you carry this? Say you have a very mature-looking twelve-year-old girl, infinitely more interested in boys than she is in studies —do you believe that repeating would necessarily solve her academic problems?

As a general rule we tend to say, "It's never too late to repeat" or "Better late than never." This would be true in the case of an eleven-year-old boy, or even of an immature twelve-year-old who has by bad luck gotten into junior high and who is floundering and lost in its complexity.

However, we agree that there can be exceptions. There are, admittedly, many boys and girls in our schools who are not academically oriented, who don't like school and don't do well in it, who will most certainly never go on to college.

Fortunately some of them will be, as the saying goes, "better at living than at learning." One's best bet may be to get them through school as quickly as possible, all in one piece.

Though we don't believe in grouping by physical size, in the kind of case you mention, we might make an exception. A large and fully developed twelve-year-old girl might indeed look and feel quite out of place back in a roomful of underdeveloped elevens.

And if because of her lack of smarts or academic interest or ability, repeating is not going to do anything spectacular for her schooling as such, we might indeed advise against having her repeat.

Instead one might hope to steer her, as soon as practical, into some kind of vocational courses. The much-maligned policy of "tracking" could, for such a girl, be very useful.

Repeating Didn't Work

We tried repeating, but it sure didn't work for us.

There is perhaps no parent more disgruntled than the one who has, against his or her better judgment, permitted a child to repeat a grade, only to find that the child still is not doing passing work.

Many parents seem to feel that some sort of guarantee does, or should, go with repeating. They feel that if they take the rather drastic step of allowing a boy or girl to repeat a grade that most certainly *then* he should start succeeding in school.

Parents, and sometimes schools, overlook the fact that repeating, like any other strong medicine, must be used judiciously. It is *not* the answer for everyone.

As, for instance, it was not the answer for Freddy. Freddy was an unusually immature little boy for whom first grade turned out to be a total disaster. Much against his parents' judgment, the school recommended that he repeat first grade. They felt that repeating would do the trick.

His parents, though not too worldly-wise in the ways of education, did have a very good insight into their own son's abilities and inabilities. They didn't exactly know *what* Freddy did need, but somehow they felt that another year in first grade was not going to solve his problems.

Fortunately, they found a children's clinic that specialized in school problems and took him there. A careful clinical examination showed that Freddy, at seven years of age and just about to start first grade for the second time around, was grossly immature and was still behaving only like a five- to five-and-a-half-year-old. He not only had not been ready for first grade the first time around, he wasn't even ready for it now.

Unfortunately, immaturity was not Freddy's only problem. He was one of those little boys who was very poorly oriented to space, and even poorly oriented to his own right and left sides. His behavior was also highly disorganized. More than that he had a very poor memory and a poor sustaining power. Unfortunately, his I.Q. measured no higher than 85, and a careful visual examination showed that he had a serious perceptual problem.

This examination indicated that Freddy was not at this time ready for a regular public-school class *at any grade level.* What he needed was a special class for perceptually handicapped children.

And so we have to give this warning: repeating is not magic and it is not the remedy needed in *all* cases of school failure.

On Learning Problems

Is Their Six-Year-Old Dyslexic?

*O*ur six-year-old son, Felix, is in first grade. I realize that he started a
little younger than you would approve of, since his birthday was not
till late December, but he is a bright boy, big for his age, and seemed to us
relatively mature.

*Now, however, things are going badly and especially with his reading.
He just can't seem to catch on. In fact his reading is almost nil and when
he does manage to spell out a word, he tends to reverse the letters. The
teacher says she thinks he is dyslexic but when I ask her what can be done,
she really does not have too much to offer. To her, apparently, my son's
future looks very gloomy, at least as far as reading is concerned.*

My advice is to relax. Your son, when the proper time comes for
him to be reading, may or may not have difficulty. It is much too
soon to tell. You are right. If his birthday wasn't till December, he
probably shouldn't be in first grade now and should not be subjected to
the teaching of reading.

If he is reversing letters, even a few, it sounds as if he is coming into
good five-and-a-half-year-old behavior and his next step, a few months
hence, will very likely be that he will be able to read, effectively, rather
simple material.

If you don't want to put him back into kindergarten now, or have him
repeat first grade next year, at least please don't assume that your boy
is dyslexic.

Even if he were older, and continued to have some problems in reading, we would not jump to that conclusion. True dyslexia—a mysterious
inability to read in spite of good intelligence and adequate maturity, is a

very rare difficulty. In twenty years of clinical practice we have met perhaps a dozen or so children so afflicted.

As a rule when children are brought to us, already classed as dyslexics, their problems are relatively simple and usually quite easily overcome. The majority are immature for the kind of reading instruction they are being given. Many started the whole thing too soon. Others just by their own nature are progressing slowly. If they could have been started later, the whole problem might not have developed. If they could, even at a later date, be taught where they are (say they're in fourth grade reading at a third-grade level), there's nothing wrong with that!

Many others have trouble reading because there is something wrong with their visual functioning. They either need glasses or visual training or both.

It would do no harm to have a check of Felix's vision, but my guess is that the main thing he needs is a little more time. Try to get the teacher to slow down on her demands of Felix and urge her, tactfully, to stop using the term *dyslexia*.

On Sex Differences and Dyslexia

Recognizing and accepting basic sex differences in behavior could vastly reduce the number of problem readers, or so-called dyslexics. So says Diane McGuiness in her sensible book, *When Children Don't Learn*.

Though some feminists insist that boys are really just as good readers as girls (and girls are just as good at math as boys but just *think* they are not—this is called "math phobia"), in truth there are real and substantial behavioral differences between the sexes. At any rate, reliable figures give it that over 75 percent of children in reading-disabled groups are males.

As McGuiness points out, this three-to-one ratio should be statistically impossible. It occurs because we figure things wrong. Children are usually selected for remedial reading help if they are two years below the norm for their age. But in making our norms, we fail to take into account the fact that, on the average, boys develop reading abilities much more slowly than do girls.

Unfortunately separate norms have not been provided for the two sexes. If girls were selected for remediation who were two years behind average reading scores *for girls,* and boys selected who were two years behind *other boys,* the sex ratio would be one to one.

Instead, remedial populations today consist of those children who are two years behind the *combined* average achievement test scores of both sexes combined. Since girls are advanced compared to boys in a number of verbal abilities, including reading, this procedure unduly penalizes boys.

In other words, if we figured our norms separately for the two sexes, a huge percentage of boys who are now considered reading disabled would be found to be slow but within normal limits. This procedure alone would reduce vastly the number of so-called dyslexic boys.

A second way of reducing the number of children labeled dyslexic would be to stop using the term as if dyslexia were a *disease* that people *have.* Our position, as expressed by Dr. Baker of our medical department, is that dyslexia merely means "reading with difficulty" or "reading poorly" and it is not possible to *have* reading poorly any more than it is possible to *have* running slowly.

Unfortunately, as McGuiness points out, in most cases she has come across, whether of parents whose children have been labeled dyslexic, or the children themselves, there seems to be a general belief that having difficulty in reading involves something wrong organically, as if having dyslexia is like having leukemia. Many people speak, and think, as if there is something wrong with the brains of children who do not read up to grade level, or so-called dyslexics.

So before any of you parents allow anybody to tell you that your boy "has" dyslexia, keep in mind that dyslexia is not something you "have." And before you go to great lengths to remedy this supposed disease, check to be sure—is your boy really all that far behind the average boy of his age in reading? Is he really in trouble, or just a trifle slow?

It seems reasonable to believe that if we could establish two sets of norms, one for girls and one for boys, *overnight about 10 percent of all boys—millions of them—would suddenly be normal readers for their age and sex.*

Some Problem Learners May Not Be Learning Disabled

There are many good reasons why children have trouble learning in school. We do not by any means intend to denigrate this fact. Our feeling about the term "learning disability," however, is simply that it is used too loosely and too often. It is used as if a *learning disability* were a *thing*, like mumps or measles—a thing for which there is a simple remedy, such as putting a child into an L.D. classroom.

Among the many reasons children have difficulty in learning are the following.

Most often, in our experience, children have trouble in school because though perfectly well endowed they started the whole thing too soon and are thus overplaced.

Some children are not very bright. Though many schools tend to ignore this fact, through mainstreaming, actually some children are not suited to the mainstream of education.

Often and this is one of the more satisfactory reasons because usually something constructive can be done about it, there is something wrong with the child's biochemistry, something that can be helped by an improved diet or by protecting the child from substances to which he is allergic.

Very often, and here again something usually can be done, the child has visual or perceptual problems.

School difficulty may result from emotional disturbance, which can often be helped by psychotherapy.

An uneven endowment can be at the root of school difficulty.

Certain children, even sometimes the highly gifted, are good in some areas of performance but woefully poor in others.

In some instances the teacher's teaching style does not fit with the child's learning style. Children are sometimes taught abstractly when their way of thinking is purely concrete.

Though in some school populations, administrators report that perhaps 30 to 40 percent of the students are learning disabled, a more correct and cautious estimate would in all likelihood put that figure at no more than 5 percent or so. Only a relatively few children actually suffer from the mysterious condition known as learning disability. Others in trouble have problems like immaturity, low intelligence, visual or hearing deficits, and specific reading problems, which can and should be specifically diagnosed and worked with.

Much So-Called Learning Disability Is Merely Overplacement

I'm a teacher in a so-called learning disability classroom. There are eighteen children in the class and a good half of them are not true learning-disability cases. They are just too young for the grade they were in and therefore, being overplaced, they floundered, floundered, floundered till they were put into my class.

I fight with the principal and school psychologist constantly. Both of them are against having a child repeat because they make that trite, untrue excuse, "It would hurt him too much in his peer relations to have him repeat." Poor children! Doomed to spend the next ten years at the bottom of the class, or to be put into a special class that most of them do not need. Just because of the principal's obstinacy!

When will these educators accept the fact that some children physiologically are not ready to play the role that their chronological age implies?

Recently I attended a fascinating seminar at Penn State where some of our top educators told us that "At age eight, some 25 percent of all boys are immature for third grade. They still make reversals and inversions!" That is, these boys are just plain not ready to be reading at a third-grade level. When will our educators ever wake up?

I'm glad to say this again in a teacher's words. Don't assume that just because your boy or girl is failing in school, he needs to be placed in a learning-disability class. Check first to be sure that his failure is not merely due to the fact that he (or she) is *overplaced* in school. It could be as simple as that.

Clues to Learning Disability in the School-Age Child

Dr. Alan C. Levin of New York City, a specialist in learning disabilities, lists fifty possible clues to this difficulty in the child from first grade through eighth. He warns that you would need to be able to answer yes to at least ten (or 20 percent) of these questions before you suspected the presence of a true learning disability.

1. Does your child have difficulty understanding what he or she reads?
2. Does he avoid sports or activities that involve catching or throwing a ball?
3. Is your child afraid of heights?
4. Is he extremely daring?
5. Does his running seem to you uncoordinated and sloppy?
6. Does he get lost frequently?
7. Is he easily distractible?
8. Does he confuse right and left?
9. Does he use one hand for some things and the other hand for other things?
10. Is he up and down from the table at mealtimes?
11. Is he a discipline problem?
12. Does he go up and down stairs one step at a time?

13. Does he seem bright and articulate but not seem to understand what he reads?
14. Is he the class clown?
15. Do people say he is not working up to potential?
16. Does he seem to "tune out" at times?
17. Is he unusually forgetful?
18. Does he find it necessary to touch everything?
19. Does he walk into things or trip?
20. Is his behavior inconsistent?
21. Does he have a short attention span?
22. Does he move his lips while reading or follow the line with his fingers?
23. Does he have frequent headaches?
24. Is he purposely destructive?
25. Does he frustrate easily?
26. Is he unusually sensitive to light, noise, touch?
27. Was he a late walker?
28. Was he a prolonged tiptoe walker?
29. Was his speech late or abnormal?
30. Is he a bed-wetter?
31. Does he have uncontrollable rages?
32. Does he complain of seeing things bigger or smaller than they actually are?
33. Does he find it hard to keep up with other children?
34. Does he have a poor appetite?
35. Does he have a history of allergies?
36. Is he irritable before or shortly after mealtimes?
37. Does he crave sweets?
38. Has he ever experienced excessive weight loss or gain?
39. Does he go outside the lines if coloring?
40. Did he have trouble learning how to tie or button or lace?
41. Was he colicky?
42. Was he a cranky baby?
43. Was he an unusually passive baby?
44. Is he a bully?
45. Is he always picked on by classmates?
46. Is he a loner?
47. Does he seek out older or younger playmates?

---

48. Does his play seem to you clumsy or disjointed?

49. When he reads out loud, does he get mixed up and lose his place?

50. Does he not complete homework assignments?

Remember, any young person may exhibit some or several of these signs. It is only if he or she shows 20 percent or more that you may suspect that a real learning disability is present.

Is Mainstreaming Fair to Problem Children?

*O*ur *school is making a big thing about the fact that this year they are going to have what they call "mainstreaming" for all pupils. No matter what the child's problem or handicap, he or she is going to be included in the regular classes. They are going to do away with all special classes.*

This all sounds very democratic and they are making a big do about it. But as the parent of a boy with very special difficulties, who has been so very well served in a special class, I am highly disturbed that our town has made this decision. My son is going to be in a regular, mainstreamed class, with boys and girls of infinitely greater capability and learning capacity. Our school says it is the only way that is fair to everybody. My feeling is that it is not fair to anybody.

My feeling is that my son, who has multiple problems, was much better off in his special class with other children who had similar problems. I realize that by myself I cannot change the school's plan, but I would like to know whether or not you support me in my thinking.

I definitely support you in your thinking. Schools and parents, too, worked for many years to set up various kinds of special classes so that children with special problems could be specially cared for, and could be freed from the demands that the regular stream of education makes on boys and girls.

Unfortunately, the 1975 Education for All Handicapped Children Act called for the integration of most children with special educational problems into the mainstream (regular classes) of our nation's schools. Since then, in a superzealous effort to demonstrate that everybody really is just as good as, or just the same as, everybody else, schools like yours are shoving everybody back into the regular classes. It is a backward step, indeed.

Not only does the special child often suffer academically from being in a "regular" class, but he may also suffer socially. A recent study by Tanis H. Bryan, reported in the *Journal of Learning Disabilities,* showed that when children voted on the popularity of their classmates, boys and girls who had been returned to the regular classroom from special classes received more votes on Social Rejection and fewer votes on Social Attraction than did the others. That is, mainstreamed children from special classes were in general less popular than children who had been in the regular classroom right along.

However, these same children were in many instances quite popular outside the classroom. It is suggested that the school failure that many experienced in the regular classroom, where they could not keep up with the others, caused feelings of anxiety and expressions of self-negation, which made these children less than acceptable to classmates.

This seems quite reasonable. Few of us are at our best in situations that are too difficult for us. Of course children don't go to school just to be popular, but extreme unpopularity can suggest that something is wrong, not necessarily with the child but with the situation.

Most bad educational ideas, based not on educational theory or knowledge but on political bias, do in the long run die of their own weight. This will undoubtedly happen to mainstreaming, but not till many boys and girls have suffered unnecessarily. So, even though one mother can't change the whole school, I hope that you and other mothers like you will continue to express your doubts.

Your own best hope, and it is not a too strong one, is to talk with your school, even with your school board. Explain to them that you agree with those educators who claim that the "least restrictive environment" mandated by Public Law 94-142 in many instances is indeed a special class and not the free-floating situation provided by a mainstreamed classroom. At least make a try to get your son back into the kind of special class where my guess is he would best be educated.

On Hyperactivity

Does Her Two-and-a-Half-Year-Old Need Drugs?

My problem is that our two-and-a-half-year-old son, Peter, is so terribly active. He is always on the go and I just can't keep up with him. I am exhausted because he never stays still.

Recently I wrote to a well-known columnist and she said to take Peter to a doctor. She said he sounded hyperkinetic and that there are drugs to control a problem like his. Bad as Peter is, I hate to start him on drugs when he is so young.

Your mistake was, perhaps, to seek help for your son's behavior from someone other than a qualified child-behavior specialist. The first part of the advice was good—take your child to a doctor. The second part was gratuitous. Without seeing Peter, nobody could know whether he is hyperkinetic or not.

The word *hyperkinetic* (or *hyperactive*)—a word that describes an abnormally overactive child—has become very popular of late and is vastly overused. Nobody who has not lived with an active preschooler could believe how active the *normal* child can be between the ages of, say, two-and-a-half and five.

Chances are your doctor will advise you that you need to schedule your son's life more carefully. Arrange, if you can, for nursery-school attendance. Arrange for more vigorous outdoor play. Arrange for more gates and locks and other controls within the house. Arrange for a good, strong, tireless baby-sitter at least a few times a week.

Preschoolers move around a lot and can be very tiring. You have to plan their days in a way that fits with your own strength and endurance.

No one person should be solely responsible for a two-and-a-half-year-old all day long, every day.

What Is Hyperactivity All About?

*H*ow does a mother know whether her child is hyperactive or not? My seven-year-old son, Kenneth, certainly is a lot more active than any of his brothers or sisters. Seems like he is never still, and he is not very well coordinated, either. Also, he has had a little more trouble in school than my others. They even talk about retaining him or putting him into a special class. Do you find a usual relationship between hyperactivity and learning disability?

On the other hand, I sometimes think he is just an unusually active boy, and possibly overplaced in school (as you so often mention). How is a mother to know?

You can't always tell for sure. But the hyperactive child characteristically is excessively active and very fidgety. He rocks, jiggles his legs, wiggles his hands, seems always to be in motion. Such a child tends to be aggressive and disruptive, both at home and at school. It is hard to divert him from an action. He commits acts that are dangerous to his own safety and that of others. He cannot seem to stay out of contact with people and objects, is always touching things.

He is also excitable, impulsive, unpredictable. Has no patience, cannot wait. His attention span is extremely short, so he finds it hard to concentrate. He flits from one task to another. He tends to be clumsy and uncoordinated. Though often of perfectly normal intelligence, it is very difficult for him to behave in school in such a way that schoolwork is successful.

You ask if there is a relationship between hyperactivity and learning disability. Yes indeed. Many hyperactive children are also labeled learning disabled. And in fact some specialists seem to use the two terms almost synonymously. The qualities they list as characteristic of one often describe the other.

However, I would like to give you just a few warnings. Any parent who fears or has been told that his or her child is hyperactive should check with a doctor or other child specialist to make sure that the child actually *is* hyperactive and not merely just active as many children, especially preschoolers, tend to be. As you appreciate, some of the difficulties you are experiencing with your son may indeed be largely caused by overplacement in school.

If it is confirmed that the problem actually *is* hyperactivity, then you will probably wish to seek medical help. A good physician should be able to help you improve your son's diet, and also help you protect him from any substances to which he is allergic. But don't expect sudden miracles even from good medical help. Sometimes improvement comes slowly.

And in the meantime try to familiarize yourself with the characteristics of hyperactivity—try to get a feeling for and an understanding of this condition. There are many good books now available that can be of help to you (see the bibliography).

Helping Your Hyperactive Child

My seven-year-old son, Jason, has been diagnosed as hyperactive. At the suggestion of our pediatrician and of friends who, like me, have a hyperactive child, I tried the Feingold diet. But it really didn't work, so now Jason is on Ritalin, a solution neither my husband nor I find satisfactory. Can you help me to help my son?

May I quote the opinion of a friend and colleague, Dr. Ray Wunderlich. He points out that the all-too-customary treatment of hyperactivity with such drugs as Ritalin, Mellaril, or Cylert is risky, since such drugs can impede a child's ability to learn, can cause blood disorders or eye problems, suppress appetite or cause insomnia.

But the most important argument against the *long-term* use of medication in treating hyperactivity is that it tends to prevent a search for the *causes* of this behavior. Of course there can be many different causes, but the one that we can often help with most is some physiological disorder, especially an allergic reaction to certain substances eaten or inhaled.

Some form of allergy is often found in hyperactive children, and perhaps the most common kind is a neuro-allergy or "brain allergy." Every child is different, of course, but foods that are commonly implicated are sugar, cow's milk, citrus products, wheat and other gluten-bearing grains, corn, chocolate, eggs, certain nuts, fish, and berries. However, literally *any* food can cause hyperactive reactions.

Clues to which foods are causing hyperactive symptoms can be gained from the child's own diet. Usually the foods he craves, or eats most every day or in large amounts are most suspect. To discover what special foods are causing the difficulty, physicians often recommend a medically supervised *elimination diet*. In choosing foods for trial elimination, one should first consider those that the child eats most frequently and in large amounts. These should be completely removed from the diet for approximately three weeks. Then reintroduce them one at a time, over five- to seven-day periods. If any of these foods is implicated as a cause of allergy or hyperactivity, it should be eliminated from the diet for at least three months.

After that a careful trial of this food in the diet can be attempted. If no symptoms develop after introducing the specific food, it can then be returned to the diet providing that parents and physician remember that the food could cause trouble if eaten in too large amounts or too frequently.

Dr. Ben Feingold was in my opinion correct that much overactivity is a result of artificial coloring and flavorings in food, drink, even medication. All food additives must be considered as potentially allergic or toxic troublemakers for the hyperactive child. But many physicians and parents have discovered that simply following the Feingold diet is often not enough to calm down the hyperactive boy or girl. It often takes real detective work on the part of you and your doctor to find out what special foods are dangerous for your particular child. And of course it may not be food at all that is at the root of the trouble. It could be something in the house itself, as formaldehyde.

One mother told of her wonderful success with a hyperactive and allergic child when she tried the special diet approach. "Our formerly extremely hyperactive son, Raymond, age nine, had been on Ritalin for some time, without appreciable results, when we took him to a clinic that practices what they call orthomolecular medicine.

"It changed the course of all our lives. We no longer eat sugar or refined foods of any kind. The clinic said Raymond's hyperactivity was just a reflection of his allergies and occurred at a certain period in the metabolic process.

"Though his fine motor behavior is still not all that it might be, he most certainly is responding very positively to this homeopathic treatment, which, as I understand it, is aimed at strengthening his basic constitution and improving some of his chemical imbalances."

Some No-Nos for Parents of Hyperactive Children

As the mother of an extremely difficult hyperactive son, David, age eight, I have read with great interest anything that comes along on hyperactivity. Do you have any good books to recommend or any new advice to offer?

I do, indeed. I strongly recommend two by Dr. Lendon Smith—*Feed Your Kids Right* and *Feed Yourself Right,* and one by Ray Wunderlich and Dwight Kalita, *Nourishing Your Child.* All of these discuss in detail the ways in which one can reduce the allergic reactions that often lie at the basis of hyperactivity. Another especially helpful book for parents of hyperactive boys and girls is Dr. Doris Rapp's *Allergies and the Hyperactive Child.*

With effective medical advice, much effort, and good luck a child's hyperactivity may be eliminated. Here are some practical suggestions for handling the hyperactive child from some excellent books on the subject.

• DON'T try to change all your child's undesirable behavior at once. Pick on some one, possibly rather small and specific thing that you can work on together.

• DON'T say one thing one day and something different the next. And don't disagree with your spouse in laying down rules. With the hyperactive child, consistency is essential—consistency and clearness.

• DON'T tell your child everything he has done wrong. Emphasize the things he may have done right. Do this right away, as his memory tends to be short and if you don't mention these good things right away he may have forgotten that he did them.

• DON'T expect him to make decisions. You make the decisions for him. However, when his choice doesn't matter, you can give him a choice, say between two acceptable things or courses of action.

• DON'T avoid letting him do things because he mostly does them wrong. That is, don't do everything for him just because you can do most things better and faster than he can.

• DON'T, if you can help it, shout, scream, talk through your teeth, or threaten. Try a calm, relaxed voice. If you can, smile as you speak.

• DON'T complain about everything. Expect a little breakage and a good many general disasters.

• DON'T embarrass your child in front of his friends by telling him he's acting up again and needs another pill.

• DON'T pick a time when the house is hectic and he's not paying attention to give him directions.

• DON'T assume that he understands what you say. After you have given directions, ask him to repeat to you the jist of what you have said.

That's a good many don'ts, but I hope you will find them helpful.

On Gifted Children

Gifted Is Fine; Precocious Not So Fine

O *ur twenty-month-old daughter, Madeline, seems to us unusually gifted. Though she crept and walked on schedule (nine months and fourteen months respectively), her talking is way ahead of that of any child in the neighborhood.*

She talks in sentences and even uses words like "also." Thus if I fasten my seat belt and then fasten hers, she will say "Daddy fastened my seat belt for me, also." She is a constant source of joy and amazement to us.

Just as a sort of parlor trick, and to astound our friends, we have taught her to recognize the pictures of foreign diplomats. Needless to say, they are amazed.

So many parents write to you with complaints about their children that I thought you might enjoy hearing about a little girl who is totally satisfactory.

I t is fine to be gifted, and quite naturally giftedness is a source of pride to a child's parents. But there is a rather fine line between gifted and precocious. *Precocious* is defined by the dictionary as "too forward." I can't help thinking that teaching Madeline to recognize pictures of foreign diplomats for your friends is a wee bit show-off.

This kind of exploitation tends to do a bright child no good. Certainly you will wish to provide your apparently very gifted daughter with an enriched environment. And certainly it is fair to applaud her accomplishments. Just try to downplay the fact that she really is quite unusual. Try to think of her as a nice child and not just as a bundle of very advanced capabilities, of which you are quite reasonably proud.

How Do You Identify the Gifted Child?

Most everyone agrees that it is fine to be gifted, but many people are not at all certain how one recognizes giftedness. The most customary measure, of course, is the possession of a high intelligence. (Many put that figure at an I.Q. of 140 or more.) Creative ability is a second clue, even though that is a hard thing to measure. Leadership qualities can in some individuals be so strong that they amount to giftedness. Abilities in the visual or performing arts can also amount to giftedness. Unusual athletic ability is another measure.

In her informative and useful book *The World of the Gifted Child,* Priscilla Vail, herself the mother of a gifted child, lists further traits of gifted minds.

To begin with, for many gifted children new material seems almost more to be recognized than learned. It is as though the information, or concept, was already there and merely waiting to be quickened to life by being mentioned.

Another way in which a gifted mind reveals itself is in noticing patterns—intervals in music, shape and space in sculpture, ratio in numbers, repetitions in history.

A third characteristic of the gifted is energy, both physical energy and psychological energy.

Curiosity, though sometimes hard to live with, especially in the very young, is another characteristic of the gifted child—as are drive and concentration.

Most gifted children also seem to have unusually good memories. They often, though certainly not always, have the gift of empathy. The genuinely sympathetic person seems to understand others intuitively.

Gifted children tend to have heightened perceptions, a trait that is definitely a mixed blessing. These children usually set very high standards for themselves, and their heightened perceptions can throw a painfully bright light on the discrepancy between what they would like to accomplish and what they can accomplish. (Gifted children also tend to have very high standards for other people.)

And lastly, the gifted child is often characterized by divergent thinking. He not only does not necessarily go along with the crowd but he definitely enjoys open-ended, unanswerable questions—seeing the infinite as a treat, not a threat.

The Best Way to Educate the Gifted Child

Our daughter Amanda is a very bright little girl. She has been right from the beginning. The school recognizes this fact. In fact they have even suggested that we skip her from first grade, where she now is, to second. She definitely reads at a second-grade level and in many ways seems too advanced for the work that first grade offers. What is your opinion about skipping a grade, when the child in question seems unquestionably gifted?

The three most popular ways of providing the gifted child with the academic stimulation he or she needs are acceleration, segregation, and enrichment.

The first of these, just plain acceleration, is what your school is now considering for Amanda. This is possibly the most customary solution of the problem and at the same time perhaps the most damaging.

The second possibility is segregation, having the child in a special class for the gifted. This is a popular solution in some schools. And of course some very special private schools provide segregation by the very nature of their staff and curriculum.

The third possibility, and the one we favor, is enrichment, which can be provided by means of independent projects available during school hours as part of the curriculum or outside of school.

There are, of course, many activities that a gifted child, with a little encouragement or suggestion, can pursue on her own. These include reading, television (which, contrary to many opinions, is not necessarily all to the bad), radio, puzzles, and collections.

Or the child will often enjoy very special projects such as learning to play a musical instrument, drawing, painting or sculpting, writing, gardening, photography, and handicrafts.

Some educators believe that optimum education for the gifted and talented should combine both enrichment and acceleration. We ourselves admittedly are very doubtful about acceleration. No matter how gifted a child may be in some respects, other things being equal, he or she does best if in the same class with other children of his or her own chronological age (or, perhaps best, behavior age), with arrangements for giving the individual special opportunities in whatever area he or she is gifted.

Programs for the gifted and talented, which many schools provide, are certainly very popular with parents, but it is very hard to be sure they are best for the child. In our own experience, a really good public school system, and certainly many good private schools, can much of the time fully meet the needs of even the rather highly gifted.

A good school situation, public or private, providing opportunities for gifted children to carry out special projects and to find use for their high abilities should be possible in the so-called mainstream of education. (Unless of course the "mainstream" includes children suffering from defect and deviation. Then, admittedly, these superbright children would, I fear, need some special classes of their own.)

As one mother of a very bright ten-year-old once told us, "My son is so interested in everything, so intellectually active, so emotionally enthusiastic, such a seeker for information and experience, that if his formal school education stopped tomorrow, he would still learn. He is like a sponge, soaking up everything that comes his way."

What Becomes of Bright Children?

We have been told by the school that our son, Gilbert, I.Q. 142, is a genius. We know that Gilbert is a smart kid, but the school's emphasis on his high intelligence makes us feel responsible—as if we should perhaps do something very special for or about him.

Also may I ask what is the future for these supposedly very bright children? How do they usually turn out?

Y our best bet is to remain very calm. Be happy that you have a bright son. Provide as enriching a home and school environment as you can but don't press and don't expect too much.

As to how these bright children turn out—here are the in-the-know findings of former Quiz Kid Ruth Duskin Feldman, from her book *Whatever Happened to the Quiz Kids?* She checked as to how the other Quiz Kids actually did turn out when they grew up. Her findings:

> We Quiz Kids, as a group, have neither fulfilled the highest hopes nor realized the worst fears laid upon us three or four decades ago. For the most part we grew up to be healthy, happy, well-rounded adults doing responsible work, earning good incomes, having stable marriages, and making substantial contributions to society.
>
> It now seems clear that exceptional intelligence does not preclude ordinary happiness or worldly success. *But neither, apparently, does it guarantee extraordinary accomplishment.* Thus none of the well-known Professor Terman's gifted children appear to have achieved the summit of true genius.
>
> Much the same can be said of us Quiz Kids, except that we do boast one Nobel Prize winner—James D. Watson, who was not a startling success on the show. I know of no Quiz Kid millionaires, nor did we turn out one Picasso.

Mrs. Feldman points out correctly that there is more to genius than having a high I.Q. And that there is no reason to assume that even very bright children will turn out to become anything more than the Quiz Kids became—intelligent, able, respected adults leading interesting, useful lives.

The term "child prodigy" has been used to mean a child with an I.Q. of at least 140 and one who seemed to be precocious. However we must keep in mind that there are approximately two million children in the U.S. with I.Q.s of 140 or more.

It is important to remember that I.Q. alone does not a genius make, and that a child who can read at three or identify hundreds of birds is not necessarily a prodigy. True prodigies are rare.

One very important suggestion, based on Mrs. Feldman's own experience, is to be very cautious about having a bright child skip a grade. As she puts it, "Having skipped made things more difficult for some of us Quiz Kids who were small, immature, and unathletic. To be labeled a size-sixteen mind and a size-six body when everybody else was size ten could be highly uncomfortable."

You may like to read Mrs. Feldman's book, and in the meantine, do relax. Be supportive but do not expect too much of Gilbert.

Parents Want Help for a "Gifted-Handicapped" Child

O *ur two children have been diagnosed as gifted-handicapped. Our local school system cannot provide adequately for them. However, at a modest cost—just a few thousand per child—there is a school they could attend. The school board says they can't afford it.*

Would you be willing to act as advocate for our children to obtain for them the rights provided for under Public Law 94–142?

D efinitely not. I admit that if I had a child with any kind of special handicap or problem, I would very probably make every possible effort to get help for that child. However, Public Law 94–142 in many instances promises a great deal more than any local community can provide or afford. There are towns in this country that are closing their local school system entirely because money is not available to keep it going. Many other communities are cutting it very, very close. My sympathy in the long run tends to be with a school superintendent who is trying to make the money stretch. Sometimes the good of the greatest number has to take precedence over the good of the individual.

At any rate, I don't approve of people suing the school board, no matter what the problem. Urge and cajole, yes. Bring legal action, no.

However, though it may sound like a contradiction in terms, I do definitely admit that there are many children who can correctly be identified as gifted-handicapped. These children give every evidence of brilliance, even sometimes genius, often in abstract thinking, or in some one of the arts, but often fail miserably at such common and essential functions as reading and writing. They do indeed need very special understanding and very special handling. I don't object to the effort to get help for such children. What I do object to is the often militant efforts of some parents to push a school system to provide services beyond those that the system can afford. The cost of a few thousand dollars for each of your children may seem "modest" to you; it may quite likely be more than your school system can afford.

I am sorry not to offer help to any parent with a serious problem. But as one of my generation, this whole area of fighting for one's supposed "rights" is not something with which I am comfortable.

On Preteens

Eleven-Year-Old Would Rather Fight Than Help

My problem is my eleven-year-old son, who gives me trouble about every chore or demand I make of him. Whatever I want to enforce, such as that he get his practicing done or wear suitable clothes when it's cold or damp, is argued as if it were a Supreme Court case.

Just for an example, he's supposed to carry out the garbage every day. Every day he makes a fuss and puts up an argument. He doesn't know that it needs to be taken out today. He doesn't think it needs to be taken out every day.

Always an excuse. It seems to be more important to him to get into an argument with me and get me upset than to do his chore.

It *is* more important to him to get into an argument with you than to do his chore. Arguing with you is fun. Doing his chore is not. It may not be too much help but it may help some to know that you and your son are going through the normal stage in which a growing boy seems to *need* to get free of his mother. He can't do this just by walking away. He seems to have to do it by staying in there and fighting.

Your problem may be either temporary or permanent. Many boys and girls who are fully cooperative at ten may argue as if their lives depended on it at eleven, even about the simplest and easiest tasks.

If you have such a child and you recognize (or think you recognize) his problem as being *eleven,* you may choose to let up a bit on daily requirements rather than going through all the boredom and exasperation of daily arguments.

As one mother expressed it, "Tasks he has done willingly for years now require from ten minutes to half an hour of arguments. It's easier to do most things myself."

There will be some fights, no matter how well you manage things. But they will be shorter and less intense if, *so far as you can,* you try to divorce yourself emotionally. You can do this partly by deciding that you are going to give up on some smaller issues. So, he gets wet. So, he doesn't have his lessons prepared. Those are *his* problems. Chances are that even if he doesn't do as you say he won't either catch pneumonia or flunk out of school. The practicing should be his responsibility. Even if money is wasted, if he can't demonstrate that he can do his practicing without your supervision, then music may have to go by the board at least for the time being.

Instead of reminding your son daily about the garbage, try to depersonalize the situation. Make a list of daily or weekly tasks. Provide a meaningful reward at the end of the week if these tasks are carried out effectively and efficiently. Provide a meaningful punishment or penalty if they are not.

Most reasonably bright children catch on to what is happening fairly quickly and soon come to appreciate that arguing and stalling get them nowhere.

Make the problem and the responsibility theirs, not yours. If your son fails to carry out his chores, that is, if he doesn't take out the garbage, take it out yourself—or get your husband to take it out—without comment, without recrimination. The penalty at the end of the week will have more effect, and less wear and tear on you, than any number of words or threats.

Should I Insist That He Wear His Sweater?

When my eleven-year-old son says, "Okay, I just won't go then," if I tell him he must wear his sweater or his rubbers or some such outside the house, should I show indifference? Or should I insist that he go and wear the sweater?

First decide which is more important—that he wear the sweater, or that he go to the function in question. If it's vital that he get there, try not to complicate matters with directives that will lead him to defy you and threaten that he just won't go.

On the other hand, if it's vital that he wear the sweater, ask him to wear it. Then, if he says, "All right, I just won't go then," pretend complete indifference. Tell him it's up to him—but if he goes, he goes wearing the sweater.

Girls Gang Up and Exclude Patricia

I would like your advice on a deplorable situation in our neighborhood. My daughter, Patricia, who is eleven, has a friend the same age. This friend in a very smooth and underhanded way talked the other children into forming a new club and they have excluded Patricia.

This bothers her but she meets it nicely. But it makes my blood boil. *I have kept quiet because Patricia has asked me to, but I would like to go over and talk to the girl's parents.*

Should I step in, or just keep quiet and let it work itself out?

Just keep quiet and let it work itself out!

Eleven is a top age, especially with girls, for ganging up against others. Jill says to Joan, "Are you playing with Jane? 'Cause if you are, I'm not speaking to you." Children seem to need to define and strengthen their friendships by being mean to and excluding others. These exclusions are often not consistent. Today's enemy may be tomorrow's friend.

Except for preaching, as we all do, concepts of friendship and fair play, there is often not too much that adults can do. This kind of behavior seems a normal, if unattractive, part of growing up.

You cannot force other children to be nice to your child! Patricia is correct in asking you *not* to talk to the parents of the other girl.

Admittedly it is hard to see other children being mean to and excluding your own. And it's bad enough when just some two or three others exclude her. (I say "her" because boys don't as a rule behave in this tiresome way. It might be interesting for those who nowadays claim that boys do not behave differently from girls, unless we grownups expect it, to think about the conspicuous differences in the play behavior of the two sexes. Why are girls so much meaner, more catty, more given to back-biting and excluding than are boys? It seems to me unlikely that we adults cause these differences.) It is especially hard to take, though, when several form a "club" and exclude your child. But the rules still hold. *You* can't solve this problem. You can help Patricia best by remaining calm and sympathetic and not acting as if the world had come to an end. Help her to continue her own calm acceptance of the situation by assuring her that this kind of excluding tends to be temporary.

Encourage her to seek new friends. Could she start a club of her own? Or could she join Girl Scouts or Campfire Girls, where there is more adult supervision and where excluding is more difficult.

Whatever you do, do not complain to the parents of the girl or girls in question.

Randy Talks Too Much

I am at a loss to know what to do about my eleven-year-old son, Randy. He is a dear boy and has always been a great pleasure to us so I feel especially guilty about the present problem.

Randy has always been a talker, but now it is nonstop and so boring to his father and me. The worst is when he has read a book or seen a movie or show on TV. He has to tell us the whole thing in complete detail. Say the movie lasted an hour and a half, it takes him almost an hour and a half to tell us about it, as he leaves out nothing.

I don't want him to think I'm not interested in what he has to say, but I can't think of any tactful way to turn him off.

This, of course, can happen at any age but admittedly it tends to be the eleven-year-old who suffers most from total recall and a need to share his every thought or experience. The trick is to make him or her feel that you are really interested without boring yourself to death. Not listening can produce a lot of guilt, yet any parent has only so much endurance.

Your best bet, when he starts to tell you about a movie (or whatever else) is to tell him that you are dying to hear all about it and you are just going to stop what you are doing and do nothing but listen to him for the next ten (or however many) minutes. Say that you'll check your watch or, if it doesn't seem too babyish, set the timer.

When this prearranged time is over, if he hasn't managed to conclude things, just say you guess you'll have to have another time together after dinner. Since it is very difficult to encourage a child of this age to gener-alize, you do have to bring in outside control (i.e., limiting your time together). Increased age on Randy's part will be your greatest ally. By thirteen he may barely give you the time of day.

On Teenagers

They're Always Off with Their Friends

My husband and I are the proud parents of four fine children, two boys and two girls. We have always had what we consider an ideal family life and we do almost everything together.

But now things seem to be going somewhat sour, especially with our two older children, thirteen and fourteen. They just seem to have lost all interest in family doings, prefer to be off by themselves with their friends. We don't object to them having friends, but their seemingly total lack of interest in our company really hurts.

Seems as if you pay for everything, doesn't it? Nearly all parents who, like you, have run a very close-knit family and who have enjoyed and counted on their children's continued interest hit a reef when their children reach their teens. It is not at all unusual for a thirteen-year-old to spend most of his time in his room, with the door shut, even locked, and perhaps a sign on the door saying GENIUS AT WORK—KEEP OUT—THIS MEANS YOU!

The sad truth is that your teenage children really don't need you to play with them. This is their world, an all-consuming fantasy universe that is an environment for trying out reality.

Even when, as is often the case, they go against or at least talk against the things you stand for, and even if they no longer seek out or prefer or even accept your company, be assured that they are still fully aware of what you do stand for.

As one teenage boy replied when his girlfriend, in an argument, remarked, "My mother says—No, we'll leave my mother out of this one," "Your mother is in *all* of our arguments, Terry."

This is true—you are always there in spirit. A young woman I know, orphaned early, replied to a relative who was trying to tell her what her parents would have wanted her to do on some occasion, "You don't have to tell *me* what my parents would have wanted. Their values are a part of me."

So, even though you and your husband may have to give up your role as playmates of your children, if you have done your job of giving them good values, you have done your part.

You may be willing to release the two younger children more gracefully. Don't be unhappy, and don't make them feel guilty because they will soon no longer want to do everything as a family. Growing away from one's parents, at least to some extent, is a normal and reasonable part of growing up.

All Janet Thinks About Is Her Hair

*M*y *daughter Janet, age thirteen, is driving us all wild. All she ever thinks about is her hair. It has to be just so and she spends hours arranging it. Then she refuses to do anything, even the smallest thing, that might disarrange it. For instance she won't zip her coat way up for fear the collar will touch her hair. She won't even turn her neck, for fear of disarranging her hairdo. She turns her whole body, stiffly, instead. It is getting to be quite a mania with her, as she spends much of her time, thought, and energy on her hair.*

Is this normal? Is there anything I can do about it?

To me it is very touching, and unless such concern persists for months and months and goes to real extremes, it doesn't seem like anything to worry about.

As boys and girls move into their teens, they become very self-conscious and often work hard to develop a sense of identity. They worry about how they look, dress, and act.

Janet obviously is identifying with her hairdo. If this is perfect it evidently gives her a sense of confidence, makes her feel that she is attractive to others.

I would not make an issue of it right now. These phases, fortunately, mostly come and go. Your daughter may always be one who cares about her looks, but as new friendships develop and new activities begin to interest her, she will almost certainly, to some extent, forget about her hair. At least I predict that she will eventually be willing to turn her neck, even at the risk of disarranging a hair or two.

Clearly having her hair look right gives her confidence, so actually even though her concern is a little extreme, it seems all to the good. How the teenager *thinks* she appears to others is an important factor in her emotional well-being. I can remember when at the age of thirteen I used to sit on a streetcar looking sad. I *thought* the other people would think, what a sad-looking little girl. Probably she has some great tragedy in her life. Chances are that they merely thought I looked cross, but it made me feel very interesting to think they were sympathizing with me.

So let Janet enjoy her hair, for a while at least. And be assured that before too long something else will take its place as a focus for her interest and her concern.

Won't Help with Housework: Room Is a Mess

E lena has not always been an easy child, but she has not been really *impossible. Now that she's thirteen and a half, one bad day follows another. She acts as if her sisters and brothers, and her parents, are absolutely dreadful people. She avoids us as much as possible. She also avoids doing any part of the household work, and this includes her own room unless I remind her twenty or thirty times. Life here is now a constant battle.*

She frequently uses a disrespectful tone of voice and sometimes words to match when she speaks to her father or me. It is hard not to get irritated or angry with her (which is what she unconsciously wants, I suppose). Sometimes things get really out of control and she shouts or slams doors. The tone of her voice is often a screech and her words are sarcastic.

She can never admit that she is wrong or has a flaw of any sort. She will fight as long as you'll stay with it to avoid admitting any error on her part.

She cannot take no for an answer—will nag and nag and get mad if you don't give in. As I say, she is impossible.

Time will be your best bet. You say that Elena has never been an easy child but has never till now been really impossible. Actually you have given a perfect description of a rather typical thirteen-year-old girl. The kind of behavior you describe often comes to a peak at thirteen, at which time the child is quite normally seclusive, critical, disagreeable, disrespectful.

If you are fortunate, and if development proceeds along the usual course and at the usual rate, by fourteen things should improve markedly. Girls and boys then become much more sociable and friendly though still, unfortunately, *very* critical of parents and worried lest their parents do some *dreadful* thing that will embarrass them forever in the eyes of their friends.

Our suggestion that for the most part you will just have to wait this out may seem passive indeed. But, you say, life with Elena is a constant battle. Your best bet, if you can manage, is not to engage in the battle, since it is hard to carry on a war alone.

You as a parent may feel that if you let up, if you don't insist on compliance, polite manners, neat room, proper personal appearance, some help with chores, that you are letting your daughter down. But she already *knows* what your standards are, what is expected of her. You don't need to give constant daily reminders.

Girls tend to enter this ugly period of hostility and rebellion earlier than do boys, and to be snippier and more unpleasant. Boys come to it later, and though they give their mothers a hard time for a year or two, it is their fathers who get the worst of it. Some father/son battles, as you know from the news reports, are actually fatal. Boys tend to be more physical in their rebellion; girls more emotional and verbal.

You say it is hard not to get irritated or angry with your daughter. There is no reason why you shouldn't get irritated and angry. Regardless of her inner motivation, or your own, there's no reason she shouldn't learn that if she behaves in certain ways, adults will respond in *their own* special ways. There is no need to handle adolescents with kid gloves.

So for the time being, make a few basic rules of what will be required around the house, and then, if you must, have your reckoning weekly, but not daily. Try to stay above this battle as much as you can. Chances are excellent that your daughter will grow up to be a perfectly normal, bearable, friendly person.

How Do You Punish a Teenager?

It's easy to punish children when they're young, but once they're in junior high school the question becomes much more complicated. By this time, the need for punishment, as a rule, is greatly reduced. Eric W. Johnson, educator and author of the helpful book, *How to Live Through Junior High,* recommends that, if possible, punishment should be self-administered, a direct result of the misdeed, and should fit the crime. And it should be neat and short.

Sometimes telling a child to spend fifteen minutes in his room alone helps to change the situation. Or withdrawing a privilege such as watching a TV show or going to a football game may help—but *not* cutting out all movies for a month or insisting a child be home from school every day at three for the next two weeks. If you really can't think what to do, ask your child. Let him figure out his own punishment!

Perhaps even more important than the DOs of punishment are the DON'Ts.

• DON'T use a punishment that brings humiliation (forced acknowledgment that you, the parent, were right; obliging the child to telephone a friend and say he can't do something because he was bad; or any public punishment).

• DON'T spank or hit a junior-high-schooler. While physical punishments have the advantage of being neat and short, twelve or above is too old for them.

• DON'T dock his allowance, which should be his (or hers) regardless. (Except of course if allowance is based on chores and chores are not done.)

• DON'T try to get good behavior by bribing with money or privileges. A bribe shows that you assume the child will be bad and that money must be paid to prevent this.

> • DON'T withhold love and appreciation. Don't say, in effect, "You were bad to do that." Rather, say, "That was a bad thing to do."

Geoffrey Is Too Conforming

My fourteen-year-old son, Geoffrey, is the most conforming boy you can imagine. He will not deviate one iota from whatever it is that his friends (the crowd) decree. Hair, pants length and style, or any other issue of clothes or deportment. I hate to see my own son being such a sheep. Can't he express a tiny bit of his own individuality?

He can and he will—*when the time comes.* To the ordinary teenager moving out beyond the family circle, winning the approval of his contemporaries is perhaps more important than anything else. One way of doing it is to do everything "right" from the standpoint of the crowd.

More than that, many teenagers quite normally feel extremely insecure. They do not have the courage or confidence to go against the traditional norms, to be different. When the time comes that you see your son starting really to do his own thing, then you will know that his self-concept is becoming, as it very probably will rather soon, more secure.

Don't forget, either, that if what your son was conforming to were your own adult concept of what is "right," of the way one "ought" to behave, chances are you would be well satisfied. So actually, my guess is that it's what your son is conforming *to,* rather than the fact that he is conforming, that bothers you. Be patient!

Fourteen-Year-Old Boy Too Interested in Sex

I don't imagine my problem is unique, but it is disturbing to me. My oldest son, Dirk, is almost fifteen and I suppose doing what comes naturally. I have discovered him smoking in his room, reading lurid literature, and hiding pictures of nudes. I intercepted a letter he had written to a pal away at school and I could hardly believe he would write such terrible things.

Dirk is a boy who has never been a problem, easy to handle, an A student. He is well liked by classmates and teachers.

I hate to sound oversolicitous but I am *concerned. I don't want him being fresh with girls and not acting as he should. I have not spoken to him about all this and he doesn't know that I found his books and pictures. Should his father talk to him or should I? Or just let it go?*

I may sound passive, but I would for the most part "just let it go." Dirk's behavior comes within normal limits for a boy of his age.

Let us hope that by now he has obtained, either at home or at school, the usual information about various aspects of sex, venereal disease and AIDS. If you really feel that these behaviors that bother you come from anxiety or ignorance on his part, you or his father could see to it that he knows all the necessary facts. But any talk you may have with him should ideally be informative and not punitive. Dirty books and pictures almost always come as a shock to parents—especially to mothers—but are quite usual, and seldom a sign that anything is really wrong.

Boys who go quite far in this direction are often shy and proper with real live girls. Boys who are already making out with girls often do not need the special erotic stimulation of books and pictures.

In other words, it is through books and pictures that many boys learn about the matters that interest them so vitally. And though it may seem passive, many mothers find that things work out best if they themselves keep out of it. If you *are* going to bring up the topic, try to do so at a time when you have gotten over your first feelings of shock and can approach the matter in a calm, reasonable way.

It's Hard On a Teenager When Family Moves

*O*ur family is in quite a turmoil about what I suppose is a fairly usual
problem. My husband is thinking about changing his job and moving
to another city. It hasn't been decided yet and he doesn't really have to
change. But our thirteen-year-old daughter is having fits about the mere
prospect.

*My feeling is that if a father's work demands that we move, the family
should not consider too seriously a teenager's objections. Am I correct?*

*Y*es, you are correct. It seems quite obvious that most families' welfare depends on the parents' work and that the family will, in most
instances, need to live somewhere near that work. It is also true that
most children, especially teenagers, do not want to move. However,
since you say your husband's job change is not essential, you might at
least like to give special thought to your daughter's point of view.

A teenager of my acquaintance explained it this way, some years after
her own family moved. She pointed out that around the age of twelve or
thirteen, your own body and feelings are changing so fast, that you feel
the need for something, such as the place you live, to stay the same.
Also, she explained, you need to talk over all these inner changes with
somebody you know and trust—that is, with your own long-time friends.

If you have to move just at this time, it seems as if you have no
stability, have nothing to cling to.

Some families who find it necessary to move allow their teenagers to
do so gradually by boarding for maybe the first year after the move with
friends or relatives in their own hometown.

How Much Obnoxiousness Must a Parent Stand from a Teenager?

*M*y problem is my fifteen-year-old son, Ron, who is definitely going
through an "obnoxious" stage. He has always used profanity to excess with his contemporaries and now it has spilled over into his language
with me. I realize that this is not unusual behavior. I just don't like it.

My husband, on the other hand, gets furious when he hears these words and even uses physical force to get Ron to stop. This gets Ron very angry and their relationship has gone from bad to worse.

Ron does okay in school and seems to have plenty of friends, but our life at home is becoming unbearable. How much of this obnoxiousness is acceptable? At what point do you decide it is excessive? At what point do you call in outside help? I have suggested family counseling but my husband will not consider it.

I wish I could help you. But nobody I know of has found a really effective way to deal with these angry, obnoxious teenage boys who can so disturb a household. In most cases, Father is totally unaccepting of ugly behavior. In most cases, Mother tries to tone things down—to get the boy to behave more acceptably and to try to get Father to see many of the boy's behaviors as problems of growth.

One's hope is that time and much patience will turn this monster into an acceptable human being. More often than not it does. Sometimes it doesn't and disaster strikes.

Though the "geographical cure" is not for every parent, some boys are perfectly nice human beings away from home, especially when—as with Ron—they are good students and do have friends. Could you afford boarding school for a year? Is there a friend or relative, even out of town, with whom he could board and go to a public school elsewhere?

If this isn't possible, do at least encourage any and all activities that keep him busy outside the house. Encourage relationships with older people (coach, teacher, parents of friends).

At what point do you decide that obnoxiousness is unacceptable? This I guess depends on your stamina. But I think that even these angry boys to some extent welcome a certain firmness on the part of their parents. If you and your husband stick together and make certain basic rules, Ron may be able to abide by them.

You speak of outside help, and this is something all of us recommend glibly. Sometimes it works; sometimes not. If your husband won't take part in family therapy, how about an adolescent-therapy group for Ron?

It is important, if you can manage, to make your husband appreciate that you are on *his* side in all this. It is very difficult for a man to endure the hostility and competitiveness of a teenage boy and also to feel that his wife is on the boy's side and against him.

Teenagers Love to Argue

S omething that my fifteen-year-old son, Tom, does drives his father and me out of our minds. No matter what we say, he has to argue about it. He would argue about the world being round if we brought up the topic. Do you think this is normal? And even if it is, is it necessary? I guess that if you could tell us "they all do it" we would be more reconciled.

I *can* tell you that they all do it, at least the intelligent ones. In fact, if a teenager did not argue, I would be surprised. As psychologist David Elkind points out, the child who is just learning to count loves to count and will do so at the slightest provocation. Teenagers who are learning to argue love to exercise *that* ability. Teenagers have the ability to marshal facts and to make a case, and they love to do it.

Also, teenagers argue just for the sake of arguing, not necessarily to prove their point. Ten- and eleven-year-olds often argue, but more in the way of answering back—"Why do I have to?" when told to do something. Twelve- and thirteen-year-olds tend to argue primarily to win their point, that is, to get permission to do (or not do) something.

But by fourteen and fifteen the majority of teenagers argue for the sake of argument. As a typical girl once told us, "I argue just about anything because it's so much fun to argue." Arguments now concern theoretical issues as much as practical ones. That is, boys and girls of this age don't just argue to get their own way, but more to prove that their *ideas* are right. As a typical boy once told us, "I never accept anything my parents say as absolute truth. It gives me *great satisfaction* to prove them wrong."

Even at sixteen, boys and girls whom we interviewed almost without exception reported that they did argue with their parents. The more mature (or more intellectual) say that they "discuss more than argue" and claim that both they and their parents enjoy it. So possibly enjoyment is just around the corner for *you.*

Are Teenage Boys Worse Than Girls?

Will you settle an argument between my sister-in-law and me? She has three girls and she insists that teenage girls are more difficult to live with and harder to bring up than teenage boys. I have four boys and there's no question in my mind that they are much more difficult than any girl possibly could be.

Obviously there are tremendous individual differences, but my guess is that most parents agree that just as, in general, little boys are harder to raise than little girls, so teenage boys are harder to live with than teenage girls.

Here are some of the differences we have observed over the years. In general when things go wrong at home teenage girls are snippy, boys are violent. Snippiness may be hard to live with but it is nowhere near as dangerous as violence. One very seldom hears of a teenage girl doing away with her entire family as some boys have done.

Since girls in general mature sooner than boys, they may go through their period of rebellion somewhat earlier than do boys. Thus, being younger, they seem less dangerous and difficult, even when rebelling.

One thing that mothers, as least, find possibly easier about girls is that when angry they tend to be more willing to talk things out than boys are. Boys are more likely than girls to go around in a sulky silence and to be, or seem to be, relatively unreachable.

Girls, unlike boys, do not seem to find it totally necessary to go through a period of strong and ugly rebellion against their fathers. Many girls, around thirteen or fourteen, are very much in love with their fathers. When they emerge from this period, they often do so quite easily. They just lose interest. This may be hard on Father but does not involve the hand-to-hand clashes (sometimes verbal but often physical) that characterize the period when the ordinary boy struggles to become free of his father's influence.

It seems to us that a girl has to be farther off the beaten track than a boy does to get into *real* trouble. Many girls have a hard time in adolescence without verging on delinquency, though admittedly there are too many delinquent girls. Many boys who basically are pretty good stuff, and who in all likelihood will grow up to be a credit to their parents, go through a really tough time in adolescence during which they may be a problem at home, at school, and in the neighborhood.

Certainly one can find easy boys and difficult girls, but in general I would vote with you—teenage boys are harder to live with than teenage girls.

When Does Your Teenager Really Need a Therapist?

My husband and I are the parents of a—to put it mildly—very difficult teenager. I feel that Josh definitely needs the help of a therapist. My husband isn't as sure. How does a parent decide when therapy is really necessary?

Some say you go to a therapist if your teenager's behavior has you *really* upset. Others say that if a problem that bothers you continues and/or gets worse, you need a therapist. Helpful rules for when to seek a therapist come from a lively book called *How to Live With Your Teenager* by Peter Buntman and E.M. Saris.

Here's a list of clues, almost any of which suggests that a boy or girl needs help.

School: When a teen is having trouble in school—doing poorly academically or expressing poor social behavior (cutting classes, for instance), especially if he has done well in earlier grades.

Law: When a teen does anything that gets him (her) involved with the criminal justice system, continually gets tickets with his car, or has accidents. If he shoplifts, burglarizes, commits vandalism, steals even from his parents. Even if he hasn't been caught, if you know he or she is breaking the law, he should be seen.

Peers: When a teen has (many) friends you don't approve of— destructive youngsters who are influencing him in ways you consider destructive. There is a specific reason and you should find out why.

Drugs: When he uses them or misuses alcohol.

Depression: If an adolescent mopes around, feels down, seems lonely and withdrawn, over any period of time.

Suicidal Thoughts or Talk: See a therapist *immediately.*

Unusually Poor Self-Image: If he seems down on himself most of the time.

Hearing Voices or Seeing Things: This is obviously *very* critical. He is really in trouble.

Severe Weight Loss: Especially if boy or girl thinks he (she) is too fat and won't eat.

Total Unwillingness to Live by Usual Family Rules.

If Your Child Is a Loner: Withdrawn teenagers with few friends, may indeed need professional help.

How to Deal with Teenagers in Real Trouble

There are, of course, teenagers who are completely out of bounds: who drink, use drugs, get pregnant, absolutely refuse to abide by house rules. Parents who have faced, and to some extent solved, such problems do exist. Among the most effective are Phyllis and David York and Ted Wachtel. They have organized a plan called "Toughlove," which has become a nationwide movement. In some ways this movement resembles Alcoholics Anonymous except that in this case it is the parents of people in trouble who band together in support groups. These groups recognize that unacceptable behavior is for the most part not the parents' fault but is encouraged by today's culture.

So they suggest ways in which parents can change this destructive cultural pattern by making their children responsible for their own negative actions and the consequences of such actions. At the heart of the Toughlove movement is a method by which parents in a community form their own support groups. They give up on searching for psychological reasons for unacceptable behavior and try, themselves, to control their child's actions. Toughlove does not encourage parents to throw their children out of the house. Only after other alternatives are attempted is the young person faced with a structured choice to change his or her behavior or leave. In such situations other parents in the group offer temporary housing, or arrangements are made with the appropriate social service agencies.

Toughlove's *Ten Beliefs* are:

1. Family problems have roots and supports in the culture.
2. Parents are people too.
3. Parents' material and emotional resources are limited.
4. Parents and kids are not equal.
5. Blaming keeps people helpless.
6. Kids' behavior affects parents. Parents' behavior affects kids.
7. Taking a stand precipitates a crisis.
8. From controlled crisis comes positive change.
9. Families need to give and get support in their own community in order to change.
10. The essence of family life is cooperation, not togetherness.

There's also an extremely frank and practical book—*How To Succeed with Your Teenager,* by Joel Wells—that discusses such hairy topics as suicide, runaways, drugs, drinking, and trouble with the law.

What to Do About Teenage Pregnancy?

*P*eople often think of delinquency in terms of young people who break the law by crimes against people or property. What about that all too common kind of delinquency that consists of unmarried teenage girls getting pregnant and producing illegitimate babies—babies that they all too often are not capable of bringing up or supporting. It just seems to me that we as a society are being excessively permissive about this whole trend.

R ight you are. Actually most of us *are* aware of the fact that teenage pregnancies are increasing. A current book, *Crises of Adolescence— Teenage Pregnancy: Its Impact on Adolescent Development,* by The Committee on Adolescence of the Group for the Advancement of Psychiatry, points out that it occurs *more often* than most people may realize. These authors tell us that each year more than one million adolescents aged fifteen to nineteen in the United States become pregnant, and two-thirds of these pregnancies are out-of-wedlock.

Unfortunately their number is steadily increasing. According to Chilman (1978) from 1965 to 1975 there was a 300 percent increase for white females. By the 1980s at least one-fourth of white males and females had had sexual experience by the time they were sixteen, while by the same age 90 percent of black males and 50 percent of black females were sexually active.

Also, unfortunately, since less contraceptive advice is available in this country than in most other developed countries, we have relatively more teenage pregnancies. Latest figures (Alan Guttmacher Institute, 1985) give it that we have 96 such pregnancies per 10,000 girls fifteen to nineteen years old, compared with only 14 in the Netherlands, 35 in Sweden, 43 in France, 44 in Canada and 45 in England.

In view of all this we must, or at least should try to, do what we can to prevent teenage pregnancy. At what point does prevention begin? This report suggests the following.

1. For some it would be a matter of abstinence from intercourse. The authors note, "No influence currently known or available has succeeded in totally discouraging early intercourse."

2. Next, if intercourse is going to take place, the focus should be on prevention of conception. Approaches that, obviously, would minimize the risk of conception include providing accurate sexual information about the body and its functioning, providing contraceptive knowledge, and making available contraceptive materials.

3. If impregnation does occur, some may consider abortion. "If carrying a pregnancy to term involves higher risks than termination, interruption of the pregnancy may be the way to lessen the risks." "Some girls will be resistant to even the best abortion counseling." "Nevertheless it is an appropriate" path to consider.

4. "If abortion is unacceptable, quality prenatal care is indicated." And "if keeping the baby would result in future harm to the teenage mother and her infant, efforts to encourage placing the baby for adoption would be both preventive and protective."

5. If the mother decides to keep her baby, efforts must be made to protect mother and child from many of the known hazards, since

mother and child are both at risk for developmental disorders. Among the obvious hazards that may be present when a teenager keeps her illegitimate child are serious health problems for both mother and baby, the danger that the mother will drop out of school, serious emotional problems for the mother, and for the child the danger of child abuse.

Clearly, efforts toward prevention through education and family involvement are primary, and for the pregnant adolescent girl abortion, if acceptable, is the least disabling choice. The potential for physical illness, psychopathology, and developmental disruption is multiplied and extended to the next generation when an adolescent girl delivers and keeps her baby.

Sex Education in Schools?

I am very upset. Recently you gave a lecture in our town and it is reported that you advocated sex education in the schools. Had I been there, I would certainly have put you straight. Are you not aware that sex education is a very delicate and private matter, and that it is the responsibility of the church and the family, not of the public schools, to give information about it? Put me down as one who is 100 percent against having the schools mess into this matter.

It is hard for me to believe that parents like you exist, yet I know they do. This topic has been kicked around for the last forty years that I know about—and likely even before that.

I suppose it is partly a matter of opinion. My opinion is that any parents who are doing a good job with sex education at home do not have to worry about the competition. Rather they should (and usually do) welcome any supplement to the advice they have already given.

We also know that many parents give this kind of information poorly. Often they do not have all the details at their fingertips. More often they are embarrassed about the whole matter, and thus shirk their duty and don't discuss it at all or only awkwardly.

We have found that in general it is those parents who are doing the poorest job at home and thus whose children most desperately need help and information, who raise this strong and emotional objection to sex education in school.

With the increasing amount of sexual activity among our high-school girls and boys, and with the increasing number of illegitimate teenage pregnancies, it seems quite obvious that somebody is falling down on giving our young people the help and advice they need. Of course the best sex education in the world is not going to keep some children off the streets. But contrary to the fears of some parents, it is not information about sex, but the lack of sex information that gets the majority into trouble.

It is conceivable that your church has caused you to take this intemperate stand. Be assured that there are many higher-ups in all denominations who go along with us in urging our schools to give all the information they can on this vital subject, and in urging parents to permit them to do so.

Psychologist Sol Gordon, in the October 1986 issue of *Psychology Today,* points out that much opposition to sex education in the schools is based on the absurd notion that if you tell kids about sex, they'll engage in it, if you tell them about VD, they'll go out and get it. He also points out, correctly, that the idea that children get adequate sex education from their parents is, in most cases, erroneous. He notes that in survey after survey that he has conducted in the past decade involving more than eight thousand students, fewer than 15 percent reported that they had received a meaningful sex education from their parents. Usually the girls were told about menstruation. The rest of the teaching could be summed up in one word—DON'T.

Should We Give Contraceptive Information to Teenagers?

As the grandmother of two teenage girls, I am much concerned about this new trend that seems to be spreading, of giving contraceptive information and even practical contraceptive help to teenagers without their

parents' consent. Isn't it quite obvious that this will increase the spread of
promiscuity and sexual activity and also weaken family relationships? Do
you approve?

As a grandmother myself I appreciate your feeling. It's hard to take
giant steps. And it is hard for some of us who grew up in a time
when people fought even the most bland sex-education courses in the
schools, to adapt to the notion of giving teenagers contraceptives, with
or without their parents' permission.

But even the most diehard have to admit that times are changing. New
York attorney Harriet Pilpel on a recent segment of William Buckley's
"Firing Line" effectively put the case in favor of giving practical contraceptive help to teenagers, without their parents' permission if that could
not be obtained.

She pointed out that such help should be given, if just from a hygiene
point of view alone. There are many more maternal deaths among teenage unmarried mothers than among married mothers. And there are
relatively many more birth difficulties or defects in illegitimate babies,
partly because their mothers, during pregnancy, do not take proper care
of themselves and of their diets.

Since it is obvious that there is more sexual activity among teenagers
today than in the past (as Mrs. Pilpel pointed out our mores, or what we
do, are often quite different from our morals, or what we preach), it
seems wise to protect them as far as we can from unwanted pregnancy.
Though some fear, or have feared in the past that having information
about contraception might increase sexual activity among young people,
most information available seems to indicate that such information does
not increase activity, nor does lack of it decrease the activity.

Our own questioning of over one thousand teenagers as to their, or
their friends', sexual activities, suggests that these activities are more
extensive, and occur much earlier, than many of us would like to believe.
We did not ask the question "Do you or any of your friends 'make out'?"
till thirteen years of age. Clearly that was rather too late since 90 percent
of both boys and girls answered yes to this question. By fourteen over
50 percent of both sexes answered yes when asked if they or friends had
"gone all the way." By fourteen 50 percent of the boys and by fifteen 50
percent of the girls admitted that they or some of their friends had
"gotten into trouble" as a result of sexual activity.

Older people may take some comfort in the general finding that increased sexual activity does not necessarily mean increased promiscuity. At least in some segments of society, quite the contrary seems to be the case.

So although it is admittedly very hard for some to go along with the new notions, we don't help young people, and don't help society, by refusing to face the new problems that confront us.

Mother, I Have Something to Tell You

"Mother, I have something to tell you!" Words to chill the blood of any parent of a teenager. Especially if they are accompanied by an expression that says "and you're not going to like this."

At any rate, this is the title of a fascinating and helpful but disturbing book by Jo Brans and Margaret Taylor Smith. It discusses problems that, unfortunately, some of you readers are going to face with your own teenagers. Also unfortunately, no parent today can guarantee that such troubling behaviors as the use of drugs and alcohol, homosexuality and lesbianism, suicide, serious crime, will not happen in your own family.

I'm hoping for all of you that they won't, but if they do these stories of the way in which other (real) parents have faced these problems may help you to face your own should they arise.

The customary stages that mothers and fathers go through when faced with any of these seemingly unhappy realities are: first, shock; second, consideration of the harmful probability— was it my fault? Third, facing the reality of the situation and taking action-seeking help. If practical help is not forthcoming or if the troubling problem continues or even worsens and the things you try don't work, then comes perhaps the hardest stage of all—detachment. You as parents are individuals, too, and not totally bound to the child you have produced. You must not let your entire existence depend on what your child is doing or has become.

Next comes the stage of autonomy—recognizing and respecting the separateness that detachment has brought you. And then comes the time when you can stop blaming—blaming society, the schools, the teen culture, yourself, your child, for what has happened. It doesn't matter whose fault it is.

Giving birth is usually not easy. Nor is this second birth—the time when you set yourself and your child free from each other. "When a mother lets an adult child go forth to his own character and his own destiny, that act, too, carries pain and peril."

At any rate some of the parents described in this truly fascinating and gripping book, as the authors point out sadly, will never see their sons and daughters reach happy, independent, productive adulthood. Instead their children may be dead, incarcerated in prison or commune, or ravaged by drugs, alcohol, or illness. Not all these children make it.

But their parents did make it. This is the heart of this remarkable book—you as a person do not have to be defeated, no matter what happens to your children.

On Drinking and Drugs

How Much Drug Use and How Young?

*O*ur son and daughter are only ten and twelve years old so it may be *soon for us to worry about drinking and drug use. But we hear such frightening things from friends whose children are just a bit older that we can't help being anxious. Some say that alcohol and drug use is increasing and extending down, even into junior high. Others tell us it is tapering off. In your work with young people, what do you find? And if what many say about alchohol and drug use is true, what do we as parents do about it?*

One set of current figures on alcohol and drug use comes from questionnaires we sent out that were responded to by over one thousand young people in schools from the East Coast to the West.

Among questions on this questionnaire, we inquired if they themselves or any of their friends smoked cigarettes, drank alcohol, or used drugs. Responses, which for the most part we assumed to be reasonably truthful, were not particularly heartening. This is what we found:

Even by ten years of age, over half of both boys and girls claimed that they or their friends did at least on occasion smoke cigarettes. By fourteen years and after this figure rose to close to 100 percent.

By twelve years of age just over half of both sexes claimed that they or their friends drank alcoholic beverages. This number rose to two-thirds by thirteen years of age and to three-quarters by fourteen. The percentages were in the nineties at fifteen and sixteen. At seventeen 100 percent of all boys and girls questioned claimed that they or their friends drank.

Since it seems rather abrupt to ask young people, "Do you use drugs?"

we hedged and inquired, "Do any of the boys and girls you know use drugs?

Thus our figures do not represent the actual number who themselves are drug users, but rather give a clue as to what is going on.

So far as our respondents admit, thirteen seems to be the time when drug use comes in rather strongly. At twelve only about a third of each sex claim that at least some of their friends are drug users. But at thirteen the number admitting such use is 46 percent of girls, 48 percent of boys.

And then, unfortunately, there comes a big jump. At fourteen, 90 percent of girls and 82 percent of boys say that they or friends use drugs, and the figures stay that high from then on through seventeen, which was the last age at which we inquired.

This doesn't sound good to us and I'm afraid it won't be much of a source of comfort or satisfaction to you, either.

Confirming the seriousness of the situation is the fact that when asked if they or any of their friends had gotten into serious trouble with drugs or drink, by fourteen years of age, half the girls, and one-third of the boys said they had. And from fifteen on, over half of both sexes admitted that at least some of their friends had gotten into serious trouble with drug use.

The community seems to make a great difference, though it's not too safe to generalize. Sometimes a small country village seems to have problems with drugs quite equal to those in the big city schools. It's not a real cheery picture.

What a Parent Can Do to Prevent Drug Use

Recognizing that drug use, other than the purely experimental, tends to occur because the person is trying to solve an emotional problem, parents are probably best advised to do everything they possibly can to raise their child so that he has a healthy personality. A strong, positive relationship between parent and child is the best safeguard against drug abuse.

At the same time, you can help your child not to become a drug abuser by maintaining open, genuine, two-way communication with him through all the preadolescent years. Talk with him, if he wishes, about drug use as well as about pleasanter topics.

Third, you can help your teenager avoid drug use by providing sound, accurate information about drugs in the years before adolescence, the years from five to thirteen. Talk about drugs, but don't dwell on the subject, in family conversation. Find out about books that he can read on the subject.

Among the important things any parent might communicate to a teenager is his or her awareness of the fact that today's older generation is also involved in the problem of drugs. It makes adolescents angry when what they consider to be hypocritical adults treat the use of drugs as a strictly adolescent problem.

If you want to keep your child away from drug use, try to see to it that he or she is involved in constructive and meaningful activities. A rich, full life does not simply develop without anybody's doing anything about it.

These are things one might do. Here are some things to avoid doing. First of all, avoid prying and playing private detective. Second, don't moralize or lecture, don't preach or carry on. If you lean on the whole topic too heavily, your boy or girl may seek out drugs simply to get even.

And, though this may be hard to do, don't be too quick to forbid your child from continuing relationships with certain friends just because you may have heard that they use drugs. The rumor may not be true, and even if it is, it is wise to let your child feel that you trust him enough not to dictate whom he should and should not have for friends.

Fourth, don't accuse any boy or girl of using drugs unless you are very certain that this is the case. And even if you find that it may be the case, don't panic and don't become hysterical. Calm down first and then try to have a reasonable and rational discussion with him during which you show him that your main concern is him and his welfare, that your concern is protective, not punitive.

What Do You Do When You Find That Your Child Is on Drugs?

You have written on this subject before, but my husband and I never dreamed that what you had to say would ever apply to us, so we didn't save the column. Now the problem is ours.

What do you do, what can you do, when you discover that your own son is on drugs? Our horror and shock are indescribable. We had known that he hadn't been himself lately and that his grades had been falling off. But we assumed that was just one of the many unattractive stages that teenagers go through.

Now it seems to us as if the roof has fallen in. Help!

By this time, you and your husband have absorbed the worst of your shock, and I hope you have begun to react constructively to what is obviously a very unpleasant situation.

Your first reaction undoubtedly was that of many other parents. You were shocked, scared, and just plain angry. "How could he do this to us?" Actually, of course, he didn't do it to you. He did it to himself. Or you ask, "Where did we fail him?" You didn't necessarily fail him. Parents cannot be held responsible for all the bad things their children do.

As to what to do right now, first of all, try not to panic (any more than you already have). Don't rush into panicky action that will only make things worse. Try to wait till you have calmed down slightly before you do anything.

Second, don't land on your son like a ton of bricks with the hope that harsh and punitive treatment will solve your problem.

Third, let your son know that it is he you are most concerned about—not what the whole matter is doing to you.

Then try to evaluate the situation. A fourteen-year-old who has experimented a few times with marijuana is obviously quite different from a sixteen-year-old who has been on heroin for six months.

Do not try the geographic cure. Sending your boy away to school or to live with relatives is not going to miraculously solve the problem.

And if you can't work things out yourselves, as you possibly cannot, don't hesitate to get professional help.

Is Alcoholism Hereditary?

I am the divorced mother of three. We do not keep in touch with my ex-husband, who was an alcoholic and treated us very badly.

Well, that is all past history. My concern now is my sixteen-year-old son, Ralph. I have a terrible feeling that Ralph, like his father, may become an alcoholic. Can you tell me if there is any evidence that alcoholism can be inherited?

Our own finding has been that alcoholism as such is not inherited. But the same kind of personality that may have made a parent alcoholic can be handed on to a child, who may then seek the same relief.

Some (though presumably not all) alcoholics tend to be sensitive, vulnerable, immature, sometimes not too terribly well coordinated. Their demands of other people tend to be so high they are continually disappointed. They often do not feel adequate or comfortable without some kind of extra support—and alcohol seems for many to give that needed support.

It seems reasonable to suppose that this basic kind of personality (or body) could be inherited. So that the teenager may be said to drink not because his father drank, but rather because they both share a vulnerable personality.

New light on this question, as well as extremely interesting reading, is furnished by Donald Goodwin in his book *Is Alcoholism Hereditary?* It is the most fascinating book about drinking that I have ever read. Here are a few of Goodwin's findings:

In a study of alcoholism carried out in Germany in 1929, nearly a thousand male alcoholics and 166 female alcoholics were examined. Alcoholism occured in half the fathers, 6 percent of the mothers, 30 percent of the brothers, 3 percent of sisters.

Most evidence suggests that alcoholism does run in families.

A recent study carried out in Denmark indicated that children of alcoholics are more likely to have alcohol problems than children of nonalcoholics, even when the children are separated from their families in early life. In fact the sons of alcoholics were no more likely to become alcoholic if they were reared by their alcoholic parent than if they were separated from him (her) early in life.

I'm afraid that neither my response nor the book I refer to will make you feel any more comfortable about Ralph, but for you or any person concerned about the problem of alcoholism I do recommend Goodwin's book highly. At least it will tell you more than you now know about the problem.

On Abuse and Abduction

Mother Sometimes Comes Close to Child Abuse

I want to say a few words about child abuse. Not that I am in favor of it, but I would like to confess, for the sake of other mothers who may feel just as I do, how close I come to it at times.

We have three children under five. You might say that was too many, but anyway we have them and we love them. But some days when something is boiling over on the stove, the doorbell or the phone is ringing, and all three of them may be crying or grabbing at once, I feel real hostility and desperation.

I wouldn't harm any of them, I know. But sometimes I come awfully close. So if any of your other readers feel as I do, I just want to say—I sympathize.

I too am totally against child abuse, but like you I often wonder that it doesn't happen more. Left briefly alone with my great-grandson, who was grabbing things off the grocery-store shelves faster than I could put them back, I advised his mother to come back quickly if she did not want to find an abused child waiting for her. That impulse to strike out and retaliate can be very strong at times.

Our best remedy continues to be—get away from your child and get away from your house just as often as you possibly can. It takes money to get a baby-sitter, but it is the best money you ever spent. Because even a good mother's patience does come to an end at times.

Dos and Don'ts of Anger

I read a lot about child abuse these days, and though I dearly love my two preschoolers, as well as my nine-year-old, sometimes I get so angry at them I can hardly stand it. I doubt that I would ever abuse one of my children but sometimes I do yank them around a bit and sometimes I say real mean things like "You little creep."

Some of my friends say they never get really angry at their children but I wonder if they are telling the truth. Am I really so abnormal?

Not at all. Most of us at times do get angry and many of us do at times utter rather dreadful threats. Here are some suggestions about anger from *Parent Awareness Training* by a rather wise woman named Saf Lerman.

1. Try not to call your children names. But it will help you to use words that express your feelings—words like "furious," "angry," "unhappy."

2. Differentiate between mild annoyance and real anger. If only slightly unhappy you could say, "I'm really a bit annoyed"; if really angry it is okay to say, "I am really furious about what you just did."

3. Try not to go overboard when you are angry. It is better to say, "I am so angry that you are banging the wall with your truck that I feel like saying no trucks in the house ever again," than to say, "I'm going to put your truck away and you can never use it again."

4. However, it is okay to think to yourself, I feel like killing that kid. (Not everyone would agree, but quite normal mothers do harbor such thoughts.)

5. In fact, do take a moment to mumble your intense feelings of anger quietly aloud, out of the child's hearing range, when thinking them silently does not give you enough relief.

6. If you feel so angry that it frightens you, put some distance between yourself and your child, approaching him or her only when you feel calmer.

7. Don't let anger get bottled up inside you. Sometimes after a situation has been resolved you still feel angry. A parent who

has spent an hour hassling with a child at bedtime needs some relief. Tell a spouse or friend, "What a drag that bedtime scene was. What a lousy hassle. I could have killed that kid!" Of course, say this out of the child's hearing.

In other words, it is quite normal to feel angry, even very angry, at your children now and then. Just try not to harm them physically or even emotionally. . . .

Where Does Child Abuse Begin?

J ust where does child abuse begin? Some of my friends and I, teenagers from presumably "good" homes, feel that we are being abused though we're not sure what happens to us would come within the usual definition.

Do you feel that hitting a person with a belt (my father does this to me) is child abuse, even though he doesn't actually break the skin or break any bones?

I do indeed consider that hitting a person with one's belt is child abuse. I don't consider it child abuse if a parent in a moment of anger lifts a hand and gives a whack. Parents are, after all, only human.

But to get a belt and use it on a boy takes a certain amount of forethought. It is an affront to his dignity as well as painful to his body. I don't know exactly what you can to prevent it, but I am definitely against it.

Perhaps if your father is basically a reasonable man, you can figure out the things that bug him the most and try to avoid doing them. The teens don't last forever, and much patience on your part might improve the situation.

Will Single Incident Mar Boy for Life?

An absolutely terrible thing has happened in our family and it has us all shaken up. Our three-year-old son, Terry, was sexually molested by our baby-sitter. Needless to say we have fired the girl and have told her parents about the occurrence, hoping that perhaps she can get some help.

But that doesn't help us. Terry being only three doesn't yet know about the birds and the bees or about where babies come from. He has a baby sister but has never asked any embarrassing questions. So far. Now this!

We don't know how to handle it. He doesn't seem much upset about it— just told us the sitter told him not to tell but he was going to tell us anyway. What should we do now? Get him to talk about it and, as they say, ventilate his feelings? Give him information, now, about sex and babies? Get psychological help? Or what? We are so upset and so confused.

Some people say that this kind of thing, if repressed into the unconscious, could ruin a person's whole life.

The first thing to do is to calm down. It is always unfortunate when something like this happens. Most parents, except the most liberated, don't even favor sex play between consenting preschoolers, let alone sexual approach to a very young child by an older person.

To begin with, try to appreciate that this is not as uncommon an occurrence as you may think. Also be assured that so far as one knows, this kind of incident does not always have lasting (and sometimes not even temporary) ill effects.

Presumably even the rather young do have some sort of feeling that sex is private and special and so we can't say that an incident like this would have *no* effect. But it could be that a young child would be more frightened and disturbed by being bitten by a large, angry dog. Who knows?

Anyway, for the time being I would as soon as practical give Terry basic information about where babies come from. He is by no means too young. One good book that might be helpful is *Making Babies: An Open Family Book for Parents and Children Together,* by Sara Bonnett Stein. Another book, which I think terrific but which might be better later on, and which you might not care for since you seem to consider talk about sex "embarrassing" is *Where Did I Come From?,* by Peter Mayle.

At any rate, whatever book you use (and books can be very helpful in telling about babies and sex), discussion of these topics will give your son a chance to talk about his own experience if he so wishes.

In rare instances, if something like this does really seem to be bothering a child, you may eventually need to get a little psychological help (play therapy) for him or her but it is altogether possible that that will not be necessary.

When Do You Believe the Child?

O ur attorney is asking us if we believe what our children say. The question, as unfortunately in so many communities, is, when a preschooler says that he has been sexually molested, and describes in quite graphic detail what has happened to him, can you believe him? Or as the courts seem to say, are children rather unreliable witnesses?

We ourselves think our son is telling the truth. We have no reason to believe that he could, or would, make up the things he has told us. Especially as he seems very reluctant to talk about the whole thing and cries when we bring it up.

It is very hard to say for sure whether or not a young child is telling the truth. But when a child describes, as you say in "graphic detail," an act committed against him that would presumably be quite beyond his imagination, I would assume that he or she was telling the truth.

Preschoolers, especially four-year-olds, admittedly are highly prone to use bathroom language. "You old wee-wee pants," "You old poo-poo," are things they often say to playmates. But their interest tends to be in elimination, its products and processes, not in sex. In most instances when children describe horrendous things that have happened to them I would believe them. And I do think that they should be allowed to testify.

I offer this in spite of the fact that it is hard to believe some of the things that have been happening recently. Nursery-school teachers as we know them are a kindly and patient lot. Certainly I can guarantee that in the fifty years during which we ran a nursery school, no child was ever molested by any of the teachers.

How to Help Protect Your Child from Strangers

I appreciate the danger that children may indeed be kidnapped, abducted, or otherwise harmed by strangers. But it seems most unlikely that this could happen in our quiet town. Don't you feel that all this public emphasis on this kind of danger—having pictures of missing children in the papers and even on milk cartons—is frightening a good many children unnecessarily? Do we really need to make quite so much of all this?

These things actually *could* happen in your quiet town. They could actually happen in your own family. Having fire drills in the schools does not, to my knowledge, frighten many children and has undoubtedly saved lives in the case of real fire.

Similarly in these very troubled times, scarey or not, I believe that every parent owes it to his or her child to give that child certain warnings and to provide certain precautions. You can and should of course do this calmly. And unless your neighborhood seems particularly dangerous to you—or you have an ex-spouse who might indeed resort to kidnapping —you should try to present this information as if the danger was not really likely to occur.

Rules for Dealing with Strangers

Here are a few common-sense rules and suggestions that should help your child protect himself from strangers. You should be able to offer them to your child without frightening him unduly.

**   1. If a stranger asks you for help or directions, just say**

politely, "I'm sorry, I can't help you," and walk away as quickly as possible. Do not accept anything (candy, a gift) from any stranger.

2. If a stranger follows you on the street, find a safe place as quickly as you can. Look out for a block mother's home. Or go to a store or a gas station and tell an adult that you think you are being followed. Never be embarrassed to ask for help.

3. If any stranger bothers you in any way, don't hesitate to run away. Drug addicts, drunks, and crazy people, or of course any who have unfriendly intentions, can indeed be very frightening. Don't worry about being friendly. Just run away and ask somebody for help. Or if you have just left school or a store, go back to where you started.

4. Never get into a car with a stranger even if this person says your mother sent him or her to bring you home.

5. Always try if you can to walk with other children, not alone.

6. If by any chance (and this would be more apt to happen in the city than in a small town) somebody tries to take your lunch money or some of your other possessions, best to give up whatever it is without a struggle.

7. If you live in the suburbs and a stranger follows you into your driveway, don't unlock your door, but go to a neighbor's house. If you come home alone and see that your door has been tampered with or if it is unlocked, or if you see *anything* suspicious, also go to a neighbor's house, to your superintendent's apartment if it is in the building, or go to a public phone and call your parents.

8. If someone rings the doorbell when you're home alone, never open the door without asking who it is and looking through a peephole if your door has one. If you don't recognize the person, never open the door, even if the person says he is the electric or gas meter man, or the special-delivery person. Never say you're home alone. Just ask him to come back later.

9. If the phone rings when you're at home alone, just say

"Hello" but don't give out any information. If the person asks for your mother or dad, just say that he or she can't come to the phone right now but that he (she) will call the person back later if he'll leave his name and number.

Any or all of these suggestions (or any others that you may consider appropriate to your situation or neighborhood), may make your child a little anxious. But obviously better safe than sorry.

And you can make the whole thing seem more safe and natural by assuring your child that most children never meet up with bad and dangerous people, but that you just want him or her to be careful and cautious in the unlikely case that it should occur.

What to Do if Your Child Is Mugged or Assaulted

Unfortunately nowadays, even in what we like to think of as "good" neighborhoods, children, as well as adults, are in a certain danger of being assaulted. Some parents, though afraid that this might happen to their children, are also afraid that they will frighten these children if they talk about it. Others, more wisely, face the fact that it might happen and consider it their responsibility to give reasonable warning.

In their helpful book *Alone After School,* Helen Swan and Victoria Houston give the following practical suggestions for parents of children who are mugged.

1. Check, first of all, for physical injury. Give your child all the reassurance you can muster. You try to keep, or seem, reasonably calm.
2. Be sure your child is certain that the incident was not his fault.

3. As time goes on, watch for symptoms that your child may continue to worry about the experience. Symptoms to watch for include sleeplessness, loss of appetite, depression. If your child is unable to forget what happened, seek professional help.

4. Do not become overprotective, but do take what steps you can to avoid a repetition of the incident, as trying to make sure that your child doesn't walk alone.

5. Discuss with him ways to get help if need be, or to stay safe. You might even consider enrolling him in a self-defense class if your neighborhood is unusually unsafe. (Some people favor this; some do not.)

6. If the threat is constant, perhaps you can work with other parents to provide a safety system such as parent patrols or group activities that will keep your child off the street unless he absolutely needs to be there.

It is hard to have to face up to these problems. When I was growing up, about the worst that happened to a child was that some other child or children would say mean things to him. The world is more dangerous now. So even at the risk of possibly frightening your child, you owe it to him to plan what he could do if some really dangerous incident should take place.

On Television

Mother Blames TV for Loss of Control of Her Three-Year-Old

I cannot get my three-year-old daughter, Tracy, to mind me. In fact I can't get her to do anything. It is all on account of television. All she wants to do is watch those stupid programs. Any effort to get her away from the set results in tantrums and tears—even when the program she is watching is way over her head.

How does a mere mother compete with the charms of what television has to offer?

Please! If you have lost control of your three-year-old, don't blame it on somebody besides yourself. Don't blame it on her father (or her grandmother) who spoils her. Don't blame in on her weak nursery-school teacher. Don't blame it on those bad children next door who set such a horrible example.

Just admit that you've lost control (if you ever had it) and proceed from there. . . . Preschoolers are not always easy to manage and sometimes, if the child is strong and you are weak, it seems like an uneven battle.

The television part of it is the easiest part of all. Either make very definite rules as to what can be watched, and when, and then stick to your rules. Or just say no TV for a day, week, month, or however long it takes.

Actually, though you perhaps don't admit it even to yourself, having Tracy watching television does give you more free time. Once you take it away, you're going to have to spend a great deal more time with her.

Try planning her day so that she has an interesting schedule, and this will involve much more time with you. Read to her, take walks with her, tell stories with her, provide creative materials such as fingerpaints and clay.

Arrange for her to go to nursery school. (Or if she already does, ask the teacher for suggestions for things that will make time at home more interesting than it apparently is.)

Some mothers are so constituted that they can actually enjoy all day long with a preschooler. If you are one of the many who is not, then arrange for a competent (and fascinating) part-time baby-sitter.

It is possible to make a three-year-old's day interesting even without television. And once you have gotten things in hand, it should surely be quite safe to arrange a very limited program of television viewing for Tracy.

But don't confuse the two things. A good disciplinarian *can* control her child even in these days of television. A poor disciplinarian cannot control, television or no.

Mom Thanks Television

I want to say something publicly that I never dreamed I would be saying. It is, "Thank you, television, for existing and for now and then taking my children off my hands."

When I was a mere mother of one I swore I would never use TV as a baby-sitter. In fact I had great scorn for those mothers who did. When I was the mother of two I still maintained this lofty attitude.

Now I am the mother of three, all under four, I can only say that anything, but anything, that gives me a moment's respite now and then is a godsend. Of course I am somewhat careful about what the children watch. And I'll admit that some of the cartoons they love are not great art. But they certainly are a help to a mother for whom there are just not enough hours in the day.

Thank you for writing. I know there are many other mothers just like you. But the ones we, and the public, hear from are mostly those who criticize rather than praise. I thank you for telling the truth—which is that television can at least on occasion be a very helpful mother's helper.

Is TV Violence Really All That Harmful?

*L*ike many another parent, I sometimes shudder at the amount of violence my children see on television. And yet I can't help feeling that the
many people who blame television violence for all the crime in the world
today are exaggerating. I often ask myself, is it television violence that
makes people violent—or do we have all this violence on television because
we as a people are violent and enjoy violence?

Good for you. I think that most parents who care, do and should
supervise the television viewing of their children, especially of their
younger children. But I personally agree with psychiatrist Ner Littner,
who comments that those who feel that TV violence is the cause of
violence in our streets and in our home make a serious mistake in logic.
One must not overlook the alternative possibility that *both* are the symptoms of something else. It is reasonable to suppose that the vast amount
of violence on television is basically a reflection of the violent interests of
the viewers, a symptom and not a cause.

Years ago we ourselves asked a group of children, ranging in age from
two through five, to tell us a story. The majority of stories told involved
themes of violence, ranging from a low of 60 percent in boys aged two
years to a high of 88 percent in three-and-a-half-year-old boys. This
study was carried out in 1966. In many of the homes involved, television
viewing was not a major activity.

We recently interviewed over one thousand teenagers from all over
the country. One of the questions we asked them was whether or not
they felt that violence seen on television affected them adversely. Possibly they were prejudiced in favor of TV and the programs they enjoyed,
but at least according to the majority television violence did not affect
them adversely or make them more violent. Fourteen years of age was

the low point for blandness on this issue. Only 52 percent of girls and boys at this age felt that television was relatively harmless. Age by age, this is what we found: At ten years, 68 percent felt that TV violence did not affect them; at eleven, 75 percent; at twelve, 72 percent; at thirteen, 66 percent; at fourteen, 52 percent; at fifteen, 77 percent; at sixteen and seventeen, 80 percent each.

And finally, in a report titled *Television and Aggression: An Experimental Field Study,* researchers Seymour Feshbach and Robert A. Singer report finding differences in aggressive behavior related to TV viewing *only* in lower-economic schools. And even in these schools they found these differences *only* among those students who were above average in aggressiveness before the study began.

What About Violence on the News?

L ike other parents, I am concerned about the things my children see on television. But when I hear other parents complain about all the violent programs available, I have to ask myself—what is the effect of regular news programs on our children?

How can we explain to them the acts of violence on the part of both man and nature? What must they think of it all?

What must *we* think of it all, for that matter? Many adults find it hard to explain to themselves that life can be so violent, let alone justify it to their children.

Your point is well taken. When children watch the more violent TV programs, it *is* possible to explain to them that this is *just* television and that in real life people don't go around shooting each other right and left. Such explanations don't hold up for the news. This is no longer *just* television. This is life.

Also, people advise, if you don't like the more violent programs, you can write to their sponsors and say you won't buy their products unless they calm the shows down. But to whom can you write when you don't like the news?

Fortunately most children under ten or eleven are not particularly interested in news programs. For those older children who do watch, there really isn't too much you can do to explain natural catastrophes. But when it comes to man-made violence, perhaps you could discuss with them ways in which all of us might at least *try* to work together to make society better.

But if a parent compares what he or she considers to be superviolent programs with the actual news of the day, it might help some of those parents who all too freely use television as a scapegoat to explain why the youth of today are violent to appreciate that we are living in violent times. Television (even when as often it exaggerates) does not so much create as reflect the way things are today.

Bibliography

Alexander, Terry Pink. *Make Room for Twins: A Complete Guide to Pregnancy, Delivery and the Childhood Years.* New York: Bantam Books, 1987.

Ames, Louise B. "Children's Stories." *Genetic Psychology Monographs,* 1966, *13,* 337–396.

Ames, Louise B. *Is Your Child in the Wrong Grade?* New York: Modern Learning Press, 1978.

Ames, Louise B. *What Am I Doing in This Grade?* New York: Programs for Education, 1985.

Ames, Louise B., and Chase, Joan A. *Don't Push Your Preschooler,* rev. ed. New York: Harper & Row, 1980.

Ames, Louise B.; Gillespie, Clyde; and Streff, John. *Stop School Failure.* rev. ed. New York: Programs for Education, 1985.

Ames, Louise B., and Haber, Carol. *He Hit Me First.* New York: Dembner, 1982.

Ames, Louise B.; Ilg, Frances L.; and Haber, Carol. A series titled: *Your One Year Old, Your Two Year Old, Your Three Year Old, Your Four Year Old, Your Five Year Old, Your Six Year Old,* and *Your Seven Year Old.* New York: Delacorte, 1976, 1979, 1980, and 1985.

Austin, John J., and Lafferty, J. Clayton. *Ready or Not: The School Readiness Checklist.* Wilmington, Delaware: Justak Assessment Systems, 1963.

Baer, Consuelo. *Report From the Heart.* New York: Simon & Schuster, 1976.

Bank, Stephen, and Kahn, Michael. *The Sibling Bond.* New York: Basic Books, 1982.

Bayard, Robert T., and Bayard, Jean. *Your Acting-Up Teenager: Practical Self-Help for Desperate Parents.* New York: M. Evans & Co., 1983.

Beck, Joan. *Effective Parenting.* New York: Simon & Schuster, 1976.

Berman, Claire. *What Am I Doing in A Stepfamily?* New York: Lyle Stuart, 1982.

Bernard, Jessie. *The Future of Motherhood.* New York: Dial, 1974.

Biller, Henry, and Meredith, Dennis. *Father Power.* New York: McKay, 1974.

Bittman, Sam, and Zalk, Sue R. *Expectant Fathers*. New York: Hawthorne, 1978.

Brans, Jo, and Smith, Margaret Taylor. *Mother, I Have Something to Tell You*. New York: Doubleday, 1987.

Brazelton, T. Berry. *Infants and Mothers*. New York: Delacorte, 1969.

Brazelton, T. Berry. *Doctor and Child*. New York: Delacorte, 1976.

Brenton, Myron. *How to Survive Your Child's Rebellious Teens: New Solutions For Troubled Parents*. Philadelphia: Lippincott, 1978.

Bruno, Anthony. *Piggybook*. New York: Knopf, 1986.

Buntman, Peter H., and Saris, E. M. *How to Live with Your Teenager*. Pasadena, Cal.: Birch Tree Press, 1980.

Burton, Linda; Dittmer, Janet; and Loveless, Cheri. *What's a Smart Woman Like You Doing at Home?* Washington, D.C.: Acropolis Press, 1986.

Calladine, Carole, and Calladine, Andrew. *Raising Siblings*. New York: Delacorte, 1979.

Cardozan, Arlene Rossen. *Woman at Home*. New York: Doubleday, 1976.

Chess, Stella; Thomas, Alexander; and Birch, Herbert. *Your Child is a Person*. New York: Viking, 1965.

Chess, Stella, and Whitebread, Jean. *Daughters*. New York: Doubleday, 1978.

Colew, Colin. *How to Raise Your Child Without Threats or Violence*. New York: Exposition Press, 1974.

Collier, Herbert L. *The Psychology of Twins: A Practical Handbook for Parents*. Phoenix, Arizona: O'Sullivan Woods & Co., 1974.

Crook, William, and Stevens, Laura. *Solving the Hyperactivity Puzzle: How to Help Your Hard to Raise Child,* New York: Random House, 1987.

Delacato, Carl. *The Ultimate Stranger*. New York: Doubleday, 1974.

DeVries-Kruyt, T. *A Special Gift: The Story of Jan*. New York: Wyden, 1974.

Dodson, Fitzhugh. *Give Your Child a Head Start in Reading*. New York: Simon & Schuster, 1981.

Dodson, Fitzhugh. *How to Discipline With Love*. New York: Rawson, 1977.

Dodson, Fitzhugh. *How to Father*. Los Angeles: Nash, 1974.

Dodson, Fitzhugh. *How to Grandparent*. New York: Harper & Row, 1981.

Dodson, Fitzhugh. *How to Parent*. Los Angeles: Nash, 1970.

Dodson, Fitzhugh. *How to Single Parent*. New York: Harper & Row, 1987.

Elkind, David. *All Grown Up and No Place to Go*. Reading, Mass.: Addison Wesley, 1984.

Elkind, David. *The Hurried Child*. Reading, Mass.: Addison Wesley, 1982.

Feingold, Ben. *Why Your Child Is Hyperactive*. New York: Random House, 1975.

Feldman, Ruth Duskin. *Whatever Happened to The Quiz Kids?* Chicago: Chicago Review Press, 1983.

Ferrara, Frank. *On Being Father: A Divorced Man Talks About Sharing the Responsibilities of Parenthood.* New York: Doubleday, 1976.

Feshbach, Seymour, and Singer, Robert A. *Television and Aggression: An Experimental Field Study.* San Francisco: Josse Bass, 1971.

Fontana, Vincent. *The Maltreated Child.* Springfield, Ill.: C. C. Thomas, 1979.

Forer, Lucille. *The Birth Order Factor.* New York: McKay, 1976.

Gardner, Richard A. *The Boys' and Girls' Book About Divorce.* New York: Bantam, 1971.

Gardner, Richard A. *The Boys' and Girls' Book About One-Parent Families.* New York: Putnam, 1978.

Gardner, Richard A. *The Parents' Book About Divorce.* New York: Doubleday, 1977.

Gehman, Betsy Holland. *Twins: Twice the Trouble, Twice the Fun.* Philadelphia: Lippincott, 1965.

Gelles, Richard J. *Family Violence.* Beverly Hills, Cal.: Sage Library of Social Research, 1979.

Gesell, Arnold; Ilg, Frances L.; and Ames, Louise B. (in collaboration with Glenna Bullis). *The Child From Five to Ten,* rev. ed. New York: Harper & Row, 1977.

Gesell, Arnold; Ilg, Frances L.; and Ames, Louise B. (in collaboration with Janet Learned Rodell). *Infant and Child in the Culture of Today,* New York: Harper & Row, 1984.

Gesell, Arnold; Ilg, Frances L.; and Ames, Louise B. *Youth: The Years from Ten to Sixteen.* New York: Harper & Row, 1956.

Gilbert, Sara. *Fat Free: Common Sense for Young Weight Watchers.* New York: Macmillan, 1975.

Gilbert, Sara. *What's a Father For?* New York: Parents Magazine Press, 1975.

Gold, Phyllis. *Please Don't Say Hello.* New York: Human Sciences Press, 1975.

Gold, Svea. *When Children Invite Child Abuse.* Eugene, Ore.: Fern Ridge Press, 1986.

Goldhill, Paul. *A Parents' Guide to the Prevention and Control of Drug Abuse.* Chicago: Regnery, 1971.

Goldstein, Sonja, and Solnit, Albert J. *Divorce and Your Child.* New Haven, Conn.: Yale University Press, 1984.

Goodwin, Donald. *Is Alcoholism Hereditary?* New York: Oxford University Press, 1976.

Grant, Jim. *I Hate School.* Rosemont, N.J.: Programs for Education, 1986.

Graubard, Paul. *Positive Parenting.* New York: Bobbs Merrill, 1977.

Grollman, Earl A., and Sweder, Gerri. *The Working Parent Dilemma: How to Balance the Responsibilities of Children and Career.* Boston: Beacon, 1986.

Group for the Advancement of Psychiatry. *Crises of Adolescence—Teenage*

Pregnancy: Its Impact on Adolescent Development. New York: Brunner/Mazel, 1986.

Hatfield, Antoinette, and Stanton, Peggy. *How to Help Your Child Eat Right.* Washington, D.C.: Acropolis Press, 1978.

Hautzig, Esther. *Life with Working Parents.* New York: Macmillan, 1976.

Healy, Jane M. *Your Child's Growing Mind.* New York: Doubleday, 1987.

Ilg, Frances L.; Ames, Louise B.; and Baker, Sidney M. *Child Behavior,* rev. ed. New York: Harper & Row, 1981.

Ilg, Frances L.; Ames, Louise B.; Haines, Jacqueline; and Gillespie, Clyde. *School Readiness,* rev. ed. New York: Harper & Row, 1978.

Johnson, Eric W. *How to Live Through Junior High.* Philadelphia: Lippincott, 1975.

Kagan, Jerome. *The Nature of the Child.* New York: Basic Books, 1974.

Kanner, Leo. *In Defense of Mothers.* New York: Dodd, Mead, 1941.

Kappelmann, Murray. *Raising the Only Child.* New York: Dutton, 1975.

Kaufman, Barry. *A Miracle to Believe In: They Loved a Child Back to Life.* New York: Doubleday, 1981.

Kaufman, Barry. *Son-Rise.* New York: Doubleday, 1976.

Knobloch, Hilda, and Pasamanick, Benjamin. *Gesell and Amatruda's Developmental Diagnosis.* New York: Harper & Row, 1974.

Kramer, Rita. *In Defense of Family.* New York: Basic Books, 1983.

Krementz, Jill. *How It Feels to Be Adopted.* New York: Knopf, 1982.

Lansky, Vicki. *Best Practical Parenting Tips.* Deephaven, Minn.: Meadowbrook Press, 1981.

Lerman, Saf. *Parent Awareness Training: Positive Parenting for the 1980s.* New York: A & W Publishers, 1980.

LeShan, Eda. *You and Your Feelings.* New York: Macmillan, 1975.

Lightfoot, Sara. *The Good High School.* New York: Basic Books, 1983.

Littner, Ner. "A Psychiatrist Looks at Television Violence." (Lecture at the Northwestern University TV Symposium, spring, 1969).

Maddox, Brenda. *The Half Parent.* New York: Evans, 1975.

Matthews, Sanford. *Through the Motherhood Maze: Survival Lessons for Loving Mothers.* New York: Doubleday, 1982.

Mayle, Peter. *Where Did I Come From?* New York: Lyle Stuart, 1973.

McCollum, Audrey T. *Coping with Prolonged Health Impairment in Your Child.* Boston: Little Brown, 1975.

McGuiness, Diane. *When Children Don't Learn.* New York: Basic Books, 1985.

Moore, Linda Perrigo. *Does This Mean My Kid's a Genius?* New York: McGraw Hill, 1981.

Moore, Sheila, and Frost, Roon. *The Little Boy Book.* New York: Clarkson N. Potter, 1986.

Norris, Gloria, and Miller, Jo Ann. *The Working Mother's Complete Handbook.* New York: Dutton, 1979.

Packard, Vance. *Our Endangered Children: Growing Up in a Changing World.* Boston: Little Brown, 1983.

Panter, Gideon, and Linde, Shirley. *Now That You've Had Your Baby.* New York: McKay, 1976.

Peck, Ellen. *The Joy of the Only Child.* New York: Delacorte, 1977.

Pitcher, Evelyn, and Schultz, Lynn H. *Boys and Girls at Play: The Development of Sex Roles.* South Hadley, Mass.: Bergin & Harvey, 1983.

Pogrebin, Letty C. *Growing Up Free: Raising Your Child in the 80s.* New York: McGraw Hill, 1980.

Polk, Lee, and LeShan, Eda. *The Incredible Television Machine.* New York: Macmillan, 1978.

Postman, Neil. *The Disappearance of Childhood.* New York: Delacorte, 1982.

Powell, Douglas. *Teenagers: When to Worry and What to Do.* New York: Doubleday, 1986.

Pruett, Kyle D. *The Nurturing Father.* New York: Warner Books, 1987.

Ramos, Suzanne, *The Complete Book of Child Custody.* New York: Putnam, 1979.

Rapp, Doris. *Allergies and the Hyperactive Child.* New York: Sovereign Books, 1984.

Reutenber, Ralph. *How to Bring Up 2,000 Teenagers.* Chicago, Ill.: Thomas More Press, 1982.

Richert, Barbara. *Getting Your Kids to Eat Right.* New York: Simon & Schuster, 1981.

Rimland, Bernard. *Infantile Autism.* New York: Appleton Century Crofts, 1964.

Rofes, Eric, and students of the Fayerweather Street School. *The Kid's Book About Parents.* Boston: Houghton Mifflin, 1983.

Roosevelt, Ruth, and Lofas, Jeanette. *Living in Step.* New York: Stein & Day, 1976.

Salk, Lee. *Preparing for Parenthood.* New York: McKay, 1974.

Schaefer, Charles. *How to Influence Children.* New York: Van Nostrand Reinhold, 1982.

Sheldon, William H. *Varieties of Temperament.* New York: Harper & Brothers, 1944.

Siegel, Ernest; Siegel, Rita; and Siegel, Paul. *Help for the Lonely Child.* New York: Dutton, 1978.

Skoussen, W. Cleon. *So You Want to Raise a Boy.* New York: Doubleday, 1962.

Smith, Lendon. *Feed Your Kids Right.* New York: McGraw Hill, 1983.

Smith, Lendon. *Feed Yourself Right.* New York: McGraw Hill, 1983.

Smith, Lendon. *Improving Your Child's Behavior Chemistry.* Englewood Cliffs, N.J.: Prentice Hall, 1976.

Smith, Sally. *No Easy Answers: The Learning Disabled Child.* Cambridge, Mass.: Winthrop Press, 1979.

Sorotsky, Arthur D.; Baran, Annette; and Pannor, Reuben. *The Adoption Triangle.* New York: Doubleday, 1976.

Stein, Sara Bonnett. *Making Babies: An Open Family Book for Parents and Children Together.* New York: Walker, 1980.

Stepfamily Bulletin. 72 Fifth Avenue, New York City: Human Sciences Press.

Straus, Murray; Gelles, Richard; and Steinmetz, Suzanne. *Behind Closed Doors: Violence in the American Family.* New York: Anchor Press, Doubleday, 1980.

Swan, Helen, and Houston, Victoria. *Alone After School.* Englewood Cliffs, N.J.: Prentice Hall, 1985.

Thevenin, Tine. *The Family Bed.* Minneapolis, Minn., privately printed.

Thompson, Helen. *The Successful Stepparent.* New York: Harper & Row, 1966.

Toman, Walter. *Family Constellation.* New York: Springer, 1969.

The Twin Mothers Club of Bergen County, New Jersey. *And Then There Were Two—A Handbook for Mothers and Fathers of Twins.* New York: Child Study Association of America.

Uphoff, James; Gilmore, June; and Huber, Rosemarie. *Summer Children,* Middletown, Ohio: J. & J. Publishing Co. 1986.

Vail, Priscilla. *Smart Kids with School Problems.* New York: Dutton, 1987.

Vail, Priscilla. *The World of the Gifted Child.* New York: Walker, 1985.

Vishner, John, and Vishner, Emily. *How to Win as a Stepparent.* New York: Dembner, 1982.

Von Hilsheimer, George. *How to Live with Your Special Child.* Washington, D.C.: Acropolis Press, 1970.

Wells, Joel. *How to Succeed with Your Teenager.* Chicago: Thomas More Press, 1982.

Wender, Paul. *The Hyperactive Child.* New York: Crown, 1973.

Wunderlich, Ray, and Kalita, Dwight. *Nourishing Your Child.* New Canaan, Conn.: Keats, 1984.

York, Phyllis; York, David; and Wachtel, Ted. *Toughlove.* New York: Doubleday, 1982.

Acknowledgments

Grateful acknowledgment is given for permission to use material from the following sources:

The Working Parent Dilemma: How to Balance the Responsibilities of Children and Career by Earl A. Grollman and Gerri L. Sweder. Copyright © 1986 by Earl A. Grollman and Gerri L. Sweder. All rights reserved. Used by permission of Beacon Press.

Help for the Lonely Child: Strengthening Social Perception by Ernest Siegel, Rita Siegel, and Paul Siegel. Copyright © 1978 by Ernest Siegel, Rita Siegel, and Paul Siegel. All rights reserved. Used by permission of the authors.

Boys and Girls at Play: The Development of Sex Roles by Evelyn Pitcher and Lynn H. Schultz. Copyright © 1983 by Bergin & Harvey Publishers, Inc. All rights reserved. Used by permission of the authors.

Excerpt from *Doctor and Child* by T. Berry Brazelton. Copyright © 1976 by T. Barry Brazelton. All rights reserved. Used by permission of Delacorte Press/Merloyd Lawrence.

How to Help Your Child Eat Right by Antoinette Hatfield and Peggy Stanton. Copyright © 1974 by Antoinette Hatfield and Peggy Stanton. All rights reserved. Used by permission of Acropolis Books Ltd.

Excerpt from *Parent Awareness Training: Positive Parenting for the 1980s* by Saf Lerman. Copyright © 1980 by Saf Lerman. All rights reserved. Used by permission of Harper & Row, Publishers, Inc.

Soundings from DDB. Used by permission of DDB Needham.

Excerpts from *Daughters* by Stella Chess and Jane Whitbread. Copyright © 1978 by Stella Chess and Jane Whitbread. Used by permission of Doubleday & Company, a division of Bantam, Doubleday, Dell Publishing Group, Inc.

Raising Siblings by Carole Calladine and Andrew Calladine. Copyright © 1979 by Carole and Andrew Calladine. All rights reserved. Used by permission of the authors.

Coping with Prolonged Health Impairment in Your Child by Audrey T. McCollum. Copyright © 1975 by Audrey T. McCollum. All rights reserved. Used by permission of Little, Brown, and Company.

Excerpts from *On Being Father: A Divorced Man Talks About Sharing the Responsibilities of Parenthood* by Frank Ferrara. Copyright © 1985 by Frank Ferrara. All rights reserved. Used by permission of Doubleday & Company, a division of Bantam, Doubleday, Dell Publishing Group, Inc.

Divorce and Your Child by Sonja Goldstein and Albert J. Solnit. Copyright © 1984 by Yale University. All rights reserved. Used by permission of Yale University Press.

Steps for Steps by Jeanette Lofas. Copyright © 1987 by Jeanette Lofas. All rights reserved. Used by permission of the author.

Ready or Not: The School Readiness Checklist by John J. Austin and J. Clayton Lafferty. Copyright © 1979, 1963 by John J. Austin and J. Clayton Lafferty. All rights reserved. Used by permission of Research Concepts, a division of Testmakers, Inc.

When Children Don't Learn by Diane McGuiness. Copyright © 1985 by Basic Books, Inc. All rights reserved. Used by permission of Basic Books, Inc.

The World of the Gifted Child by Priscilla Vail. Copyright © 1985 by Priscilla Vail. All rights reserved. Used by permission of Walker and Company.

Whatever Happened to the Quiz Kids? by Ruth Duskin Feldman. Copyright © 1982 by Ruth Duskin Feldman. All rights reserved. Used by permission of the author.

How to Live Through Junior High by Eric W. Johnson. Copyright © 1975 by Eric W. Johnson. All rights reserved. Used by permission of the author.

Excerpts from *Toughlove* by Phyllis and David York and Ted Wachtel. Copyright © 1984 by Phyllis and David York and Ted Wachtel. All rights reserved. Used by permission of Doubleday & Company, a division of Bantam, Doubleday, Dell Publishing Group, Inc.

Excerpts from *Crises of Adolescence—Teenage Pregnancy: Its Impact on Adolescent Development* by the Committee on Adolescence, The Group for the Advancement of Psychiatry. Copyright © 1986 by The Group for the Advancement of Psychiatry. All rights reserved. Used by permission of Brunner/Mazel, Inc.

Mother, I Have Something to Tell You by Jo Brans and Margaret Taylor Smith. Copyright © 1987 by Jo Brans and Margaret Taylor Smith. All rights reserved. Used by permission of Doubleday & Company, a division of Bantam, Doubleday, Dell Publishing Group, Inc.

Alone After School by Helen L. Swan and Victoria Houston. Copyright © 1985 by Helen L. Swan and Victoria Houston. All rights reserved. Used by permission of Prentice-Hall, Inc.

Index